CONDUCTING PARENTING CAPACITY ASSESSMENTS

A Manual For Mental Health Practitioners

Alexander T. Polgar, Ph.D.

SANDRIAM
PUBLICATIONS

Sandriam Publications Inc.
Hamilton, Ontario, Canada

CONDUCTING PARENTING CAPACITY ASSESSMENTS:

A MANUAL FOR MENTAL HEALTH PRACTITIONERS

BY ALEXANDER T. POLGAR

© 2001, 2005, 2019

Sandriam Publications Inc.

Hamilton, Ontario. Canada

atpolgar@sympatico.ca

www.atpolgar.com/sandriam-publications

DEDICATION

This work is dedicated to all Mental Health practitioners willing to apply their knowledge, skills and practice wisdom, to benefit children in need. As part of a multi-disciplinary team, the contribution of a Parenting Capacity Assessor constitutes a profoundly significant component to rescuing children from the dysfunctional legacy to which they would otherwise have been destined by virtue of the circumstances into which they were born.

ABSTRACT

This practical manual is intended to be used by both the novice and the seasoned Mental Health practitioner. For the novice, the manual is intended to de-mystify the methodology for conducting a Parenting Capacity Assessment and thereby to provide an entry to opportunities on which to build practice wisdom. For the seasoned Mental Health practitioner, the manual is intended to provide a standardized methodology ready to be enriched and expanded by the wisdom gained through years of experience performing clinical assessments.

The manual is also intended to be used by child welfare professionals as a source for organizing their concerns about individuals as parents and when necessary formulating the terms of reference for a Parenting Capacity Assessment. Counsels for child welfare agencies will find this manual invaluable for organizing their legal strategies. Opposing counsels will find the material equally invaluable for ensuring a comprehensive methodology was used for assessing their clients. Judges charged with the onerous responsibility for making a definitive determination, in all jurisdictions regardless of the methodology used by an assessor will find this manual to be an invaluable standard against which evidence is evaluated.

The format of this manual is a rational, logical one in which each procedure is justified by empirically substantiated theory. The manual is divided into two major components. The first part of the manual constitutes a learning experience for the user. It is also intended to instill the kind of confidence that is required to rise to the challenge of conducting a comprehensive Parenting Capacity Assessment that will potentially have profound impact on the fate of a child.

The second part of this manual constitutes a fictional report drawn from a composite of several actual cases. The report is intended to promote the adoption by all Mental Health practitioners of a standardized methodology and report format. Users of this manual are encouraged to "plagiarize" in whole the generic content of the report. The case-specific findings, conclusions and recommendations under each of the four categories of analysis arc presented in a "presentations that work" format. In the report each conclusion on which a recommendation is based is supported by a number of findings, as well as being underpinned by the logical interconnectedness of all the various sources of information obtained through the prescribed methodology. A significant premise on which this manual is based is that a Parenting Capacity Assessment is, first and foremost, produced to be read and acted upon by a judge who is not a Mental Health professional. As such, this methodology avoids the use of jargon and idiosyncratic labels and, most importantly, reliance on credentialized authority as opposed to authority that is earned by demonstrated competence.

ACKNOWLEDGEMENTS

This work represents accumulated experience reaching a critical mass, a process that was alluded to by a mentor some twenty years ago. I am certain that he will not have registered the profound significance of his encouraging words as I was lamenting my misgivings about the disjointed directions of my career, just as I was embarking on yet another seemingly unrelated venture. I was assured a synthesis would occur, producing a level of understanding that does not come through any short-cut path of least resistance or without a myriad of humbling learning experiences. This work is also the product of an even longer process of synthesis precipitated by an undergraduate Philosophy of Science professor whose name I have long forgotten and who I am certain has no recollection of me as a student in his class either. Nevertheless, it was there that I was first introduced to the most pleasurable and productive human endeavor of thinking. As opposed to my previous parochial school experiences where the motto was "don't think, do what you are told," in this short but brief educational experience, I was systematically introduced to not only the notion that one can actually learn to think, but that struggling to develop such skills can be an enjoyable endeavor crowned by positive results.

There were other mentors in my life who, in their own particular way, encouraged my unusual lateral thinking processes and, most importantly, validated the questions and issues with which I struggled. While few and far between, these individuals had a profound impact on my spirit as an individual, unwilling or perhaps incapable of being co-opted into simply going along, conforming or otherwise maintaining the status quo.

In spite of the encouragement and sage mentoring throughout my life by the various individuals with whom I had brief or extended periods of encounter, this work would never have commenced or been completed without the unconditional confidence my family has communicated to me from the beginning of this endeavor. My wife and two children, when I announced my sabbatical to embark on this project, were quite matter-of-fact about it. Without reservation, they believed that this would be accomplished and that it will be a valuable contribution to an area of practice about which I am passionate.

Paradoxically, the impetus for this endeavor also comes from a number of profoundly negative experiences with individuals who have long forgotten about their idealism and who, likely without realizing it, had become co-opted into self-serving and status quo-maintenance tactics. It is a travesty that, ultimately, the fate of children in greatest need are determined by a judicial process where winning and losing dominates everything that is done. All this in the name of some "vigorous defense" slogan, the etiology of which is far removed from principles of justice and more associated with principles of finance and "the end justifies the means". Once the Mental Health practitioner encounters the antics of lawyers, it is not too difficult to become appropriately oriented and to see what they do for what it is: far removed from what it should be as officers of the court in pursuit of justice. In my experience, it is the rare judge who intervenes in this "win at all cost" process. If more judges intervened to constantly focus on a child's right to optimal growth and development, this manual would have never been written.

INTRODUCTION TO THE 3RD EDITION

Alexander T. Polgar, Ph.D.
Hamilton, ON, Canada
18 April 2019

In the late 1990's I was encouraged to apply my evidence-based assessment approach to child welfare parenting capacity assessment. I knew it to be an adversarial process and as such focused on one side winning at the price of the other's loss. The best interest of the child was achieved, so it was rationalized, by this robust combative method. The legal refrain being "I did my job better than you did yours."

The challenge, therefore, was first to discern how best to do my job by learning the best current relevant to the task methodology. The next task I imagined would entail improving the methodology through the experience of actually applying it.

Much to my surprise, there was no existing standardized, approved, tested or validated parenting capacity assessment methodology in existence. I could only find guidelines with which everyone seemed content. Everyone seemed equally content with parenting capacity assessment reports lacking any discernible standard format and methodology. All assessors were doing their own thing.

To best prepare myself for the inevitable adversarial legal process and more importantly to optimally act in the best interest of the child at risk I prepared this manual. It was an incredibly challenging task. It was also an incredibly rewarding one.

Most noteworthy of the rewards was the confidence with which the methodology allowed me to formulate evidence-based conclusions. Whether I was testifying as an expert or submitting my report as evidence, I felt truly to be 'amicus curiae" a friend of the court. The presiding judges, without exception, sure gave the impression that they appreciated the assistance in performing their difficult task.

The other rewards accrued writing the manual were that it was approved for two days continuing education credits in the USA by the disciplines of psychology and social work. This publication, to say the least, also greatly simplified the task of qualifying me as an expert witness.

Almost twenty years later, we continue to sell manuals every year. Nearly twenty years later acting in the best interest of a child at risk continues to invoke the adversarial legal process. And almost twenty years later there appears to be no new manual advocating an evidence-based standard methodology for conducting parenting capacity assessments.

There is, however, something wonderfully new twenty years later. It is Amazon. Through its platform, it is now possible to make this manual readily available internationally. It is still relevant, and the only changes in this 3rd printing are the cleaning up of some poor spelling and sentence structures through new technological advancements. Perhaps this time around it will serve as the impetus for fine-tuning the methodology and then finally standardizing the methodology wherever parenting capacity assessments are done.

Alexander T. Polgar, Ph.D.
2019, Hamilton, Ontario

PROLOGUE

"You will observe with concern how long a useful truth may be known and exist, before it is generally received and practised on."

Benjamin Franklin

For a long time, I have been fascinated by Hans Christian Andersen's fairy tale about the Emperor's New Clothes. I am also fascinated by the play of children who can create, using the simplest of objects, fanciful, intriguing and engaging games. I am fascinated by the virtually unspoken manner in which children can share their imaginative play, easily fancying things to be different from what they are, joyfully and co-operatively entertaining themselves for hours on end. I have been even more fascinated and intrigued by the collusion that exists amongst adults pretending how magnificent the Emperor's New Clothes are and being quite convinced that, should they speak otherwise, it would be to their dire distress, if not demise. Initially, since English is not my first language, I attributed my failure to understand to my own shortcomings. I either became discouraged or resolved to work harder so I could have the same level of comprehension as my peers. I do not recall exactly when it dawned on me that we were all, more or less, on the same level, struggling to understand concepts, systems and the process of synthesizing information into something that was useful. When I discovered this commonality, it became liberating for me to ask questions, seek clarification and explanation. I did this in person and I did this in academic fashion through research and experimentation. By natural inclination, I was leery of all concepts, especially once I recognized that even the most common ones were differentially understood and used by similarly trained professionals. Recognizing this as a reality served to produce in me a firm resolve to employ practical language that described in qualitative and quantitative terms what I was expressing in person or in document form. Admittedly, this has often led to verbose communications, but hopefully also useful ones that produced an understanding that was intended.

When I started doing Parenting Capacity Assessments, I was not shy to ask to see an example of a "state of the art" report. This was never forthcoming. I was also not shy to ask for a definition of what constitutes a Parenting Capacity Assessment. This, too, was not forthcoming in any meaningful way. It should be acknowledged, however, that there were some guidelines and general schemes produced by courageous groups of individuals from time to time, each, for various reasons, never really accepted as a standard methodology to be generally adopted. I systematically attacked the problem in the only way I knew how: acknowledging that to do this competently required research, and the creation and application of a methodology that was, first and foremost, logical and informed by "state of the art" knowledge concerning human development and functioning.

During most of my almost thirty-year career as a Mental Health practitioner, I have been regularly involved in the preparation of forensic assessments. This experience taught me that all offenders had longstanding histories of dysfunctionalities of varying severity. While I have always believed in, and found empirical support for, natural innate propensities to be significant variables in human growth, development and functioning, environmental circumstances, in my experience, were always far greater determinants of an individual's self-actualization than any other factor.

In conducting forensic assessments, I also became exquisitely aware that any and all behaviours can only be understood in context. Without the contextual component, the interpretation of any phenomenon I knew to be extremely limited in every respect. In my seeking a contextual understanding, the personal histories of individuals invariably revealed horrific childhood experiences proportional to the degree of their adult dysfunctionalities (e.g., criminal offences). I have never encountered a case in which the etiology of an adult's problem could not be traced to disturbed early experiences, most notably events that occurred during the most crucial formative stage of development in that person's life. Often, especially with the most horrific forensic cases, I wondered and asked "where were the adults when the atrocities were being committed against the person when he was a child?" How could adults be oblivious to the pain and suffering of the child during his time of limited or protracted victimization? Where was the other parent? Where were the neighbours, the teachers, the clergy, or any other adult who had some contact, even if only in passing, with a family where there was one or more children in need? On the rare occasions when I actually looked for historical information one or two decades old, the result was always a stonewalling of my efforts.

Against my better judgment, and because of my complete and utterly profound disagreement with the application of an adversarial process where the welfare of children is concerned, reluctantly agreed from time to time to conduct what are archaically referred to as "Custody and Access Assessments". Instead of producing reports that pronounced one combatant as the Custodial Parent (winner) and the other as the Access Parent (loser), in my reports I talked about Parenting Plans determined by the circumstances, strengths and weaknesses of the individuals involved. In spite of the escalating acceptance of this approach in a variety of jurisdictions and among a growing number of Mental Health professionals, my approach was met with considerable resistance, sometimes from the bench and often from the lawyers representing the parents.

For over a decade in Canada, "no fault divorce" has been in effect circumventing tardy and protracted efforts to blame one or the other for the demise of a marriage. Certainly, the Family Law Reform Act had a deleterious financial impact on private investigators in pursuit of surreptitious photos of romantic or sexual liaisons. These were presented as evidence of blame and as a rationale for the offending partner being worthy of some punitive measure imposed by the Court. In spite of advances in this respect, there is a tenacious resistance by the legal profession to relinquish totally the adversarial component inherent when a family unit breaks down. Throwing gasoline on a fire, especially when the combatants are in a heightened emotional state with diminished rational capacities, is not at all difficult. Unfortunately, many Mental Health practitioners become inadvertent abettors of acrimony, co-opted into a system that is incompatible with the basic tenets of ethical conduct and moral principles. Whether co-opted or not, Mental Health practitioners willing to conduct so-called "Custody and Access Assessments" constitute a small number of select individuals. They invariably have a waiting period as long as six to nine months before they can begin a new referral. Time to complete an assessment may take as long, if not longer, in many instances.

Frustrated, disillusioned and constantly having to resolve the Emperor's New Clothes paradigm in my mind, I had absolutely no interest in expanding my practice into the domain of child welfare, although each year I became increasingly more convinced that remedial intervention with adults is a poor use of scarce resources that could be better and more cost-effectively utilized in preventative measures.

My involvement in conducting Parenting Capacity Assessments began with a benign, friendly conversation with a senior Children's Aid manager. Our conversation regarding the plight of children eventually escalated from a reiteration of my often-asked question "Where were the adults?" to a challenge to me to become a responsible adult (professional): the kind I had been asking about when wondering how it is possible to perpetrate abuse on a child without someone intervening. Reluctantly and with a great deal of misgiving, I agreed to conduct a "few" Parenting Capacity Assessments.

My first task was to determine what exactly constitutes a Parenting Capacity Assessment. This practical manual represents the results of my literature research, personal communications and review of Parenting Capacity Assessments reports prepared by clinics, as well as by Mental Health private practitioners. I also reviewed the efforts of committees and professional organizations with respect to what invariably were described as "guidelines" for conducting Parenting Capacity Assessments.

This practical manual is not intended to be a guide. It is intended to be a user-friendly prescribed methodology. A template to be used persistently, its focus is on protecting a child's right to optimal growth and development accepted as a universal principle that applies in all jurisdictions where there is a socially mandated Child Welfare Agency. As such, the methodology is intended to be a template relevant to any jurisdiction in any country where child welfare laws are in existence.

Use of the template is intended to give both the novice and the seasoned Mental Health practitioner the confidence to become involved in this area of practice: an area of practice which is in vital need of courageous, competent Mental Health practitioners committed to ethical conduct based on moral principles. At least in theory, this prescribed method should also protect you from becoming easily co-opted by an adversarial legal system.

For those already conducting Parenting Capacity Assessments, working toward standardization through this prescribed methodology hopefully will make sense, as well as help to improve the data collection and analysis on which conclusions and recommendations of profound consequence are based.

While it is inevitable that both the novice and the seasoned practitioner will impart their personal touch to the prescribed methodology and, indeed, through this effect improvements; hopefully the integrity of the method will remain. This is imperative for establishing an international acceptance of a standard format, albeit constantly evolving and improving over time. It would not be unreasonable to make the analogy that this prescribed methodology represents the clinical use of a standardized instrument. Once developed, standardized instruments invariably evolve but essentially relieve most practitioners from the burden of reinventing the wheel, freeing them instead to develop the skill with which they use the standardized instrument creatively, scientifically and with increasing competence for the purpose it was intended.

In all honesty my objective in writing this practical manual is to entice, encourage, or otherwise convince more Mental Health practitioners to become involved in this area of ever-increasing need. Not only is there an exponential growth in the population of children at risk but also an increasing acceptance and recognition of the absolute need to intervene in a child's best interest during the first two to three years of life. There is an emerging professional and general consensus that the formative stage in a child's life is the most powerful determinant of development, success, quality of life and contribution to the human condition.

My encouragement of colleagues to become involved in my practice conducting Parenting Capacity Assessments was greeted with polite but firm refusal. The primary reason for their unwillingness was described as an absence of will to become involved in an adversarial system with each case potentially going to trial. While all areas of clinical mental health practice are potentially litigious, admittedly child welfare is more so. The refusal to become involved, therefore, is quite probably based on a fear of the unknown and a belief that this is a highly specialized area of practice. Reading and applying this practical manual is intended to dispel this myth and impress upon practitioners that their clinical assessment skills, when formatted by the template of this method, will make a profound contribution to stemming the exponentially growing tide of children at risk.

There is an ulterior motive to my interest in increasing the number of Mental Health professionals in this vitally important area of practice. The more professionals are involved, the less likely the legal system will be able to co-opt them by diverting their attention from the content of a report to a preoccupation with the potential for impeachment of their professional credibility based on methodological criticisms. The tactic of isolating the practitioner is relatively simple in the absence of standardization in conducting Parenting Capacity Assessments. Standardization in analytic method and report format, especially as an increasing number of Mental Health professionals adopt it, will create support for the independence and professionalism of all Parenting Capacity Assessors.

Finally, this Manual represents an independent work not sanctioned by any organization or credentializing body. It has not been influenced or mandated by any other agenda than mine. I have tried to candidly describe my motives and rationale, as well as my biases. Admittedly, at first glance, it would be easy to attribute to cynicism some of my views, which I prefer to characterize as realism acquired through persistent reflection on experiences. While I have not stated it so far, I affirm that I remain eternally optimistic that most people will rise to the occasion and strive to do what is ethical: preferring moral principles over a rationale of situationally determined convenience. The field of Child Welfare could and will benefit profoundly by the infusion of an expanding, intellectually rich, morally principled array of Mental Health practitioners. Practitioners who are aware of the risks and who are unwilling to succumb to the insidious socialization that comes from constant involvement in a system that is essentially adversarial in nature. Unco-opted and uncompromised, the Mental Health practitioner's ability to positively influence an outcome, I anticipate, will explode exponentially and will bring about a long overdue reform in a flawed process.

I will, therefore, not make any disclaimers or feign that this methodology is recommended only as a guideline. On the contrary, my intention is purely to advance this manual as a prescriptive to be applied and improved upon as our knowledge and collective practice wisdom evolve. It is up to you to judge the methodology on its own merit, regardless of whether or not it is sanctioned by any formal organization. While resistance to change is inherent in the human condition, it is more so when it is institutionally based. If, indeed, this methodology becomes accepted as a standard, it will be as a result of you, the Mental Health practitioner, having been convinced and, on the basis of this, being committed to its application.

CONTENTS

PART ONE

Defining the Rationale for the Methodology

Part One in the manual is divided into two separate but vitally related components. It starts with prerequisite information about the magnitude of the problem and the use of the manual as a means with which to bring about timely determinations in the best interest of children at risk. In this context fundamental premises on which the rationale for the Assessment methodology is based are delineated. Part One continues with explaining the rationale for the methodological approach to conducting a Parent Capacity Assessment as well as the organization of the written report.

INTRODUCTION

Scope of the Problem

Media interviews, statements by elected officials and quotations from Child Welfare Executive Directors essentially convey politically correct problem definitions invariably related to diminishing resources. Hidden in this formulation, and implied for anyone wishing to read between the lines, is the reality of an exponential explosion in the population of children at risk and in profound need of intervention. Seldom do the media explore the etiology of exponential growth in the population of children at risk. The reasons are numerous and beyond the scope of this work. Suffice it to say that the reasons as they are elaborated are invariably determined by ideological, religious or political perspectives.

Criminologists with an epidemiological bent for the last decade have conducted extensive actuarial calculations demonstrating the enormous social and financial cost of responding to the escalating dysfunctionalities of children as they grow older. To say the least, this is interesting data that reveals astronomical costs created by a problem that could have been prevented with much less costly and less resource-intense measures. This is not an unusual paradigm and applies to virtually all aspects of life, including physical health and simple maintenance of our automobiles. Expending resources on preventative measures, however, has never been, and is unlikely to be in the near future, an appealing endeavor. It is certainly not associated with the glory and glamour that is inherent in heroic responses to a problem. Moreover, preventative measures, with the exception of promoting empirically unsupported deterrence initiatives, seldom, if ever, garner political votes, let alone justify the allocation of tax dollars. Some also argue that simply throwing money at an old problem seldom, if ever, produces a solution, especially if it entails doing more of the same. Therefore, to allocate increasingly more financial resources, as for example to diminish caseload responsibilities, is resisted by funders and enlightened agency directors before examining systematically the potential of this tactic to address the obviously escalating demands on Child Welfare agencies.

We must remind mindful of the Emperor's New Clothes paradigm: reality must be acknowledge, regardless of how politically incorrect it may be viewed in many circles. The fact is that the number of children bearing children is exploding exponentially into numbers impossible to accurately and directly track in a timely fashion. At best, only data one, two or more years old are available. Data which fail to reveal the magnitude of the problem by the time the statistics are made available. For example, in 1998, the Children's Defense Fund reported that three years previously in the United States, over a half-million babies were born to teenage girls. Just over 12,000 of these mothers were younger than fifteen. More often than not, children identified at risk are the offspring of teenage mothers who themselves are the product of teenage, or in many cases, even younger parents. These same ill-prepared young mothers tragically continue to procreate well past their teenage years even as the fate of their one or more apprehended children remains unresolved. The intergenerational perpetuation of family legacies is tragic evidence of a failure to intervene in the cycle. In fact, the statistics and clinical experience reveal the normalization of legacies whereby each successive generation of unwed, ill-prepared and dysfunctional mothers bear more children than the previous generation. In almost every case, by the time decisive action is taken with respect to an identified child at risk, much damage already has been done. The formative stage in a child's life is very brief. While legislation in various jurisdictions acknowledges this, the ponderous, painstakingly slow legal process fails to implement the principle underlying the legislation prescribing timely action on the child's behalf. It is the norm rather than the exception that decisive intervention may take as long as three or more years to occur as a result of a contested application for a Parenting Capacity Assessment, a period of time to begin the process, an equally if not more protracted period of time to actually produce a Parenting Capacity Assessment, postponements with respect to bringing the matter to trial and scheduling difficulties with respect to actually having the trial.

It would be tantamount to embracing social constructivism if we were, as a society, to pursue the prescription of who should or should not bear children. Let us hope we will never regress to such base social interference as has periodically marked the history of mankind. An alternative is to advocate fundamental and thereby potentially powerful preventative strategies whereby children through primary and secondary education are exposed to experiences that promote healthy relationships, responsible procreation and a desire to develop knowledge and skills pertaining to parenting, recognizing it to be an onerous responsibility that entails promoting the optimal growth and development of a child.

In the interim, this prescribed, standardized methodology for conducting a Parenting Capacity Assessment is intended to address a limited, albeit significant, reason for the explosion in the number of children at risk. The methodology is designed and intended to better direct Child Welfare Agencies and Parenting Capacity Assessors with respect to the assistance provided to families in crisis, or alternatively enhance the timeliness with which definitive action is taken in the best interest of a child.

While the problem of children at risk is exacerbated by an often protracted adversarial judicial process, it is difficult, if not impossible, to imagine that the judicial system will willingly or readily relinquish its involvement in Child Welfare issues. Especially an adversarial process that has come to be perceived by many (at least in part as a result of socialization) as justifiable. This fundamental social problem will be elaborated in a separate companion publication. Suffice it to say, that eventually, as was accomplished by the no-fault divorce legislation, it will be the exception rather than the rule that Child Welfare cases will require a protracted, adversarial process before definitive action can be taken. Standardizing the methodology is submitted to be a essential prerequisite step toward achieving timely determinations when children are at risk.

Organization of the Manual

This manual has been organized into two parts. Part One constitutes the rationale and elaboration of the what, why and how pertaining to every aspect of conducting a Parenting Capacity Assessment and preparing the actual report. It begins with the premises that are the basis of each assertion in this manual. The premises support assertions that are then presented in a manner as to convey both their relevance and empirically supported validity (truthfulness) with the view of enhancing your confidence in the application of this methodology.

The rationale and elaboration provided in the first part of this manual would be far too much to include in an actual report.

Part Two of the manual constitutes a report that is a composite case example. In the interest of standardization, the prescribed format requires that you use, verbatim, the non-case-specific, generic introductions to each category of analysis in the report. I suspect it will be a long time before judges tire of reading the preambles. In the event that this desirable state occurs, my preference would be to continue applying the format, leaving it to a judge's discretion to read or not read the generic parts of the report. Furthermore, insofar as the generic preamble will likely change over the course of time and use, incorporating the latest research findings and your own fine-tuning of the information presentation, in the interest of standardization which this effort is intended to achieve, the preamble to each category of analyses should never be excluded from any report.

The composite case example in the second part of this manual is organized to establish the interconnectedness of the various findings produced by the methodology, as well as to contextualize the case in a logically coherent fashion. Specifically, the findings are presented in a format that constitutes a logical argument, with one, and in most cases several, findings in support of the formulation and concomitant recommendations under four separate but related categories of analysis.

How to Use This Manual

Time is always of the essence for every practitioner. The more seasoned we become, the more we are inclined to rely on unconscious/automatic thought processes to guide our data collection, analysis and formulations. More often than not, these tactics serve us well.

Given the enormous complexity of the issues, the interconnectedness of the information and most importantly mindful of the one for whom the report is ultimately intended, a non-mental health professional, a judge, it is imperative at least initially that you approach the task of conducting a Parenting Capacity Assessment in a deliberate, systematic manner.

The manual will be most useful to you if you first familiarize yourself with Part One. The next and ultimately the most productive strategy will be to review sequentially each section in the first part with the corresponding sections in the second part.

In the second part of this manual, the rationale is provided for each category of analysis that is of tolerable length for readers of your report. You may, however, choose to elaborate or be more concise to suit your own personal style. Notwithstanding this discretionary prerogative, to reiterate, too much variance among Parenting Capacity Assessors will seriously compromise the move to standardization of the methodology and report format. I would, therefore, urge you to keep the changes to a bare minimum, recognizing that it is better to leave the reader with the discretion as to the care with which the rationale is read than to pre-empt this prerogative. At the risk of sounding sophomoric, experience, personal and with clinical associates, dictates that I urge you to spend time producing an outline before composing your Parenting Capacity Assessment report case-specific formulations. Eventually, in time and with practice, the need for this may diminish, but not likely entirely. Ultimately, this practice, instead of being tedious, will save you time and effort and most importantly make the difference between a comprehensive and thoughtful report and one that enumerates a seemingly unrelated myriad of findings that do not clearly reveal the basis of your conclusions and recommendations.

It is insufficient, for example, to simply provide factual information in the background history of the individual being assessed. This methodology requires that you make connections between an individual's history and current state of functioning with a view to explaining not only the etiology of worrisome findings but also the chronicity and thereby the amenability of certain conditions to intervention. The delay in which changes can be expected is always a crucial consideration, especially given the brief window of opportunity defined by the most crucial formative stage in a child's life. Therefore, while a potential primary caregiver being assessed could benefit from intervention, background history information will serve as a powerful indicator of the time frame in which gains can be accomplished.

In my experience, even seasoned Mental Health practitioners benefit greatly from regularly developing outlines prior to embarking on the task of composing a report. Using the presentations-that-work format which will be documented subsequently under the four categories of analysis will ensure that your conclusion and concomitant recommendations are clearly supported by findings. In so doing, it will be impossible for you to ever make the unforgivable, although all too familiar, proclamation "in my opinion". Instead, any conclusion and formulation will be supported not by your status as an assessor but by your demonstrated competence in collecting and interpreting valid and reliable data and reporting your findings as evidence in support of your formulations.

Your outline will serve as the backbone of your report. This can then be enhanced by the prose in which you write the assessment, making it easily read and understood by the non-mental health professional judge.

In a final note, I would urge you to curtail the need to distinguish yourself in favour of strengthening the position of the Parenting Capacity Assessor. This will be best achieved by adopting this format. Moreover, direct benefits can be derived from standardizing the methodology and reporting format. Regardless of your expertise, competence and seniority, your efforts will be better utilized if they are focused on data collection and analysis, thereby ensuring that every conclusion and concomitant recommendation is clearly and comprehensively supported, leaving nothing to be read between the lines. Do not suppose that the generic preamble of the prescribed report format are best postponed until you are giving your evidence and supporting your conclusions in court. Making your report as complete and as solid as possible will hasten the conclusion of the proceedings. It behooves us, as Mental Health practitioners, not to be co-opted into a protracted adversarial process but instead to work towards what we know is in the short-and long-term best interest of a child.

A Word About References

Part One of this manual is followed by references cited in the preceding text. The references are by no means exhaustive.

While the cited references provide what I believe is sufficient and go beyond simple orientation, it is strongly recommended that you review in entirety at least one source publication under each category of analysis. The objective is to further enhance your confidence and the authority with which you formulate conclusions and recommendations. Once you have completed this task, my next recommendation is to structure yourself to ensure that on an annual basis, you review the most current "state-of-the-art" information under each category of analysis. This, too, will not only ensure your currency but also facilitate the continued development of your confidence as an assessor.

It is difficult to recommend one work above another. While continued innovations and refinements will be reported indefinitely, the discriminations most often likely will be of an academic, as opposed to a practical, interest Nevertheless, it is imperative that you confirm this for yourself regularly.

The second part of this manual, which is the composite case example, is also followed by a list of references cited in the actual report. Some of the references cited will be the same as those cited in the first part of this manual. The reason for listing them separately is to simplify your task with the view to channeling your energies into data analysis, formulation of conclusions and recommendations, and reporting these in an optimally comprehensive manner.

Legislation

The existence of a Child Welfare agency in a jurisdiction is considered to be indicative of a collective commitment to protecting the inalienable rights of children. The basis for such a commitment is universally grounded in fundamental givens. While the following is in no way presented as an exhaustive list, the existence of a Child Welfare agency implies an acknowledgment of children as the current culture's hope for the future and an investment in facilitating the optimal actualization of each child as essential for optimizing the collective's quality of life. As opposed to properties to be done with as a proprietor parent pleases, in societies where Child Welfare agencies exist, children are viewed as responsibilities that are onerous and should not be lightly undertaken. Moreover, as a dependent, evolving entity, a child's right to optimally realize his or her potential is considered to be of a higher order than parents' competing rights to be in custody and control of their offspring. In support for the existence of Child Welfare agencies, there is an emerging body of financial actuarial information that clearly demonstrates the enormous escalating social and financial costs posed by troubled youth. According to this line of investigation, there is absolutely no doubt that the earlier intervention occurs, the earlier expert and financial resources are provided, the more likely a child is to develop to his or her full positive potential. Clearly, the converse is also true, a fact that certainly explains the exponential growth in the number of child welfare cases and the demands placed on Child Protection workers.

Legislation is now also reflecting (both generally and specifically) the even more fundamental reality that timely intervention is absolutely necessary to safeguard the best interest of the child. The formative stage in a child's development is considered to be the most crucial time in life and a far more powerful determinant of future functioning than any genetic or innate potentialities with which the child is born. Moreover, there is an emerging consensus that this crucial formative stage in a child's life is far briefer than previously thought. Most scholars in the field of human growth and development now believe that life enduring characterological traits are fixed by the time a child is three years old. Furthermore, there are equally compelling findings with respect to brain development, namely that environmental conditions are the essential determinants of the child's brain development from birth to three years. This will be discussed later in this manual. Suffice it to say that these facts have culminated in legislation that is intended to impact on policy and practice.

In many jurisdictions, legislation affecting child welfare has included neglect, as well as abuse, as grounds for intervention by a Child Welfare Agency. In many jurisdictions, Child Protection workers are required by law to follow new standardized reporting systems intended to ensure children are protected. The standardized documentation required in many jurisdictions includes the use of risk assessment tools designed to ensure that Protection Workers explore all aspects of a case.

The legislative requirements as reflected by the prescribed use of risk assessment tools by Child Protection workers recognize, however, the reality that risk is not and cannot be determined by any single factor. Invariably, risk is determined by a systemic interaction between several factors. Many scholars, most notably Miller, et al. (1988) have underscored this perspective by identifying that4 risk can only be measured through a careful fluid holistic consideration of many interconnected factors". This prescribed methodology reflects both the legislation and state-of-the-art thinking by not only considering four categories of investigation, but also the dynamic interaction between them in the context of the assessed person's history.

Standardized Instruments

It stands to reason that confidence in conclusions and concomitant recommendations is exponentially increased by not only the number, but by the kind of findings that support them. Some clinicians rely essentially on clinical interviews as the basis of their formulations. Others rely primarily on the interpretation of a variety of standardized instruments. This observation is admittedly an exaggerated example of extremes along a continuum intended to make the point that neither does justice to a task that potentially can have profound consequences on a child's future. Under each category of analysis, specific tools (standardized instruments) are recommended to enhance and augment clinical formulations. The objective is to promote a balanced methodology with respect to data collection and, more importantly, analyses and interpretation that synthesizes all that is known about a case. Formulations that are based on a synthesis of information are your responsibility as an assessor. It is not the responsibility of a non-mental health practitioner, namely the judge who will make the ultimate determination about a case. The challenge is how convincingly you can synthesize the information available to you; a challenge that, at least in part, is determined by your approach to data collection.

Quantification

It is important to keep in mind a distinction between a Parenting Capacity Assessment and a Risk Assessment Scales, even those legislatively mandated to be used by Child Protection workers. First of all, many Risk Assessment Scales are not empirically tested, let alone validated. Their use is essentially a method that structures the assessment made by a Child Protection worker using a pre-determined list of potentially worrisome areas in the manner in which the child is being raised. Risk Assessment Scales can also be classified on a continuum of scientific merit, some better constructed than others. For example, the Levels of Supervision Inventory (LSI) used with correctional clients has both acceptable reliability and validity standards in spite of the fact that the ratings require the subjective judgment of the assessor (Andrews and Bonta, 1995). Recognizing that assessors who use the LSI have varying levels of skills and experience, the instrument is constructed in such a manner as to minimize the confounding influences of these factors. While not without limitations, the LSI as a risk indicator is widely accepted as a useful tool in the management of correctional clients. This is encouraging insofar as it establishes the possibility that the findings of a Parenting Capacity Assessment may eventually be quantified with criterion levels that will define the nature of a determination required in the best interest of a child. As it stands now, the weighting attributed to any single or combination of findings under the four categories of analyses and pertaining to the background history of the person being assessed is a clinical judgment required by the assessor. Your clinical judgment as the Assessor is especially challenging when not all findings point to one outcome as in the best interest of a child. Nevertheless, you will be required to make a decision and recommendation that resolves the contradictory findings. To do so, complex mental processes will be required which must be operationalized. Taking these processes out of the realm of "intuition," will not only increase the confidence level in your formulations and concomitant recommendations, but will eventually lead to a degree of scientific rigor that can justify the quantification of a Parenting Capacity Assessment finding.

We are committed to such a quantification endeavor and invite all interested practitioners to make contributions to this process by whatever means available. Our vision is that the elaborate comprehensive assessment report will eventually include a rating system that is reliable and valid and of further assistance to making a determination that is ultimately the responsibility of a judge who is a non-mental health practitioner.

Immigrant Families

This prescribed standardized methodology applies to all Child Welfare cases, including children at risk in immigrant families. When a child is identified as "at risk" and the risk is substantiated, the fact that such a determination is in part or in whole attributed to cultural differences or the trauma associated with immigration is only relevant with respect to the nature of the intervention that is judged to be necessary by the findings of the Parenting Capacity Assessment. The same issue of timeliness is germane and will be determined by the nature of the family's "adjustment/socialization" problems and the availability of facilitative resources.

The salient issue in a case that involves an immigrant family cannot be, and must not be, the allowances often made with respect to parenting practices, regardless of how acceptable and normalized they were in the families' place of origin. In some societies, child labor is acceptable, as well as the mutilation of female infants, among many other practices that are completely unacceptable in jurisdictions where Child Welfare Agencies exist.

Immigrant families with children at risk, therefore, are subject to the same scrutiny as all other families. Support of, and value placed on, cultural diversity does not include parenting practices which contravene Child Welfare legislation in a particular jurisdiction.

Immigrant families pose a specific clinical challenge for an assessor with respect to the skills and sensitivity required to obtain information on which to base formulations and recommendations. Apart from such considerations, the Parenting Capacity Assessor need not be an expert in the area of immigration- associated adjustment problems insofar as the task requires identification, not intervention, by the Mental Health practitioner.

Language and literacy competence must be taken into special consideration with immigrant families. A general rule of thumb is that immigrants from non-English speaking countries, after five years of work and living experience in their new, adopted country, can be in most cases administered standardized instruments which are usually written at a grade five to eight level. In jurisdictions in which there is a disproportionate number of immigrant Child Welfare cases, the assessor would be prudent to seek training in communication skills with people whose first language is not English. Such training is usually provided to police and social assistance workers and could be of benefit to both the seasoned and novice Mental Health practitioner in this area of practice.

Logic and Critical Thinking Revisited

Invariably, both the novice and seasoned practitioner, in a relatively brief period of time, integrate the formal principles of critical thinking and logic into an unconscious process which is automatically applied, most of the time. The operative term is "most of the time". As such, and given the profound impact a Parenting Capacity Assessment potentially has on the destiny of a child, it is worthwhile to revisit briefly these fundamental principles that are consistently applied in our work as Mental Health practitioners. In Appendix A there is a brief review of the essential principles involved in critical thinking, as well as in formulating a logical argument. Should this brief review prove to be insufficient, I would strongly urge that you revisit more comprehensively what for most of us was undergraduate course material likely taken without full appreciation of how invaluable these skills would prove to be as the nature of our work became more complex and of greater impact on the lives of others.

CHAPTER 1

Defining the Basic Premises Applied in Conducting Parenting Capacity Assessments

"How seldom we hear of any high or holy preparation for the office of parenthood! Here, in the most momentous act of life, all is left to chance. Man and woman, intelligent and prudent, in all other directions, seem to exercise no forethought here, but hand down their individual and family idiosyncrasies in the most reckless manner."

Elizabeth Cady Stanton (1858-1902) American Suffragist

Statements that are made as evidence in support of an assertion are called "premises". Insofar as there are no set number of premises that every argument must have, practical considerations dictate how many are provided. To produce an exhaustive list would simply be impossible. The premises for each assertion are intended to convey the underlying rationale and more importantly are intended to be sufficiently convincing to elicit confidence in the use of this methodology.

Defining What Constitutes a Premise

In the language of formal logic, this manual represents an argument supported by a number of explicit premises (facts) and implicit premises (facts) that will be made explicit under this subheading. This manual also represents a group of statements standing in relation to each other. There are several levels of relationships and all are associated with each other in a logically coherent manner. Each argument made in this manual constitutes one statement or a conclusion. A conclusion can also be thought of as an assertion that the reader is intended to accept, believe or otherwise "buy into". There are several levels of assertions. The first and most prominent assertion is that this prescribed methodology should be accepted as a standard in conducting Parenting Capacity Assessments and that the pursuit of standardization will ultimately benefit children in need of intervention. There are several related sub-assertions, most notably the four categories of analysis. As assertions, they represent an argument that this is a sound, empirically based rational approach to conducting a Parenting Capacity Assessment. The main and sub-assertions of this manual, according to the rules of logic, are supported by one or more premises (statements which are presented as facts relevant to the specific assertion being made).

For the purpose of clarity, this section in the manual constitutes a list of premises that are the fundamental building blocks of the prescribed Parenting Capacity Assessment methodology and report format. They are listed separately and, in fact, represent in themselves an argument insofar as each premise is presented as an assertion followed by supportive evidence to convince you of its "truthfulness". The task, therefore, for you the user of this methodology, is to evaluate the extent to which you agree with the relevance of a premise and the extent to which the premise supports an assertion.

Your task, is to critically evaluate the following list of premises. First you must ask yourself "Do believe the premise to be true?" Second, you must ask yourself "Are the premises relevant to the assertion?" If I have presented the material adequately on both accounts, your answer will be in the affirmative. Even if you are not totally convinced on each account, a critical examination can have a profoundly positive impact with respect to raising to a level of consciousness issues previously not examined. A critical analysis may also produce insights that confirm a premise previously not considered or generate an alternative better premise than that which is presented. Regardless of the outcome, such constructive critical analysis can only lead to greater confidence in your ability to conduct a Parenting Capacity Assessment.

It would have been impossible to order the premises in any hierarchical fashion. Depending on the specific, unique aspects of a case, emphasis and importance of the various premises are likely to vary, some being more important for one case and less important for another. Suffice it to say that the list represents relevant facts which, I believe, support the approach to conducting Parenting Capacity Assessments and give me the confidence to prescribe it as a standard methodology regardless of jurisdiction and the specifics of the law (rules) that apply to protecting a child's inalienable right to optimal growth and development.

First Premise: Who Will Read the Report?

The primary intended reader of a Parenting Capacity Assessment is a non-mental health professional, specifically a judge.

Although the intended reader of a Parenting Capacity Assessment is a non-mental health professional, Child Welfare Protection workers, supervisors and managers will be the first to review the report. Nevertheless, it is incumbent on an assessor to identify and present in the report the theoretical basis used for conducting the assessment. This will serve to ensure that all readers have a shared understanding of the rationale for the methodology, as well as a common orientation to the relationship among the findings, conclusions and recommendations.

This approach prescribes, therefore, that the theoretical basis for the methodology be made explicit and be included in each and every report. Even in small jurisdictions where the same child welfare workers and judge receive the report, at worst, the theoretical content of the document may be skipped over after a while, but will always be on record in case of some unforeseen future event

The reason such elaboration is prescribed is because a Parenting Capacity Assessment constitutes a significant body of information that will be used in determining a child's disposition. A disposition that, in spite of a range of variations, either removes a child from a primary caregiver or allows a child to remain in his or her care and control. The decision is an onerous and complex undertaking which ultimately a judge is sanctioned legislatively to do: a judge who by training and experience is a lawyer either promoted or elected to the bench based on a variety of considerations. None of the criteria include any consideration with respect to training or experience as a Mental Health professional.

In spite of this reality, assessments prepared by Mental Health professionals are most often written as if they were intended to be read by other Mental Health professionals who are assumed (most often unjustifiably) to attribute the same meaning to Mental Health jargon, especially diagnostic labels. Moreover, reports are written in such a manner as to leave undefined the assessor's rationale for the methodology and the literature that supports the approach taken. The absolute worst examples of this type of report writing are instances where "opinions" are rendered without supporting evidence beyond the "credentials" of the assessor.

Some assessors unwittingly become a part of the problem that negatively impacts on a child's welfare by taking the position that elaborations are to be provided in trial during cross-examination. In so doing, these assessors contribute to unnecessary delays in reaching a disposition with respect to the child's status. Moreover, such a practice contributes to the need for a trial (to ascertain the rationale of the assessment method) as opposed to promoting the possibility of a timely settlement through the comprehensiveness of a report. Often a comprehensive, well-prepared report where all that is relevant is articulated can serve as an impetus for all parties to reach a resolution without the costly and time-consuming initiation of a trial process. A well-written, comprehensive report also can be invaluable to a pre-trial judge in jurisdictions where such practices are in place. Often a comprehensive report can be a significant factor in a pre-trial judge recommending a settlement that can be timely and consistent with acting in the child's best interests, especially if that child is in the most crucial formative stage of life.

In contrast, traditional assessment report formats often inadvertently circumvent a child's right to optimal growth and development by obstructing that which would produce timely determinations. Such reports abet the judicial process in taking priority over the provision of timely intervention critical at any stage in a child's life, but especially more so during the formative one to three years.

Unfortunately, judges too often allow their expertise in jurisprudence to be generalized unjustifiably to areas outside of their knowledge base. Indeed, they loathe to acknowledge not being able to discern the rationale for the assessor's methodology or, for that fact, the meaning and relevance of Mental Health jargon, especially diagnostic labels. Instead, all too often, they make attributions about appearances (resumes), degrees, credentials, and years of experience and, on the basis of these, accepting an opinion and recommendation at face value. This practice perpetuates the writing of reports that fall far short of the potential of which the assessor is capable.

In brief, given that a Parenting Capacity Assessment is conducted in a child's best interest and has profound potential consequences, it demands the same scientific rigor as a journal article or a dissertation.

Second Premise: The Meaning of Capacity

By definition, a Parenting Capacity Assessment focuses on parents. While it is conducted in the best interest of a child, it is not about assessing the child. Assessing a child with respect to developmental delays or special needs requires specific expertise. Once a child's special needs are determined, the question remains the same: what is the primary caregiver's capacity to optimally parent that child?

It is, therefore, imperative that a clear distinction be made between parenting ability and capacity.

The impetus for conducting a Parenting Capacity Assessment, is almost always founded in a perceived absence of ability. Ability is defined as existing parenting knowledge, skills and competence in their persistent application. Moreover, parenting ability is a constantly evolving process in response to the developmentally evolving needs of the child. Existing parenting ability in most cases predicts that the parent will continue to develop his or her abilities. Prediction in this respect is based on the empirically recognized reality that past behaviour predicts future behaviour unless there is a profound or significant intervening event that has disrupted the established pattern of functioning. Therefore, competent parents at any given time were also highly likely to have been competent before and are equally likely to continue to develop knowledge and skills and apply them in a predictably effective manner.

Such parents are not the subjects of Parenting Capacity Assessments.

The subjects of Parenting Capacity Assessments are individuals who, for a myriad of reasons, lack ability. The effect of such deficits accumulate and reach a critical mass that precipitates intervention by a Child Welfare agency. This most often occurs early in the life of a child. There is an increasingly emerging trend to apprehend a child at birth. The actions are precipitated by a Child Welfare Agency risk analysis that defines criterion levels of concerns as to justify intrusive interventions in a child's best interest. The reason for apprehending a child at birth is a conclusion that the parent is significantly unlikely to have the ability to meet the primary needs of the infant and, therefore, that the child is concluded to be at fatal risk.

These are the cases that become subjects of a Parenting Capacity Assessment.

Capacity defined, therefore, is an individual's potential to acquire parenting knowledge and skills. Of equal importance in determining capacity is the parent's potential with respect to applying, with predictable competence, the knowledge and skills required to optimally promote a child's development at each phase. A determination with respect to learning and applying knowledge and skills is based on separate considerations. Essentially, learning is a function of cognitive intelligence and application a function of emotional intelligence. The potential of individuals in these respects are influenced by many factors and as such are essential to determine. For example a potential for learning may be obstructed by 'emotional' factors and a potential for application by limitations in cognitive intelligence.

A Parenting Capacity Assessment constitutes a probability determination with respect to a primary caregiver's potential to learn that which is required and a probability determination with respect to the mental and emotional functioning of prospective caregivers known to be correlated positively with the application of what they learn. A probability determination is also required with respect to the assessed individual's capacity to relate to and establish a positive social support network consistent with that which is known as conducive to the actualization of parenting potential.

Furthermore, while a Parenting Capacity Assessment is to determine a primary caregiver's potential, it should also be recognized that the potential must be in relation to the needs of a child. Assessing children, especially those with special needs, requires an area of expertise best left to specialists in this field. Identifying special needs children is extremely relevant insofar as even greater parenting capacity is required in such circumstances. Tenacity, high frustration tolerance and creativity are a few of the attributes that are especially important to successfully face the challenges posed by a special needs child.

Whether an individual's capacity/potential is absent and compensatory strategies are required or whether an individual's capacity/potential is obstructed by any myriad of conditions, ultimately the issue in each and every Assessment will be the timeliness with which discernable improvements can be realized to of benefit to a child at risk.

Third Premise: The Need for Autonomous Objectivity

A Parenting Capacity Assessment is not a "rubber stamping" of a Child Welfare Agency's decision to implement intrusive measures based on the agency's determination of risk. In spite of the resentment of some Child Welfare workers with respect to having their conclusion and intervention verified, given what is at stake, objective comprehensive methods are an absolute necessity. Moreover, a Parenting Capacity Assessment is not redundant since it goes far beyond that which can be determined by even reliable and valid risk assessment tools.

In most jurisdictions, there is a legislative prescriptive that the application of a principle of least intrusive measures must supersede an intrusive final determination of a child's status. This legislative requirement is based on the tenet that whenever possible, it is in the best interest of children to be parented by biological caregivers. An objective, comprehensive Parenting Capacity Assessment, therefore, is a significant means by which to determine what intervention strategies could be introduced through which parents could be facilitated to actualize their potential. This determination is especially important in light of the fact that, in many cases, the imposition of requirements by a Child Welfare Agency or a court have been unsuccessful. Without a systematic, empirically based problem definition, the individuality of a prospective primary caregiver is lost and the undifferentiated imposition of requirements becomes an act of desperation in lieu of knowing what else to do.

A differential, empirically enhanced formulation that informs intervention not only is not a "rubber stamping" of a Child Welfare Agency's identification of a risk but also can be a significant contribution pertaining to what constitutes relevant intervention through which the best interest of a child can be achieved.

What may appear to be a "rubber stamping" of a Child Welfare Agency conclusion invariably is not. It is not so because an internally logical and coherent methodology produces operational statements rather than the conceptual formulations with which front-line practitioners often function. Notwithstanding the increasing use in a progressively expanding number of jurisdictions, of Risk Assessment Scales, operational statements generated by a Parenting Capacity Assessment (by the fact that they quantify and qualify observable behaviours) are still more reliable and valid indicators on which to base determinations and implement a disposition in a timely manner. Furthermore, while hope can prevail for every individual being assessed, quantified and qualified findings provide more robust information as to how long and with what effort a prospective primary caregiver can be expected to make changes in time to be of benefit, especially for a child in the most crucial formative stage of life. The same can be said for a special needs child or, for that fact, any child at a particular stage of cognitive, emotional and physiological development.

Fourth Premise: The Need for Empirically Informed Intervention

The principle of least intrusive measures, which is a legislative prescriptive in many jurisdictions requires that Child Welfare Agencies make available to parents of children at risk a variety of resources. For a resource to be optimally beneficial, the intervention must be relevant and it must be informed by comprehensive data. Sometimes these resources are offered and utilized voluntarily and, on other occasions, the use of resources are court imposed. Often a Parenting Capacity Assessment referral is preceded by such impositions. The interventions provided by the resources generally can be classified into two broad categories. The first entails clinical/counseling intervention. Most often, however, the imposed requirements entail participation in some learning experience. These intervention strategies assume that the primary caregiver of a child at risk is capable of exercising choices of an order that is required to participate and constructively use that which is offered to them. Alternatively, requirements are imposed by enlightened agencies to ascertain the extent to which a parent can make appropriate choices and act on these in a consistently constructive manner. Furthermore, the imposed requirements especially assume that, that which is learned through didactic instruction will be applied in a predictably consistent and competent manner. A parent's failure to constructively use that which is made available more often than not is interpreted as willful non-compliance and as indicative of escalating risk to a child.

The prescribed Parenting Capacity Assessment methodology, by integrating background information with the findings under the four categories of analysis, is capable of identifying a parent's inadvertent intergenerational perpetuation of dysfunctionalities. For example, by identifying an attachment disorder, the need to compliment with specific expertise existing traditional resources is also defined. The assessment process also can reveal the use of denial as a function of marked cognitive developmental deficits, which can predispose primary caregivers to engage in a vindication oriented acrimonious process rather than in constructive pursuits with which to become better parents. This, too, requires specific expertise to ameliorate.

While a futile approach, a parent's non-compliance is invariably responded to by doing more of the same. That is, imposing further requirements on an individual clearly unable to do that which would alleviate concerns about the person as a parent. An objective, comprehensive Parenting Capacity Assessment, therefore, is also a means by which to better determine what are appropriate intervention strategies, especially in light of the fact that the imposition of traditional requirements has been unsuccessful. Without a systematic, empirically based problem definition, the individuality of the prospective primary caregiver is lost. More importantly, without the objective definition of the problem that prevents the potential primary caregiver from constructively using resources, intervention strategies fail to accomplish what is desired.

Fifth Premise: Maintaining the Integrity of the Methodology

The challenge to maintaining the integrity of the prescribed methodology is to remain unperturbed by the legal strategies and concomitant questions posed by counsel in the employ of a Child Welfare Agency. The questions may be few and concise or many and rambling. Rarely, if ever, are the questions specific to a case. Moreover, rarely, if ever, are the questions informed by sound theory or empirically determined findings pertaining to optimal strategies with which to act in the best interest of a child at risk as a function of primary caregiver dysfunctionalities. Rather, in most instances, the questions posed by counsel in the employ of a Child Welfare Agency are based on legal strategy. The questions are often disjointed, conceptual notions regarding what constitute significant variables in a determination process. Examples of such questions are provided in Appendix A, Part Two of the Manual. A process which, from legal counsel's perspective, is focused on winning a case as opposed to seeking a just resolution between the competing rights of a primary caregiver and the inalienable rights of a child.

Insofar as a Letter of Referral and Terms of Reference (question posed) really cannot be ignored by an assessor, there are limited options available with respect to approaching the task of responding to a Court sanctioned mandate to prepare a Parenting Capacity Assessment. The first tendency for many assessors is to approach the task by responding specifically to the Terms of Reference. In so doing, the assessor's methodology changes from case to case and, to a large extent, is determined by the legal process or, specifically, how counsel for a Child Welfare Agency approaches the task. This may explain why past efforts with respect to defining a methodology for conducting a Parenting Capacity Assessment were invariably developed as guidelines as opposed to as a prescribed format. Furthermore, this likely also explains the relative absence of standardization in the methodology in spite of an obvious and persistently nagging need.

Instead of allowing the referral Terms of Reference to compromise the prescribed methodology, it is far more advisable to deal with the questions posed by counsel to a Child Welfare Agency separately in an appendix. This is the approach that is presented in this manual. Using this tactic, the assessor can prepare concise responses to each question. This will minimize frustrating, often negative reactions to non-case specific, generic or redundant questions and, in general, counsel's rather uninformed approach to pursuing that which is in the child's best interest. The tactic in this manual provide the assessor with a constructive way to respond to all Terms of Reference questions without diverting attention from the real issues. Moreover, by addressing the posed questions in an appendix it is possible to prepare concise responses referring the reader to the body of the report in which elaboration and justification are provided for conclusions and recommendations based on a comprehensive, empirically informed, best practices methodology.

Hopefully, as this prescribed methodology becomes more common and increasingly better understood, eventually all Letters of Referral will pose questions pertaining to the four categories of analysis and the manner in which they are enhanced, elaborated and informed by the background history of the person being assessed.

Exerting energy unnecessarily by reinventing the proverbial methodological wheel in response to the often-frustrating questions posed by legal counsel diverts the assessor's efforts, which would have been better spent on data collection, analysis and interpretation.

This methodology, therefore, is designed to protect the clinical integrity of the assessment process by prescribing a format that is ultimately capable of answering any number of lawyer-posed questions. When lawyers become better informed and pose questions consistent with the four categories of analysis, instead of working at cross purposes, the synergy created will better serve the child in question rather than serving the legal process.

Sixth Premise: Professional Objectivity

In spite of the contradictory conduct of some judges, and in spite of the conduct of legal counsel in the employ of a Child Welfare Agency or in the employ of a parent being assessed, it is imperative that the Mental Health practitioner conducting a Parenting Capacity Assessment be consistently mindful of the reality that the assessment is being prepared for a judge. As such, by agreement and by court appointment, the assessor is a friend of the court. Court-appointed, agreed upon by opposing legal counsel, an assessor is immune from lawsuits launched by discontented subjects of an assessment. This, however, does not generalize to include immunity from scrutiny, initiated by the complaints of a discontented subject of an assessment, by the various credentializing professional bodies to which an assessor may belong. The assessor's defense in such instances can only be grounded in the clear application of a standardized methodology.

The issue of objectivity also is crucial and often obscured by the fact that, in most jurisdictions, Child Welfare Agencies contract with the assessor and are responsible for the fees of the Mental Health practitioner conducting the Parenting Capacity Assessment. Notwithstanding these realities, it is imperative that the assessor be persistently mindful that the primary alliance is to a judge.

The implications, in spite of the often contrary reality, of the fact that an assessor is essentially a friend of the court (there to assist the court, not one or the other side) are profound and must be strictly adhered to. If at the completion of a Parenting Capacity Assessment, opposing counsel are willing to meet with the assessor to review findings, conclusions and recommendations with the view to doing everything possible to reach a timely determination, this is quite acceptable and encouraged. It is, however, totally unacceptable for an assessor to meet separately with either counsel. Equally unacceptable is for an assessor to engage in any trial preparation process with either counsel which, in most cases, entails meeting with the representative of a Child Welfare Agency. Not only will this create a perception of bias, alliance or allegiance, but also will lull the assessor into a false sense that he or she is not alone in an adversarial process; a process that can range in severity from courteous professionalism to an out-and-out degradation and profound assault on the very person of the assessor. The extent to which the acrimony plays itself out along this continuum is determined by the judge in whose court a trial takes place. To a lesser degree, it is also determined by the assessor's accurate perception of the trial process and the functions of all the participants.

It is noteworthy that this premise in the methodology contravenes common practice and, indeed, is contrary to the ways I have sometimes allowed myself in the past inadvertently to become involved. Nevertheless, the mistakes of the past can be insights for the future. Hopefully, assessors will increasingly recognize the folly of being co-opted by the judicial process or the equal folly of seeking some comfort in an adversarial process by an ill-conceived alliance with one or the other legal counsel. It is far more constructive and adaptive for an assessor to be constantly mindful of their vulnerable, isolated status and to conduct themselves accordingly. This includes having no expectations of alliance with a judge for whom the assessment report is intended. Civility and professional courtesy, when afforded by the bench, should be viewed as a rare occurrence, seldom expected but always welcomed when it occurs. The only allies reliably available are the assessor's objectivity, scientific rigor, sound methodology and uncompromised focus on championing what is in a child's best interest.

It is noteworthy that, throughout this manual, the term opposing counsel can refer to either the representative of the Child Welfare Agency or the representative of the person being assessed. In tenaciously guarding your objectivity you will alienate, from time to time, one or the other or both. On many occasions, you will also alienate the judge, in spite of your role as a friend of the court mandated to assist the determination process. To better understand this the user of this manual is referred to a separate but related publication pertaining to understanding the judicial process from a Mental Health Practitioner's point of view. This level of understanding is imperative to avoid becoming co-opted and intimidated by a system that is mired in rules and procedures, as opposed to being focused on arriving at a determination that is just.

Seventh Premise: In Pursuit of Justice

A Parenting Capacity Assessment is performed in order to assist in the process of arriving at a disposition that is just. This is in direct contradiction to the legal approach that has evolved to entail the unmitigated pursuit of winning a case. Lawyers for some time now have uniformly subscribed to the principle that their function is to vigorously advocate their client's position. Instead of focusing on justice, they focus on procedures, rules and regulations almost exclusively (with the exception of their effort to impeach the assessor's credibility or expertise). To the legal profession, this is the path of least resistance and that which is most comfortable since it is consistent with the adversarial process into which they are all socialized.

For the legal profession, the goal is to win. This applies to both the defense and the plaintiff representatives. It is easy for a Mental Health professional to become co-opted by this mentality and thereby abandon the potential to be part of the solution as opposed to being part of the problem: a problem that is manifested through a protracted legal process that ultimately prevents meeting the needs of a child at risk in a timely fashion.

The Mental Health professional, therefore, must understand what constitutes an issue of justice. While often used, this term is seldom understood and, at best, is interpreted to entail an unbiased (fair) application of rules. The best analogy of this simplistic interpretation is a sport event whereby opposing sides pursue a win within well-defined parameters of conduct that is fully or partially enforced by a referee.

Justice entails far more than what is involved in a sport competition or, for that fact, any event in which the goal is to win.

Justice is a concept that defines a process by which a resolution is sought for competing claims (conflicting needs) in a way that respects (takes into consideration) the legitimate desires of all parties. Resolution operationally defined is a solution, not a partial measure, but an end to a problem. In Victor Hugo's Les Misérables, the protagonist stole bread out of a need to feed his family to save them from starvation. The baker's competing claim (need) was to protect his property that was his livelihood. While both the protagonist and the baker have legitimate (real) needs, the challenge of determining a just solution requires an ability to apply a framework capable of ranking the "legitimate" needs of each party in the context of the goal of maintaining social order. This is no simple task and, indeed, requires the Wisdom of Solomon. Or at least, it requires an individual who has reached a cognitive moral perspective that is post-conventional. Since few people achieve such a cognitive developmental perspective (or they are quickly corrupted by socialization into a profession), the pursuit of justice is replaced by the rule-driven, win-at-any-cost mentality of the legal profession.

No wonder observers and legal practitioners talk of a "Court of Law" as opposed to a "Court of Justice".

It is imperative, therefore, that the Mental Health practitioner understand that laws are rules and that as rules, laws represent agreed-upon formulations as to what is acceptable and unacceptable conduct. As such, laws change, just as any other consensually agreed-upon practices change from time to time. Therefore, it is not unusual to find in history that the crime of today may become the heroic deed of tomorrow or visa versa.

The application of the law in the Parenting Capacity trial is most often manifested in what is and what is not acceptable conduct in court. There is a myriad of rules that can easily discombobulate the Mental Health practitioner. Efforts to become familiar or, indeed, comfortable with the rules exacerbate the focus on law and will invariably leave the assessor dismayed with the process. Instead of contributing to achieving a solution, the assessor becomes an inadvertent/unwilling participant in perpetuating a problem. Therefore, rather than exerting effort to learn to play along with the "Emperor's New Clothes" paradigm, the Mental Health practitioner will be better off exerting effort to understand the legal process and through this avoid becoming co-opted by it.

To reiterate, the challenge in arriving at a just determination is to decide whose competing claim takes precedence.

This prescribed methodology holds that a vulnerable child's right to optimal development of his potential takes precedence over a parent's right to have custody of that child. A Parenting Capacity Assessment, by virtue of it being conducted, acknowledges the legitimacy of both the child's and the parent's claims.

If the Assessment and other information determine that a parent is capable or more likely has the capacity (potential) to parent with facilitation and/or provision of resources, a just solution is to implement such a disposition since it has an empirically established probability of being in the child's best interest.

If the assessment finds the parent as highly unlikely to develop his or her parenting potential in sufficient time to be of discernable benefit to a rapidly developing child, especially one in the most crucial formative stage of life, a just solution is to seek, in a timely manner, alternative measures.

While admittedly difficult, if not impossible to achieve, the premise of this methodology is that at least the assessor must be an advocate for justice. Focus on this goal is imperative. The methodology is designed to ensure that the integrity of conducting the assessment is predictably maintained, thereby freeing all parties to focus optimally on the real issue of competing rights and arriving at a just solution as opposed to focusing on the application and interpretation of rules and regulations.

(This complex, vitally important issue is also addressed in the same separate publication referred to previously. The Mental Health professional is strongly urged to review this other publication in order to leave the business of law to the lawyers and, without distraction, apply his or her skills to the best interest of the child.)

Eighth Premise: Use Descriptions and Explanations, Not Labels

The prescribed methodology is a Parenting Capacity Assessment, not a mental status examination. In other words, it is not intended to generate diagnostic labels comprised of idiosyncratic Mental Health specific jargon. Moreover, the premise is that diagnostic labeling is antithetical to all that is implied by conducting an assessment in the best interests of a child. A comprehensive literature review reveals a consensus among all Mental Health practitioners who conduct Parenting Capacity Assessments that a Diagnostic and Statistical Manual of Mental Disorders, 4th edition (DSM-IV) label should not automatically disqualify a parent. Moreover, there is consensus among Mental Health practitioners that no label is able to convey the specific individual manifestations of a disorder, nor can a label accurately describe the severity of a disorder or the conditions under which symptoms are likely.

Rather than relying on a diagnostic label, the premise is that the assessor must define and explain the nature of a dysfunctionality in the content of what precipitating factors elicit the behaviours that are contraindicated to optimal parenting. The chronicity, thereby the resilience, of the disorder is another crucial consideration, as well as the parent's motivation to seek assistance. Considerations with respect to what supports or resources are available to a parent and how remedial is the disorder are also vitally important.

This premise also embodies a principle that, in general, labeling in Mental Health is antithetical to helping troubled individuals. At best, labeling is a manifestation of the destructive elements inherent in elitism, advanced and supported by credentialism. At worst, diagnostic labeling, indeed the DSM, represents an essentially political document not derived through scientific rigor as it would lead the uninitiated reader to believe. Instead, what it includes or does not include is the result, mostly, of intensive campaigning, lengthy negotiating, infighting and power plays by physician specialists in psychiatry.

Assessors, especially practitioners enamored with the practice of diagnostic labeling, are strongly urged to read Armstrong's And They Call it Help (1993) and Caplain's They Say You are Crazy (1995); comprehensive treatments of this phenomenon also addressed decades earlier in The Myth of Mental Illness by Thomas Zsazs (1961). It is the efforts of these few unco-opted scholars that mitigate the best efforts of elitists and exclusionaries, and encourage the detractors of the mysticism involved in labeling to refuse to fade away. Besides this point, what use is a label to a judge, trained as a lawyer without sufficient knowledge or expertise in understanding what exactly is implied and what exactly is the significance associated with a particular label, especially in reference to parenting?

Ninth Premise: The Essence of Expertise

The premise is that expertise required to conduct a Parenting Capacity Assessment is not based on credentialism. Instead, it is based on expertise gained through formal education or continued studies (guided or self-directed) and practice wisdom that comes from years of varied but related experiences. Moreover, the premise of the methodology encompasses a general principle that, given the complex and systemic nature of the undertaking, exclusive/specialization (that is practice restricted to conducting Parenting Capacity Assessments) is quite probably contraindicated.

This premise is consistent with one of the objectives for writing this manual, namely, to demystify the process and thereby encourage increasingly more Mental Health practitioners to venture into this area of high need. The broader the perspective of Mental Health practitioners, the broader and more meaningful their contribution to battling the perpetuation and exponential growth of dysfunctionality among successive generations. Each child, through the efforts of many, when rescued from a dysfunctional destiny can and will become an optimally actualized, autonomous, independent, adaptive individual.

This premise postulates that there is no exclusionary expertise required to apply and constructively use this prescribed methodology. Notwithstanding this position, over time the benefits of applying the methodology can be expected to have incrementally positive results, mostly with respect to the ease with which the assessor manages the process. Therefore, this premise holds that a Mental Health practitioner's expertise in conducting Parenting Capacity Assessments is grounded in training and experience-acquired knowledge and skills with respect to conducting individual assessments. Although previous assessments were most likely conducted for other purposes, with the use of this prescribed methodology an assessor can readily translate the relevance of findings and concomitant conclusions to an individual's potential to acquire in a timely manner, and use with predictable confidence, parenting skills that will meet a particular child's needs. Furthermore, the standardization of the methodology will not only free the assessor to focus on the challenges of data collection, interpretation and conclusion formulations, but will also free the practitioner from substantiating expertise traditionally believed to come from specialization. That is to say, while the expertise of a supervisor, trainer or mentor can go far to support the expertise of a novice assessor in a court of law, the reliance on a recognized and increasingly broadly accepted methodology can also accomplish the same outcome.

This premise identifies the potential for making false attributions regarding competence on the basis of a practitioner's credentials bestowed by a self-regulated professional organization. As an antidote, this premise prescribes that expertise in each and every case should be determined, as opposed to assumed by status, title or, for that fact, length of experience in a particular area of professional practice. For example, deciding on a court-appointed assessor should take into consideration whether ten years of experience constitutes one year repeated ten times, or a broad and rich range of ten separate but related years of experience that, when integrated, will ultimately positively impact on the practitioner's knowledge, skill and wisdom with which a Parenting Capacity Assessment is conducted.

Tenth Premise: The Benefits of a Comprehensive, Integrated Approach

Regardless of the discipline to which an assessor belongs, this premise holds that a comprehensive Parenting Capacity Assessment requires an integrated approach informed by a variety of data sources. Clinical formulations made on the basis of interviews and review of documentation must be enhanced and elaborated by objective findings derived from the administration of standardized instruments, and visa versa. While this prescribed methodology uses a specific array of standardized instruments, some based on self-reporting and others not, there are other options as defined by the practitioner's ability to integrate the findings of standardized instruments with formulations derived from clinical interviews and other sources.

Since the assessment is intended to be used by a non-Mental Health professional, a judge, it is imperative that the assessor clearly demonstrates a discernable logic with each formulation supported by evidence that includes behavioural observations, clinical formulations, as well as the results of standardized assessment tools.

If you do not routinely use standardized instruments in your practice, especially when doing an assessment, it is essential that you invest some time and money in learning to administer and interpret tools in which you have confidence and tools that you believe will enhance your expertise as a Parenting Capacity Assessor. Initially, some ongoing supervision in this respect is also advisable.

There is a mistaken belief that the use of standardized instruments is restricted to certain credentialized groups of Mental Health professionals. In some jurisdictions, there may be a restriction with respect to the use of diagnostic labels. As long as you refrain from the use of diagnostic labels, which has already been discussed, as antithetical to conducting a Parenting Capacity Assessment, the only restriction with respect to the use of standardized instruments is that you have knowledge and skills to administer and interpret the results of that particular tool. The knowledge and skills required depend on the instrument is question. The use of some can be readily mastered while others take time and practice, aided by supervision or support by a knowledgeable mentor.

Standardized instruments used in this methodology are listed and explained in this manual. Other potentially useful instruments are also listed along with information as to how they may be obtained. This list, however, should not be considered as exhaustive. It is only meant to be an example on which you can expand.

Eleventh Premise: Presentations that Work Format

The prescribed Parenting Capacity Assessment report format encompasses the "presentations that work" approach to persuading the reader to accept and act on that which you have concluded and recommended. While the "presentations that work" format is widely utilized in the business world, reports prepared by Mental Health practitioners often still rely on the Agatha Christie mystery novel style whereby all is revealed to the reader in the last page of a lengthy presentation of seemingly disjointed facts, characterizations and events. While your prose may be excellent, a Parenting Capacity Assessment does not constitute a novel. Moreover, in spite of your excellent prose, the assumption you can keep the attention of the reader until the very end of your discourse may be quite unwarranted, especially given all that a judge is required to review in a particular case.

The "presentations that work" format prescribes that the conclusions you want the reader to believe and act on be prioritized and presented in descending order. Under each conclusion, evidence in support of the formulation is also prioritized and presented in descending order of importance. The prioritization of conclusions and the prioritization of evidence in support of each conclusion, as well as the number of pieces of supporting evidence you present, to a large degree constitutes the creative/artistic component of report writing. Practice vastly improves this skill which also is enhanced and developed by the unavoidable prerequisite of first developing an outline before applying your prose skills to writing a report. Familiarity with the literature that is provided in this manual will also be of assistance to you with respect to choosing which supportive evidence has the greatest weight and importance. Moreover, your experience will help to decide which finding is the most valid and reliable of the various data sources available to you. For example, your direct observation and interpretation of behaviour precedes someone else's observations, about which you then make attributions.

An optimally constructive report, therefore, (the one in the best interest of a child) is comprised of the most important conclusions placed first, each supported by evidence in a descending order. By the time the reader, specifically a judge, finishes reading your report, there should be no doubt with respect to what would be the best disposition of a child at risk. Moreover, by organizing your material in this manner, there should be no doubt in your mind as to what is in the best interest of the child and why.

Twelfth Premise: Assume the Optimal About Alternative Dispositions

A Parenting Capacity Assessment cannot be based on reservations about foster care or reservations about adoptions. While abuse and tragedies occur in both and are well reported in the media, ultimately you must assume that every non-parental disposition will be optimal.

While the legislative requirement of least intrusive measures is based on sound evidence concerning the benefits being derived by children being raised by biological parents, heroic efforts in this respect often are misplaced and unnecessarily protract the child's negative circumstances. It is especially tragic when considerations for permanence planning are compromised by an assessor's isolated negative experiences with alternative caregivers.

Given that as you can choose your friends but not your family, a conscious, deliberate choice of alternative caregivers must be assumed to be ultimately better than the negative life legacy to which a child would otherwise be destined by virtue of his or her birth. This is especially true if the child's legacy entails an ambivalent, rejecting or abusive parent unable to meet even minimal primary developmental needs. A substitute environment comprised of competent adults has been empirically demonstrated to be infinitely better for the child (Tizard and Rees, 1974; Fanshel and Shimm, 1978; Wald et. al., 1988) than prolonging the child's drift within a natural family.

Thirteenth Premise: Avoiding Countertransference

Unfortunately, the psychoanalytic notion of transference is gradually losing its stature in the Mental Health field. Perhaps if we do not talk about it, it will no longer occur. This is not only an erroneous conclusion but a dangerous one. Transference issues are potential confounding variables in all that is done by Mental Health professionals and can be especially problematic in conducting Parenting Capacity Assessments if not recognized and systematically controlled by the Assessor. The prescribed methodology is intended to provide the structure with which to minimize the negative effects of transference.

Specifically, countertransference is the unconscious process against which a Parenting Capacity Assessor must be particularly vigilant. This entails the occurrence of unconscious feelings that cause the Assessor to make clinical formulations before all data has been collected and analyzed. Moreover, this unconscious process can also inadvertently cause the Assessor to not only formulate hypotheses that are consistent with the unconscious countertransference experience, but also cause him or her to inadvertently engage in biased data collection that supports the unfounded formulation.

Assessors can have positive countertransference to a parent or to a child or to both. In the process of unconsciously over-identifying with one or the other, the risk is that the Assessor overlooks the worrisome features of a parent or a child and thereby acts less than optimally in the child's best interest.

Negative countertransference to a parent or a child entails unconscious negative feelings by an Assessor about one or the other or both. This can be the source of over-estimating the inadequacy of a parent and perhaps even becoming uninterested in the welfare of a child.

The application of a standardized methodology that requires the collection of data to address specific issues under the four categories of analyses will minimize the unconscious influences of either negative or positive counter-transference experiences by an assessor. Nevertheless, countertransference will invariably occur. It is the degree to which it occurs that is the responsibility of an Assessor to control. Conclusions based on historical data, reliable observations made by Child Welfare workers, collateral information, clinical formulations, systematic observa-tions and the interpretation of standardized instruments all mitigate against the occurrence of powerful counter-transference effects.

The natural countertransference response also affects others involved in a family system, such as Child Welfare workers, lawyers and judges. While the prescribed methodology is designed to be comprehensive and thereby avoid unwarranted/unsubstantiated conclusions as a function of unconscious positive or negative feelings, this phe-nomenon warrants persistent vigilance. Indeed, under the second category of analysis, this phenomenon requires clinical formulations pertaining to the feelings/emotions aroused by a parent or a child as a function of how they present themselves during the assessment process. The emotional experience of the Assessor may be quite similar to the emotional experience of, for example, Child Welfare workers involved with the family, and perhaps will also reflect the unconscious feelings of a judge hearing the case. As such, an objective reflection on a very subjective experience will serve to enhance the confidence with which decisions are formulated and actions implemented in the best interests of a child.

Fourteenth Premise: Decisive, Timely Action

The prescribed methodology does not lend itself to being interpreted as a time-specific (snapshot) perspective of an individual's capacities warranting further delays in making a decisive determination regarding a child's status. The prescribed methodology also mitigates unfounded beliefs that, even without the occurrence of a significant event, people can change drastically, simply as a function of time.

A snapshot interpretation of a Parenting Capacity Assessment is guarded against by the prescribed requirement that all findings be contextualized in terms of explaining the etiology of dysfunctionalities, as well as what concom-itantly can reasonably be expected of a parent with or without intervention.

Insofar as a Parenting Capacity Assessment will seldom focus on acute disturbances and most often will focus on characterological traits that compromise an individual's ability to meet the complex needs of a child, there is a need to clearly distinguish between what reasonably can be expected to be eradicated from a person's current cognitive, emotional and behavioural functioning and what only can be brought under control through the predictably consistent and competent application of well-defined strategies. While in most instances, a Parenting Capacity Assessment is not initiated to determine the impact an acute mental illness has on an individual's parenting abilities, an acute state may however, require temporary apprehension of a child until such time as a "cure" is effected, usually by a physician specialist in psychiatry. An assessment of Parenting Capacity invariably is required when the acute state becomes chronic, likely exacerbated by dysfunctional characterological traits. In this event, the issue is to determine what impact a chronic "mental illness" may have on an individual's ability to parent, as well as the individual's capacity to improve parenting skills as required and demanded by the developmental stage challenges posed by a child.

While the legislative prescriptive of "least intrusive measures" is well-founded and based on good empirical evidence, its indiscriminate application by well-intentioned Child Welfare workers and other Mental Health professionals can inadvertently compromise the welfare of a child at risk. For example, non-contextual views lead to the justification of futile intervention strategies and thereby unnecessarily delay a child being placed in an environment capable of optimally promoting his or her growth and development. It is the consensus of Parenting Capacity Assessors that once a child has been apprehended, the absolute worst that can happen is for that child to "drift in care." This is especially true for a child who is in the most crucial formative stage in life. It is particularly unconscionable if the child "drifts in care" due to legalistic procedural requirements or court scheduling problems.

Permanency planning, therefore, is greatly facilitated by the comprehensive contextual format prescribed by the assessment methodology. This is intended to minimize the time a child remains in limbo and thereby serves to protect the child from developing life-enduring negative consequences. This premise especially recognizes the profound negative consequences delays have on infants and toddlers who are in the most crucial formative developmental stage of their lives (Goldstein, Freud and Salnit, 1973).

There is an initiative to quantify the findings generated by the methodology of this prescribed format. As opposed to time-limited (snapshot) Risk Assessment Scales, the quantification objective is to produce criterion levels that support a specific determination such as: Society Wardship with Access until the benefits of intervention are realized; Supervision Order until the benefits of intervention are realized; Crown Wardship without Access with a view to placing a child for adoption.

Fifteenth Premise: Determining Sexual Abuse

The prescribed Parenting Capacity Assessment is not designed to investigate or determine the probability, of child sexual abuse. Nevertheless, the four categories of analyses in the context of historical factors can reveal the presence of variables empirically known to be associated with instances of intrafamilial sexual abuse. The prescribed method can also reveal personality factors of primary caregivers associated with failure to protect a child from sexual exploitation or abuse by perpetrators outside of the family structure.

Notwithstanding these capabilities, it is, in fact, considered as inappropriate for a Parenting Capacity Assessment to be mandated to establish the occurrence of child sexual abuse. Such determinations require an immediate expert response to a disclosure or suspicion beyond the time availability of an independent Assessor, even one with expertise in this highly specialized field of practice.

A Parenting Capacity Assessment where child sexual abuse is an issue is prescribed by this method to include information obtained and interpreted by allied professionals who are specifically trained in the most current investigation methods. Methods which recognize that an optimally competent first response to disclosure or suspicion produce the best results and that multiple reassessments profoundly contaminate data to the point it becomes virtually meaningless, lacking both the reliability and validity criteria to take definitive action.

It is noteworthy that most, if not all, jurisdictions require that professionals and all others report disclosures, as well as suspicions of abuse to a Child Welfare agency and/or the police. By law, all reports must be immediately investigated by designated authorities. In the event that a disclosure occurs during a Parenting Capacity Assessment or if there is a suspicion that a child has been sexually or physically abused, it is the responsibility of the Assessor to report such findings to the appropriate authorities without delay and then to incorporate the findings of the specialized investigation team in the Assessment report.

Sixteenth Premise: The Baseline Data Imperative Regarding Development

One of the most important data sources potentially available to an Assessor is the status of a child when apprehended. The developmental status of an apprehended child can be the source of profoundly important formulations, especially if contextualized in the background history of the primary caretaker and further informed by the four categories of analyses used in this methodology. The same premise applies to apprehended newborn infants. It is therefore imperative to determine toxicity and other prenatal indicators of neglect or abuse when the child is born. While the latter determination is relatively easy to obtain in hospital, the former is more difficult since it requires observational and interpretative expertise that is usually not readily accessible to a Child Welfare agency.

In lieu of an immediate determination of a child's status when an agency becomes involved with a family, other than a newborn infant, it is imperative that systematic observations of the child's behaviour be collected. The observations of child care, medical and educational professionals can be useful data sources for child developmental specialists in formulating a conclusion of the child's status at the time of apprehension. It is, therefore, imperative that whenever possible, child developmental specialists determine developmental delays and other problems related to negative environmental factors. Where such resources are readily available, invariably such determinations are significant factors is precipitating the requirement for a comprehensive Parenting Capacity Assessment.

The extent to which a Parenting Capacity Assessment can be definitive regarding a correlation between a child's developmental status and the parenting the child received is determined by how soon a baseline measure can be obtained; obviously, the sooner the better. Developmental gains made by a child with alternative caregivers can then be attributed with more confidence to improved environmental conditions/parenting. Confidence in such attributions is especially enhanced by the empirical methods and expertise of developmental specialists assessing the child at the time of apprehension and subsequently.

The resources of developmental specialists can also be useful in determining the cause of delays other than neglect, and inconsistent and/or inadequate parenting. There are rare cases where developmental delays are caused or exacerbated by factors such as deafness or chronic illness. Nevertheless, even in such cases, the issue of parenting competence remains the same, namely the question concerns the parent's timely and consistent use of medical resources and the parent's compliance with referral and remedial services. A parent who fails to use medical services or fails to identify a problem or fails to follow through with a referral to a remedial service is as worrisome, if not more so, than a parent in whose care an otherwise "normal" child is failing to thrive.

Given the vitally important implications of developmental delay findings, it is imperative that every effort be made to assign this task immediately to an expert in this highly specialized area of practice. To augment a determination of developmental delays, special attention and systematic reporting of a child's behaviour should be undertaken by the Child Welfare agency involved with the family. Ideally, a referral for a Parenting Capacity Assessment should include these vitally important findings and should constitute a significant reason for the undertaking.

Seventeenth Premise: The Baseline Data Imperative Regarding Attachment

It is imperative that the nature of the child/parent interaction be observed and systematically documented immediately upon a family becoming involved with a Child Welfare agency. This will serve as vital information for the classification of the attachment category that best defines the bond the parent has been able to create with the child. Once a child is apprehended, observations of interaction patterns with the parent will be confounded by a number of possible factors.

For example, a child's reaction to a parent after being apprehended may be in part due to the negative effects of separation, bonding with a foster parent, or an instinctive defensive reaction characterized by distancing from others. Furthermore, an observation may well be indicative of a child on his or her way to becoming what Bowlby (1951) described in "young thieves" as "affectionless" as a function of instinctive defensive reactions to traumatic separation.

It would be ideal if the interaction between a child at risk and the parent could be videotaped and later reviewed by the Parenting Capacity Assessor. This is unlikely to occur in even the best-funded jurisdiction. In lieu of obtaining such pure, objective, non- contaminated information, the next best thing is observations conducted as soon as possible. In fact as part of a first contact protocol, observations of parent-child interaction patterns should be made and documented. It is imperative that the observations be restricted to descriptions void of interpretive formulations pertaining to attachment. Attributing emotional states to behaviour being described is, however, imperative as long as the observer provides reasons (frown, smiles, stiff body, etc.) for the particular emotional label used.

To augment documented behavioural observations, it is imperative that the Parenting Capacity Assessor interview the child protection worker who produced the descriptions of the child-parent interaction patterns at first contact with the family. Moreover, in the interest of establishing baseline data regarding attachment, the assessor is prescribed by this method to interview, whenever possible, the Child Welfare agency staff who had first contact with the family even if observations of interactions were not documented. While the inclination is to devise a structured methodology for making observations for this purpose, the tactic is likely to be counterproductive. An imposed format is highly likely to be restrictive and will thereby impede as opposed to facilitate the observer's task.

The most useful baseline data regarding attachment, therefore, is to describe what was seen and heard along with what behavioural manifestations were the basis for concluding a particular emotional state was being experienced by the parent and the child at a given time during the contact.

Eighteenth Premise: The Semantics of Abuse

A fundamental premise of this prescribed methodology is that all treatment that does not promote development of a child constitutes abuse. While some jurisdictions engage in semantic differentiations, and some even specify physical risk as the criteria for intrusive intervention, physical maltreatment, neglect, lack of appropriate stimulation, failure to seek appropriate medical attention and a myriad of other incompetencies all constitute abuse.

While abuse is abuse, objectively it must be acknowledged that there are degrees of abuse and mitigating factors that must be taken into consideration when determining a parent's capacity to act in a child's best interest in a timely manner with the provision of appropriate resources. The degrees of abuse may be defined by the nature, frequency and magnitude of the maltreatment perpetrated on a child.

Therefore, instead of differentiating between abuse and neglect, the premise of this methodology is that the nature of the maltreatment must be operationally defined and related to the findings pertaining to the dysfunctionalities of the child's parent (e.g., neglect, related to substance abuse). In so doing, the child's right to optimal growth and development remains paramount. Also, unwarranted apprehensions can be avoided and apprehensions, when they do occur, can be empirically supported. Invariably, the issues pertain to determining the implications of situational/acute variables regarding parenting or to manifestations of dysfunctionalities that predict escalating chronic patterns of maltreatment: maltreatment which can precipitate physical, emotional and developmental later-life negative consequences on the child.

This premise mistakenly can be interpreted as supporting social constructivism whereby behaviours become prescribed by one group onto another. This would be the case if the prescribed behaviours were based on culturally determined values. While values invariably play a part in Child Welfare, by the very fact that socially funded agencies exist to protect the rights of children, this premise, is based on what is empirically known to promote a child's optimal growth and development to become independent, autonomous, adaptive adult.

Along a continuum of gravity, invariably an assessor can recall worse and better cases. Such experiences could possibly lead to countertransference-like issues and thereby compromise the potential optimal benefits of a Parenting Capacity Assessment. Comparative analyses need not, however, lead to any deleterious effects. Rather, comparative analyses can be very useful with respect to defining what interventions work for what group of individuals, as well as predicting the timeliness with which individuals in a particular group respond to intervention. Notwithstanding these realities, while the often-heard protest from parents being assessed is that there are far worse cases than theirs, the fact remains that the assessment is of them and not others, and their capacity may still be found wanting, albeit not as severely as some others'.

Nineteenth Premise: The Need for Compassion

It is possible to recommend intrusive measures without having to "decimate" the parent being assessed. Moreover, it is possible to prepare a most unfavorable assessment report and still maintain the report's therapeutic potential for caregivers who were not vindicated for their protracted conflict with a Child Welfare Agency.

To achieve these vitally important results requires objectivity evidenced by recommendations that have logical connections with conclusions that, in turn, are supported, ideally, by several observable and measurable findings.

The tone of the report is also vitally important to achieving therapeutic benefits from a Parenting Capacity Assessment. Compassion does not negate the presence of dysfunctionality, although some lawyers will try to use your compassion as the "thin edge of a wedge" to impeach the credibility of your conclusions and recommendations or worse, your competence. Compassion also does not compromise formulations regarding dysfunctionality insofar as compassion is inconsistent with value-laden blaming of a parent, and especially insofar as maladaptive behaviours are placed into the context of the assessed individual's history, concomitant development and personality structure.

In spite of your best efforts, unfortunately at times the appearance of cruelty toward a parent being assessed will be unavoidable. This can be a problem especially, when a lawyer elects to focus on this issue as a means by which to garner sympathy from a judge for a client. The risk is especially prevalent in instances when formulations are taken out of context by a defense lawyer with the intent of discrediting your objectivity as an Assessor. It is imperative, therefore, that the child's best interests remain a paramount theme in the assessment and the most negative of findings be presented always contextually and never in a blameworthy manner. This is possible even if responsibility to address a dysfunctionality lies within a parent who, for a variety of reasons, has not been able to do that which is required.

Twentieth Premise: Implications for Child Welfare Workers

While this prescribed Parenting Capacity Assessment methodology is primarily intended to be used by Mental Health professionals functioning separate and apart from a Child Welfare Agency, the format is also intended to be used by front-line Child Protection workers and agency managers.

First and foremost, the format defines for a Child Protection worker the vitally important function of collecting baseline data in the form of systematic observations. The observations pertain to the functioning of a child at first contact. Such systematic notations will constitute a significant database for child developmental specialists who, as soon as possible, should be assessing a child whether the child remains or not with a worrisome parent. Observations should also be made concerning the pattern of interaction between a parent and a child as soon as the Child Welfare Agency becomes involved with the family. Such systematic baseline observations will be information used during a Parenting Capacity Assessment to classify the nature of the attachment between the child and the parent.

Additionally, the prescribed format is intended to provide child protection workers with a basis on which to petition the court to impose various degrees of intrusive measures. In the event that initial interventions fail to produce desired outcomes, the format will serve to provide the basis on which to petition the court to order a Parenting Capacity Assessment. It will be a significant source of information with which to pursue a timely disposition of a child perceived to be at risk as determined with or without the use of a standardized Risk Assessment tool.

Once a Court-ordered Parenting Capacity Assessment is initiated, the prescribed format is intended to inform the Terms of Reference that mandates the Mental Health professional receiving the referral. Ideally and eventually the Terms of Reference articulated by a Child Welfare Agency will become standard, although elaborated by the specifics of each case. While ambitious, this expectation is not unrealistic insofar as the model reflects the current state of knowledge in the field and is consistent with legislation in all jurisdictions in which there is a consensus commitment to protect the rights of all children.

Twenty-First Premise: Artificiality Created by the Need for Clarity

Clarity and readily perceived logic necessitates the artificial creation of four separate categories of analyses in this prescribed methodology. Clearly, there are overlaps in the dynamically systemic relationship among the four categories of analyses. Any attempt to report this as it actually occurs would serve to confuse the judge, other non-Mental Health professionals, many Mental Health professionals and most probably, even the Assessor. Moreover, any attempt to report what actually defines the dynamics of a particular case without the artificial creation of categories of analyses would seriously compromise whatever therapeutic benefit a report could have for the person being assessed and, most importantly, inadvertently place the expert Assessor in the role of contributing to the confusion that was the impetus for conducting a Parenting Capacity Assessment in the first place.

It is imperative, therefore, that the utmost precision be applied to reporting findings, conclusions and recommendations under the category of analysis where they belong. Similarly, it is imperative that interpretations of the background information that establishes the contextual basis of the case be clearly organized, and implications of the individual's background be clearly presented as the later-life consequences of childhood experiences as they are manifested under one or more of the four categories of analyses. The discussion part of the report constitutes a concise synthesis of the findings.

The prescribed methodology, therefore, is designed to a large degree to facilitate clarity in the reporting format. Of equal importance, the methodology is also designed to free the Mental Health professional from stylistic/report organization concerns, to focus on the interpretation and implications of the findings.

Twenty-Second Premise: The Issue of Grandparents

Grandparents can and do play a vitally important role in the development of their grandchild. They can be the source of validation of the child's special, unique nature by conveying their affection and pride in a consistently and predictably unconditional manner. In the role of grandparents, even individuals who were previously marginal parents can perform an incredibly positive service in promoting the optimal growth and development of children.

These same grandparents, however, need not be as promising an influence on a child's development if they are placed by circumstance in the role of parents. This is especially true in cases where the dysfunctional parent of a child at risk is the product of their parenting efforts. Therefore, while positive and competent as grandparents, the probability is significant that they will be just as incompetent as parents with the grandchild as they were with that child's parent.

When grandparents become primary caregivers, when they assume the responsibility of parents, they are no longer acting in the capacity of grandparents and therefore their past parenting patterns are most likely to be repeated. In fact, this may not be exactly accurate. As a function of their diminishing physical capabilities, it would not be unreasonable to predict that their abilities will be even further compromised than they were in the past, due to their being less energetic and physically capable with the passage of each year.

In spite of what is commonly believed, rarely do people learn significantly from their experiences. Rarely do they reflect on what they have experienced to the extent that they are actually able to predictably and with competence enact new patterns of behaviour. Sometimes, there may have been a significant event in a grandparent's life that served to precipitate positive changes (for example, achieving and maintaining sobriety by long-term involvement in a community-based, twelve-step self-help program such as Alcoholics Anonymous). Given these possibilities, therefore, even if at first glance grandparents may or may not appear to be viable alternative primary caregivers, it is imperative that the prescribed Parenting Capacity Assessment methodology be applied fully. In such instances the Terms of Reference should include a mandate to identify what, if any, event has precipitated marked changes in their functioning, as opposed to them becoming even more like themselves with the passage of time.

CHAPTER 2
Achieving a Psychosocial Systems Perspective

This chapter is designed to delineate the psychosocial systems approach to contextualizing the implications of your findings as well as the underlying rationale for those sections in the prescribed report format that precede the four categories of analyses. To state the obvious, a rationale is nothing more than a reason or justification which, in this case, is informed by practice experience and a comprehensive literature review. The intent is to save you from having to guess what was the reasoning for prescribing a particular assessment behaviour and, more importantly, having the consumers of the report do likewise. Rather than having to guess, it is better that your reasoning be clearly and concisely revealed to the reader of your report. By definition, your authority as an Assessor is essentially determined by the extent to which you can provide reasoned elaboration for your methods, conclusions and recommendations. If there are disagreements with the methodology and the underlying rationale, this need not undermine your authority as an expert, especially if there are no alternative/better methods offered. If there are, improved approaches offered, so much the better, since a hallmark of competence is a will and desire to constantly develop knowledge and skills.

The First Page

The first page of your report should be printed on your letterhead, clearly defining who you are, who your associates are, your address, and any institutional affiliations. There is nothing more frustrating than trying to determine who conducted a Parenting Capacity Assessment and what his or her organizational affiliations are. Dating the Assessment is also crucial and something overlooked in many instances. This can be a further source of frustration in the near, as well as the distant, future when the content of the report may once again be scrutinized.

The first page of your report should also include the names of the various other individuals involved in a case and their specific roles (e.g., Child Welfare supervisor, counsel for the parent, etc.) insofar as these, too, can change relatively quickly and such changes could have significant impact on many aspects of the determination process concerning the status of a child at risk.

While the style of the first page prescribed by this methodology is likely not an unfamiliar one, it is unfortunately not one that is uniformly used by Assessors. What is provided on the first page of your report therefore should constitute at least basic descriptive information.

Précis

Reading a Parenting Capacity Assessment report is not intended to be an arduous experience, albeit it can be time-consuming. As such, to place a judge into the position of having to "work" to understand the conclusions and supportive evidence is not advisable. Therefore, borrowing from a well-established business practice, an executive summary is prescribed as essential for providing concise, definitive conclusions and concomitant recommendations as to what determination would be in the child's best interest.

Also borrowing from business practice, the presentations that work format requires that the most important conclusion and recommendation be stated first, followed by the four categories of analyses which support them. Insofar as the précis should ideally be no longer than a page, evidence in support of your conclusion and recommendations is not provided.

A précis is also intended to immediately orient the reader to the argument you are making. This strategy quickly focuses the reader on how you substantiate the position you have taken with respect to the child's disposition. This tactic is contrary to the mystery novel approach which "teases" the reader to guess, on the basis of gradually revealed information, what will be the outcome of a book. The prescribed format requires you to abandon the traditional style of report writing whereby conclusions and recommendations are stated last and supporting evidence, to various degrees, is lost in the prose of the text. In this prescribed methodology, the précis serves to focus the reader to be consistently looking for supportive evidence and the contextual dynamics of the case.

In complicated cases, where there are several potential primary caregivers, I have used a précis for each individual to parallel the organization of the body of the report.

A précis in no way constitutes a revelation of biases, although I have been accused of such by a lawyer solicited second opinion provider who likely did not understand the meaning of the concept. This is noteworthy, since there is a high probability that, even among professionals, this shortcoming is not unheard-of (along with a lack of will to consult a dictionary).

Caveat

This one-page statement is intended to orient the reader to how you approached the task of conducting the Parenting Capacity Assessment. It is also advisable to further orient the reader immediately to focus on how the Assessment fulfills the goals that the author has set for him or herself. This is far from mundane, insofar as many assessment reports I have reviewed do not reveal a standard according to which the Assessor did the work, leaving the reader to make an enormous leap in faith, essentially based on the Assessor's title, credentials or academic degree. This prescribed Parenting Capacity Assessment methodology requires that the entire process be transparent. In contrast, the use of mystique or power tactics constitutes fodder for an adversarial process. Such ill-advised tactics also represent an inadvertent co-option into the adversarial process that is invariably protracted and, as such, contraindicated to a timely disposition that is in the best interest of a child.

Not surprisingly, if one were to survey a random sample of non-Mental Health professionals, their views as to how an Assessment is conducted would be profoundly misinformed. To a large degree this same finding could be replicated among allied professionals, including the judiciary.

The caveat, therefore, is intended to orient the judge to the fact that you, the Assessor, approached the process in an informed, deliberate manner: that you were cognizant of potential misrepresentations, deliberate or inadvertent, and that confidence in formulations and recommendations was essentially determined, not only by the quantity and quality of information obtained, but also by the internal logic revealed by the data sources in relation to what is known about the dynamics of various dysfunctionalities, personality structures and behavioural patterns.

In essence, the caveat establishes your expertise and reveals the standard against which you apply your theoretical and practice-gained knowledge and skills. Moreover, the caveat also sets the stage for the identification of logical inconsistencies, and the need to explain these in a manner that will facilitate a timely and decisive determination in the child's best interest.

Reasons for the Referral

This section in the report is intended to convey your understanding as to why a Parenting Capacity Assessment was deemed to be necessary by a Child Welfare Agency and what was sufficiently compelling to justify a Court Order to do so.

Under this subheading, the task is also to reveal to the reader what information you were provided which may or may not be complete, deliberately or inadvertently. It is imperative that a judge understand that you are cognizant of how the case is viewed by the referring Child Welfare Agency. This also contextualizes any Terms of Reference which are included in a Letter of Referral.

It is worthy of note that opposing counsel often does not agree with a need for a Parenting Capacity Assessment and if "poorly done" the Terms of Reference can be a source of protracted litigation and concomitant billing opportunities for less-than-scrupulous lawyers.

It is necessary to articulate the reasons for the referral since this will serve as one source of information with respect to formulating an opinion about the relationship between a Child Welfare Agency and primary caretakers who are being assessed. Moreover, by defining the reasons for the referral from the perspective of the Agency and as supported by the court, you will have an opportunity to comment on past problem definitions, especially as the definitions relate to the lack of success any previous intervention strategies have had with the subjects of your Assessment.

Instead of listing any Terms of Reference, they are simply acknowledged under this subcategory and the reader is referred to Appendix A, which also constitutes concise responses based on the findings produced by the assessment methodology. To reiterate an earlier point, hopefully and eventually, Child Welfare Agency Terms of Reference will adopt the format of this prescribed methodology, asking general and specific questions pertaining to the four categories of analyses with a request that the answers be contextualized into the developmental and life experiences of the person being assessed. When this occurs, there will no longer be a need for an Appendix A in the report format.

The Rationale for the Method

This section is intended to convey to the reader in a concise manner the methodology that was used and the conceptual framework for choosing the approach. Under this subheading, the direct focus on primary caregivers is identified. Experience has taught this to be necessary in order to diffuse opposing counsel's strategy to discredit an Assessor on the basis of a lack of expertise assessing the status of children. As already noted, such a task is best left to experts who specialize in this area of practice. Furthermore, even when comprehensive information is available with respect to possible special needs of a child on whose behalf an assessment is being conducted, the question remains the same. Is the potential primary caregiver, the person being assessed, capable of, or does he or she have the capacity to learn and apply specialized knowledge and skills for competently parenting the child. The more profound the needs of the child, the greater will be the demands on the potential caregiver. Specific demands on a potential caregiver may have to be spoken to in certain cases (e.g., potentially fatal medical condition). On even rarer occasions it may be necessary to produce a report of considerable specificity to address several special needs a child has been found to possess.

Under this subheading the rationale is clearly stated. It declares the Assessor's conceptual framework that emotionally adjusted, cognitive developmentally mature individuals are more adaptive and competent parents than parents who are dysfunctional in any number of areas including being developmentally delayed and thereby maladaptive as adults.

Equally, the intent also is to convey to the reader that a Parenting Capacity Assessment is only an assessment of parenting capacity. It is not a mental status examination or a DSM label-generating process. As with respect to determining the status of a child, if for some unimaginable reason there is a specific request for a diagnostic label, this, too, is better left to specialized experts, specifically physician specialists in psychiatry. From the perspective of this prescribed methodology, a useful Term of Reference posed by a referring Child Welfare Agency is a request to explain the meaning and relevance of a diagnostic label, and especially the implications this has on the individual's parenting capacity.

As in any scientific scholarly report, under this subheading, the intent is to clearly identify the theoretical perspectives incorporated in the methodology. Personality theory and social learning theory speak not only to the development of characterological traits that have profound implications with respect to intervention strategies and what can be expected, but also to the time frames required to bring about improvements that could positively impact on a child. By declaring this perspective, the intent is to convey that this leads to a better understanding of possible variances between an individual's capacity to learn and apply that which is learned. This approach can also be extremely useful in explaining obstacles to learning, especially for an individual who has innate intellectual capacities that remain unrealized.

Taking into consideration the assessed person's cognitive developmental perspective can provide a great deal of understanding of the person's reasoning and behaviours. This also has implications for addressing the person's use of denial and concomitant resistance to doing that which could ameliorate a dysfunctionality. Such dynamics need to be clearly explained, especially to a non-Mental Health professional reader, but in many instances also to Child Welfare workers and allied Mental Health professionals who may be involved in the case. This type of information will never be redundant even if it simply serves to confirm for the reader that the Assessment methodology is consistent with beliefs to which the reader subscribes.

The rationale and theoretical frameworks applied in the methodology of this prescribed format are by no means presented as exhaustive. They are, however, meant to represent at least what is considered to be necessary and what constitutes the basic standard for conducting a Parenting Capacity Assessment. You may wish to incorporate additional conceptual/theoretical perspectives as long as they meet the criterion of explaining in a logically consistent, coherent manner your conclusions and recommendations as to what is in the best interest of a child.

Care should be taken not to venture too far afield from focusing on the parenting capacities of potential primary caregivers. Therefore, references to a child's needs and how these may be satisfied should be restricted to the assessed person's potential to learn about the special needs and to use the specialized knowledge and skills in a predictably competent manner. While some Child Welfare Agencies, in their Terms of Reference, may request identification in a Parenting Capacity Assessment of a child's various special needs, unless there are child developmental and intervention specialists in your practice and organization with the expertise to speak to this, the best suggestion you may make is that a specialized assessment is required with respect to defining the child's special needs. Of equal importance, it is imperative that you recommend that resources be made available to address these in a timely manner. The findings of the Parenting Capacity Assessment will determine the extent to which the person being assessed has the potential to co-operate and facilitate expert remedial efforts with the child.

While you may not have extensive or well-defined expertise in child development and the treatment of childhood disorders, this level of specificity is not a prerequisite to understanding the fundamental conditions that promote optimal development in a child, nor to understanding that which promotes the escalating emergence of dysfunctionalities. It is, therefore, stated under this subheading that a Parenting Capacity Assessment focuses on the assessed individual's capacity to create an environment that is conducive to a child's optimal development. This is quite different from having the clinical expertise to define the nature of a child's developmental delays or of the specific anomalies manifested by a child. Moreover, you need not have the expertise to recommend possible intervention strategies known to be ameliorative of the child's specific condition. To glean the complexity and expertise required consult the most recent work of Randolph (2001).

The intent is to avoid being trapped by a superfluous effort to discredit your work on the basis that you have little, if any, direct experience assessing and working with children. In fact, a specialist in child development and treatment of dysfunctional children is highly unlikely to have the expertise required to conduct a Parenting Capacity Assessment as prescribed by this format and as required in order to intervene optimally in a child's best interest.

Under this subheading, it must also be conveyed to the reader that the methodology is not culturally specific. That is to say, the same universal conditions are required for the promotion of optimal growth and development. This is a process that is separate and apart from the acquisition of knowledge and skills necessary for adaptive survival in a specific culture. The work of cognitive developmentalists has empirically established this universal phenomenon, as well as the reality that psychosocial conditions to a profoundly significant degree determine the rate and degree to which development occurs in cognitive perspectives as reflected by concomitant behaviours.

The purpose of this section in the report also is to orient the reader to the format that will increasingly be self-evident in the body of the report. Constantly orienting the reader is not a redundancy, but a necessity intended to convey that, you are cognizant of the intricate and complex interplay between a myriad of variables in an individual's make-up. Moreover, it is imperative that the reader be reminded frequently that the four categories of analysis represent created simplifications for the purpose of clarity in the presentation of what otherwise would be overwhelming and incomprehensible information.

Sources of Information

It is common practice among virtually all Mental Health practitioners when producing an Assessment report to carefully list all the information taken into consideration in formulating conclusions and recommendations. How this is done, to a large extent, is a stylistic decision. In the prescribed format, the primary information analyzed is listed in the body of the report. The documentations that were reviewed are listed separately in an appendix. The reason for this is simply to reduce tedium and it is often irrelevant for the reader to see what can be an extremely long list of affidavits, motions and forms idiosyncratic to a referring Child Welfare Agency. Notwithstanding these comments, it is imperative, that every piece of information reviewed be clearly identified since this, too, can potentially be used as a strategy by one or the other counsel to discredit you and/or your conclusions and recommendations. For example, what you read, when you read it and in what sequence you read it may be the basis of an accusation of bias. This issue could also be the basis of a visceral attack on your intelligence, professionalism and clinical assessment skills. In the same vein, it is imperative that you protect yourself by listing precisely what documents you reviewed since there may be instances where, deliberately or inadvertently, vitally important information was withheld from you. The objective is clearly to define the basis of your formulations insofar as your accountability is limited to what documentation you were provided, as well as what information you pursued and obtained.

This subheading section is restricted to listing what you did. That is to say, who you talked to, what observations you made, and what standardized instruments you administered, interpreted and so on. It does not and should not venture into any dialogue as to what you did not do, with some very well-defined exceptions. For example, if you administered a standardized scale to one parent who is literate but not to the other parent who is illiterate, this will be important to explain. Beyond this, there is absolutely no obligation or value in broaching the myriad of things you did not do. This is mentioned to alert you to yet another strategy used by opposing counsel to viscerally or professionally discredit you on the basis of failing to do any number of things with respect to pursuing and collecting information.

This subheading in essence defines your clinical judgment as to what you examined and thereby what you used as the basis of your formulations. In this section, for example, you reveal a clinical judgment that you decided to interview the person being assessed, one, two, three, or four times, as opposed to eight or nine times. Under this subheading you also reveal clinical judgment with respect to how long the interviews were, what collateral sources of information you sought and what efforts you went to in order to prepare an optimally comprehensive report to be used by the court. This subheading section in your report also serves to implicitly acknowledge that at some stage you decided that there would be diminishing benefits to continue collecting information. When there are diminishing returns to your efforts and a consequence that entails exacerbating the "limbo" status of a child, it is prudent to move to the next step in the prescribed methodology, namely analysis followed by formulations and concomitant recommendations.

Commonly, Mental Health professionals in their assessment reports simply use the title of the standardized instrument that they employed in the data collection methodology. If the report is intended to be used primarily by other Mental Health professionals, in most instances this is an acceptable practice. Insofar as a Parenting Capacity Assessment is not intended to be read by a Mental Health professional, but by a judge, this is an unacceptable practice. The prescribed format of this Parenting Capacity Assessment methodology therefore requires that you not only list the tools that you used, but also your rationale for using them, as well as the information that is provided by the results obtained with each tool. In fact, you may want to elaborate beyond what is prescribed, perhaps differentiating between self-report measures and measures that provide information with respect to actual abilities. Ultimately, the consideration is the same as above, namely at which point does your elaboration produce diminishing returns.

This subheading section will force you, the assessor, to reflect on the strategy which you have taken with respect to data collection and, more importantly, cause you to reflect on what you are not doing and the reasons that justify the parameters you set with respect to achieving confidence in your clinical formulations and concomitant recommendations.

Documentation Review-Findings

This subheading constitutes your analysis of the information obtained and your formulations as to the meaning and relevance of the information with respect to the assessed individual's capacity to parent a child considered to be at risk. The prescribed report format requires from you, however, a brief introduction with respect to your strategy for including the documented information as part of your database. The prescribed format is intended to ensure that the reader understands you are cognizant of the possibility that documentations could represent deliberate or inadvertent distortions. This may be relevant, especially regarding the interpretations of observers.

The introductory comments, therefore, are intended to orient the reader to recognize that your focus was on the observations/descriptions of behaviours concerning the person being assessed. The interpretation of the reported observations is yours. Moreover, the introductory comments are intended to also orient the reader to the fact that you noted and sought to explain any inconsistencies with respect to the behaviour patterns revealed by the person being assessed.

The introductory comments under this subheading also are designed to convey in no uncertain terms that all the documentation reviewed was done so with a measured, constructive, critical perspective. As such, the information was not taken at face value. Nevertheless, you need to convey that all documentation was treated as potentially relevant to broadening the basis on which your conclusions were made.

This section is not intended to reiterate the information revealed by the documentation, especially since the materials have most likely been filed in the court as evidence and are readily available to the judge assigned to the case. Rather, the material under this subheading is provided to support the clinical impressions created by the documentation. The task is to delineate, for example, impressions pertaining to the characterization of the person being assessed, as well as pertaining to the nature and the dynamics of the differences of opinion between a Child Welfare Agency and the parent whose capacity is being questioned. The documented behaviour of the person being assessed can, in most instances, enhance the confidence of your clinical formulations under one or more of the categories of analysis, strengthening your position that the assessment findings do not constitute a "snapshot" view of the individual but rather a contextual formulation that is relevant over time. The documentation can also serve to broaden your clinical formulations, as for example, by providing the behavioural manifestations of characterological dysfunctionalities. These manifestations may pertain to documented instances of inebriation consistent with identified addictive propensities or documented instances of profoundly violent outbursts minimized or denied by the assessed individual as a function of cognitive developmental deficits that can support the creation of "fantasy".

Under this subheading, conclusions are restricted to orienting the reader to make connections between the various sources of information which constitute the basis of your formulations. This section in the report begins to establish the contextualization of the Parenting Capacity Assessment's findings, conclusions and recommendations.

Background Information

Since the early days of psychotherapy, a basic assumption has been made that an individual's early development (Freud 1963, Mahler et. al. 1975, Piaget 1932) or life stages (Erickson 1980) give insight into present personality and behaviour. Since change through developmental stages is determined by physiology, experience and a myriad of other variables, an adequate assessment of a person's past and its relationship to present circumstances is essential.

It is common practice among Mental Health professionals to obtain a personal history from the individual being assessed. Less common, but often seen if circumstances permit, a corroboration of the assessed person's report is obtained through, for example, a criminal record check or interviews with a significant other.

As common as this practice is, it is equally uncommon to find in assessment reports a synthesis of an individual's historical experiences and the clinical findings. It is as if the Assessor expects the reader to intuitively make the connection, as for example between the finding of an attachment disorder and that individual's descriptions of a chaotic, hostile environment during the most crucial formative stage of life. To make such connections is the responsibility of the Assessor, even if the intended recipients of a report are other Mental Health professionals, let alone a non-Mental Health professional such as a judge.

This section of the report, therefore, is the contextual grounding of the findings produced by the prescribed assessment methodology. Consequently, reporting the background history of the person being assessed is not intended to stand alone. On the contrary, it is intended to be integral to the conclusions and recommendations under the four categories of analysis and to provide the clinical, logical coherence for your formulations.

How and what the assessed reports, whether consistent or inconsistent, corroborated or not, is all profoundly significant and must be taken into consideration, explained and its relevance clearly delineated with respect to the individual's capacity as a parent.

At the risk of being sophomoric, collecting and reporting background historical information about the person being assessed is prescribed to follow a systematically logical pattern starting with the individual's recollection of events and progressing to the current circumstance in the person's life. As such, the report begins with the individual's descriptions of parents, their strengths and weaknesses, the home environment they created and the nature of the relationship they had with the person being assessed. Insofar as the most crucial developmental time in an individual's life is the formative stage which takes up the first three years of life, as much information as possible should be ascertained about the family circumstances of the person at that time. The objective is to learn about the person's environmental circumstance in order to characterize it along a continuum of functionality. The same criterion applies with respect to the person's recollection of the quality of relationships with primary caregivers. This will be significant with respect to establishing the confidence in your formulation pertaining to the attachment experiences of the person being assessed.

Therefore, there should be significant effort exerted to ascertain from the person being assessed their memory, view and description of how they were parented. This is crucially important insofar as early-life experiences of the person being assessed are likely to have a major effect on his or her ability and capacity to establish a secure attachment. This issue is especially significant if the person being assessed has been clinically identified as having sustained an attachment disorder but is unaware of it and as a consequence is not addressing it in any persistent or assisted manner.

The experiences of siblings are significant and must be included in the background information. The finding of dysfunctional siblings as reported by the assessed and corroborated whenever possible can serve to confirm the presence of a dysfunctional environment and strengthen the hypothesis of intergenerational perpetuation of dys-functionalities, especially of an attachment disorder.

The reported academic performance of the person being assessed is vitally important to ascertain the emerging later-life consequences of formative life experiences. Insofar as most individuals being assessed are found to have at least average innate intellectual potential, school performance and behaviour will be additional sources of informa-tion with respect to strengthening a possible formulation about the deleterious later-life consequences of formative stage experiences. School experiences can also begin to reveal information about the assessed individual's capacity to relate and become involved in a social network. This information is profoundly relevant for the third category of analyses in the prescribed methodology. Peer experiences can also provide invaluable information with respect to the individual's development of sense of self and concomitant identification or alienation from the norm.

Employment history can also be informative about the later-life manifestations of formative stage experiences, especially if juxtaposed with unrealized intellectual capacities.

The relationships of individuals, especially romantic liaisons, are profound later-life indicators of early life experi-ences. Both romantic and social patterns of interaction reveal much about the unmet needs of the person during the most crucial formative stage of life. Progressively dysfunctional, abusive, serial relationships are profoundly strong indicators of inadequate parenting as well as negative environmental circumstances in an individual's early life. This is also consistent with the development of dysfunctional characterological traits that pertain to inter-personal skill propensities. Such findings predict with significant probability the perpetuation of dysfunctional relationships of a romantic nature, and more importantly, dysfunctional relationships with the person's child and thereby the perpetuation of negative family legacies.

Physical health, nutrition, lifestyle, substance use and abuse, past and current, will confirm or negate formulations pertaining to the logical clinical emergence of dysfunctionality which will be the basis of your hypothesis that will be tested under the four categories of analysis.

A positive self-report pertaining to current circumstances that is inconsistent with that which would be predicted by the individual's negative early-life experiences gives cause to explore what, if any, significant intervention/event precipitated positive changes in the functioning of the person being assessed. Alternatively, in the absence of such significant intervening events, inconsistent self-reports give rise to hypothesize and investigate the possible reliance on fantasy with which individuals avoid the emotional pain of their circumstances. The same considerations hold true if a person reports current dysfunctionalities but describes an idyllic childhood.

The collection of background history is best done in the spirit of absolute curiosity. There is no need to approach the data collection with any preconceived notions beyond the fact that an individual's current functioning represents the sum total of his or her life experiences, the most profound determinant being what occurred during the most crucial formative stage. Curiosity and skill to explore all possibilities is not difficult to maintain, especially if you, the Assessor, tenaciously and consistently remain mindful of your mandated role to provide information that will be one criterion among many used by a judge to make a definitive determination in the best interest of a child at risk.

Approaching the task of collecting background information with genuine curiosity is the means by which to prevent asking "leading questions" that produce the kind of negative results that explain why that person is the subject of a Parenting Capacity Assessment. A genuine clinical curiosity, can in fact, be quite reinforcing and thereby self-perpetuating, especially if the person's self-report does not produce a clinically predictable coherent picture. Such instances are most intriguing and engaging for an Assessor, although in reality they seldom occur. Therefore, it is difficult to imagine an argument of bias being valid with respect to soliciting only information that is detrimental to the person being assessed as is often advanced by that person's legal counsel. In fact, knowing what to ask and how to ask is by no means evidence of bias. Instead, it is invariably evidence of the Assessor's competence in obtaining, in a systematic and efficient manner, information profoundly useful for the formulation of conclusions and recommendations in the best interest of a child.

Salient Issues

While reasons for the referral entail the conceptualization of concerns about a parent from the perspective of a Child Welfare Agency, this section in the report requires the conceptualization of the problem from the perspective of the person being assessed. The conceptualization of the problem by the assessed provides significant information that will be incorporated into clinical formulations and concomitant recommendations. Individuals reveal much about their emotional state and cognitive developmental perspective through how they conceptualize their differences of opinion with a Child Welfare Agency.

Seldom, if ever, will you find persons being assessed agreeing with the concerns expressed about them or having insight into the nature of their dysfunctionalities or accepting responsibility for having created through their actions concerns about their ability and capacity to competently parent a child. By the time they are going through a Parenting Capacity Assessment process, individuals are no longer in a state of crisis. As such, whatever crisis experience they encountered has long passed. Instead of realizing the opportunity that was initially inherent during their crisis, they will most likely manifest the danger component that was also inherent in their crisis situation. The danger is manifested by the marshalling of considerable defense mechanisms, often exacerbated by marked cognitive developmental deficits.

If this was not the case, there would be no need for a Parenting Capacity Assessment.

In collecting information for this subheading, the assessed will reveal to you an array of defense mechanisms, including projection, minimization, and most often, the use of denial. Much can be learned about an individual's functioning from the psychodynamic defenses that he or she employs. The best example of this is the creation of pleasing fantasies about themselves and their circumstances. This is the basis of denial. Developmentally deficient individuals, not unlike children, are capable of sustaining elaborate fantasies that bear little resemblance to reality. To understand this phenomenon, we need only reflect on our own experiences of progressively decreasing ability to engage in daydreaming or fantasy with the passage of time. This declining ability is largely attributable to cognitive developmental advancements (maturation) that provide us with the ability to understand and appreciate the immediate, broad and long-term implications of our actions. This attribute is incompatible with sustaining beliefs and interpretations of events that have minimal, if any, relationship to reality. In contrast the creation of a fantasy that is pleasing and protects the individual from adverse emotional experiences is inconsistent with doing that which is required to bring a dysfunctionality under control. This is best exemplified by the person addicted to alcohol. In spite of several criminal convictions, perhaps even including vehicular homicide, the person can still be in denial about their alcohol abuse problem and thereby resistant to engaging in strategies with which to bring this debilitating propensity under control.

Ascertaining from the perspective of a potential caregiver their views with respect to the nature of the acrimony with a Child Welfare Agency can also be invaluable information with respect to understanding the reasons why interventions were either not complied with or did not produce the desired benefits expected. For example, as opposed to finding the assessed as petulant and willfully defiant, his or her view of the problem will often be as a disagreement that is grounded in marked cognitive developmental limitations that prevent the person from understanding and/or accepting the legitimacy of the concerns their lifestyle/behaviour create with respect to their ability and capacity to promote optimally a child's development.

To a large extent, the conceptualization of the problem by the person being assessed will explain the person's maladaptive and dysfunctional strategy for pursuing vindication through an Assessment and through the court as opposed to pursuing the less demanding and upsetting strategy of working toward alleviating the concerns of a Child Welfare Agency. Since the assessed do not understand, or cannot relate to the conceptualization of the concerns about them as parents, the only strategy available to them is an instinctive defensive tactic, regardless of its unproductivity. Unfortunately, their legal counsels can be exacerbating influences on this dysfunctional strategy as a function of a distorted interpretation of their role as vigorous defenders of their client as opposed to being officers of the court.

Under this subheading, the prescribed format requires that the Assessor also formulate from a clinical perspective what constitute the salient issues in the case. Such a formulation will be based on the Child Welfare Agency's Terms of Reference, the review of documentation, as well as the assessed person's conceptualization of the nature of the conflict with the Child Welfare Agency. The reason for making a statement with respect to what constitute the salient issues in the case from a clinical perspective is consistent with the previously elaborated rationales, namely to orient the reader to the Assessor's line of investigation as the Assessment questions become increasingly better formulated in the data collection process.

A brief commentary on problem formulation/assessment is warranted in this discussion regarding salient issues. From time to time, the unique, individual characteristics of a case will require an additional line of investigation. The need for this, in my experience, has always been identified through a discussion about what constitute the salient issues. That is to say, why the Parenting Capacity Assessment is being done, from the perspective of the person being assessed. The point, therefore, is that whatever additional lines of investigation you pursue, your decisions in this respect should be based on information you collect up to this point in the assessment process. If additional lines of investigation are warranted by the information, to maintain the integrity of the methodology it is imperative that the additional line of investigation be allocated to one or more of the four categories of analyses. There are a few examples that come to mind in this respect. The most remarkable are instances in which expected patterns are not found and significant variances need to be explained. An example of this is a predicted addictive characterological trait not being found and an individual's substance use and abuse being determined to be essentially situationally based. On further investigation, it was revealed that during the most crucial formative stage in that individual's life, primary care was given by competent and nurturing grandparents in the absence of profoundly dysfunctional parents. Therefore, while the prescribed Parenting Capacity Assessment is analogous to testing experimentally well-formulated hypotheses, a hypothesis which is unsupported rather than being relegated to the discarded category of insignificant results as it is done in research, can be a clinically profound source of elucidating information.

CHAPTER 3
Categories of Analyses

The following constitute elaborations that are beyond that which is required in terms of introductory comments to be included in your Parenting Capacity Assessment report. The elaborations are intended to provide you with greater insight as to the importance of each category of analysis and their interrelationships with each other. The following is also intended to provide you with the confidence necessary for making formulations and recommendations that will profoundly impact on the disposition of a child. In the event that you may have to testify in court, the following also will be of benefit to you with respect to providing greater elaboration beyond that which is in your report, as well as demonstrating your substantive knowledge in this particular area of clinical practice.

The First Category of Analysis: Attachment

"No one has the right to block development of another: that is a spiritual crime"

James Hollis, 1993

This category of analysis examines what is uniformly accepted by Mental Health professionals, especially those involved in the practice of conducting "child custody and access evaluations" and "Parenting Capacity Assessments", as the most important determinant of what disposition would be in the best interest of a child. Attachment success or failure during the most crucial formative stage in life (the first three years) will define for the duration of the life of all individuals their personality structure, behavioural propensities, in brief, their functionality. Insofar as primary caregivers determine the child's attachment success, the focus is primarily on the attachment experiences of the person being assessed.

Findings

Start this and all subsequent categories of analyses with a statement that defines your conclusion and concomitant recommendations as supported by the information you collected and analyzed. Instead of a stylistic flaw, redundancy is necessary to dispel any doubt and to structure (force) a decisive timely determination in a child's best interest. Redundancy of course does not mean repeating the same conclusion, or evidence in support of it. Rather, redundancy means proving your conclusion in as many ways as you can, for each proof using valid and reliably data. Your interpretation of the assessed person's own attachment history is a crucial variable under this category of analysis followed by information concerning the parent-child interaction patterns.

The Importance of Attachment

As so eloquently described by Hollis (1993), the far-reaching effects of early-life experiences, indeed the experiences during the most crucial formative stage of life, impact on us even as we enter the middle passage of life which usually encompasses the fifth decade. Even at this stage, the imperative is to find one's own authority as opposed to the authority of the parent. Otherwise the second half of the individual's life will remain dominated by the vagaries of childhood. According to Hollis, at mid-life there are several aspects of the parent complex that one must work through. At the most visceral level, the infantile experiences of the person being assessed was a primal lesson about life itself, how supportive or hurtful it was and how warm or cold the person's welcome was into the life of his or her parents. How well or poorly the assessed person's parents mediated their natural anxieties as children is the basis of all individuals' attitudes and behaviours for the remainder of their lives.

This is not a culturally specific phenomenon. While there are cultural variations in the forms of attachment behaviour, as well as differences in approach to caregiving and expectations of an infant (Takahashi 1990), there are well-established universal factors. The universal factors are that an infant needs to have an attachment to a primary caregiver (or in many cultures, to a set of primary caregivers) who are consistently sensitive and capable of contingent responsiveness. In all cultures, secure attachment in infancy and toddlerhood has empirically been demonstrated to predict social competence, good problem-solving abilities and other personality qualities associated with successful adaptation in later life. A myriad of longitudinal studies have demonstrated this (Sroufe 1989).

The anthropologist, Margaret Mead (1910, 1913, 1934), preceded and influenced the work of John Bowlby by proposing that young children learn about themselves from the responses of important others (usually parents) to their social acts. That is to say, children learn to understand themselves through the responses significant others make to their social behaviours. Mead spoke of the direct correlation between what an infant does and the response that infant receives. For example, if an infant's gesture of holding up the arms to be picked up is habitually ignored by a parent, this particular way of signaling will, according to Mead, lose meaning for that infant.

Later attachment theory expanded on Mead's insights about loss of meaning with respect to a particular way of signaling to define more profound consequences on the development of a child. Insofar as infants intuitively expect caring parental responsiveness to attachment signals, parental ignoring of an infant's attachment signals does not render the infant's communication meaningless, but rather conveys rejection. Verbally, this rejection can be expressed as "your signals do no count". Eventually, such parental responses, if pervasive and consistent, are incorporated into an internal working model of self that can be articulated as "my needs are not important" (Bretherton 1990). Therefore, meanings derived from attachment interactions hold tremendous significance for the child's developing working models of self, first in relation to attachment figures and later in relation to people in general.

Following the work of Margaret Mead in the 1940s and 1950s, John Bowlby and James Robertson used films of young children undergoing separation to demonstrate the importance of attachment relationships. The films highlighted the emotions that accompany disruptions of the attachment relationship. It was apparent to observers that the children experienced the separations as a fundamental threat to their wellbeing. The films documented the significance of this threat by showing the young children's emotional reactions, including fearful expressions, angry protests, and desperate efforts to find the missing parent. The more extreme emotions of fear and anger that were immediately evident following the separation gave way to more subtle expressions of sadness and despair.

After prolonged periods of sadness, the infants regained some composure and became detached and less emotionally expressive.

From a cognitive developmental perspective, progress through an invariant hierarchical sequence of reasoning is based on and stimulated by attachment to the primary socialization of the individual to "belong" to and with social agents. This is the process by which the individual organism becomes an acculturated person. Without the development of affective and cognitive orientation to other people, the motivation (drive) to incorporate a system of morality defined and directed by social agents will likely not arise (Garbarino and Bronfenbenner 1976). In fact, studies of the long-term consequences of early social neglect indicate a pattern of psychopathology which may be characterized as amoral (Bowlby 1946). Not surprisingly, therefore, an attachment disorder has invariably been found to undermine the capacity to trust, for empathy, for achievement of impulse control, positive identity formation, self-esteem, the development of conscience and successful socialization (Schneider-Rosen and Cicchetti 1984; Steinhauer 1990).

How parents describe their childhood attachments can be used to predict the predominant pattern of their children's attachment to them in more than two cases out of three according to the findings of Main and Solomon (1990). In the Strange Situation, whereby contact between a child and primary caregiver is involuntarily disrupted, the nature of a child's primary pattern of attachment was found to be predictable entirely from a complex analysis of the children's primary caretakers' descriptions of their relationship with primary caretakers as they remembered them.

It is noteworthy that by the time children reach the age of three or four years, physical separation no longer presents as serious a threat and consequently does not produce the same kind of emotional reactions.

The early observations of Bowlby gave rise to his often quoted phrase, "the provision of mothering is as important to a child's development as a proper diet and nutrition". Furthermore, Bowlby postulated that institutional/foster care could not substitute for the attachment bond with parents. The position of Bowlby was always that "the services which mothers and fathers habitually render their children are so taken for granted that their magnitude is forgotten" (Karen 1994). Moreover, it has long been believed that in no other relationship do human beings place themselves so unreservedly and so continuously at the disposal of others as in a parent-child dyad. To a large extent, the conclusions of Bowlby and subsequent research in this vitally important area of human development are the basis of the legislative principle of "least intrusive measures". Recent legislation serves to underscore the point that it is crucial to pursue timely adoption or repatriation with parents insofar as secure attachment provides an irreplaceable context for emotional development.

Bowlby (1969-1982) also acknowledged that most young infants, especially in some cultures, form more than one attachment. As such, many children have more than one figure to whom they direct attachment behaviours. In most cultures, this means the biological parents, older siblings and grandparents. Bowlby clearly notes that the father is also a particularly significant attachment figure very early in an infant's life. Although there is usually more than one attachment figure, the potential number is not limitless (Bretherton 1980) insofar as infants have a "small hierarchy of major caregivers". Therefore, while most infants have multiple attachment figures, it is important not to assume that an infant treats all attachment figures as equivalent or that they are interchangeable. Bowlby (1969-1982) was very clear about this stating that infants prefer a principal attachment figure for comfort and security, a phenomenon that he labeled as "monotropy".

Attachment Defined

At this juncture, it is vitally important to establish a shared definition or understanding of the concept of attachment and what constitutes an attachment disorder.

An attachment bond is a specific type of a larger class of bonds that Bowlby and Ainsworth referred to as "affectional bonds" (Ainsworth 1989). There are five criteria for an affectional bond to exist. The addition of a sixth criteria expands the affectional bond to constitute an attachment bond. The first five criteria for an affectional bond entail:

1. an affectional bond must be persistent, not transitory;
2. affectional bond involves a specific person, a figure who is not interchangeable with anyone else;
3. an affectional bond involves a relationship that is emotionally significant;
4. an affectional bond must involve a wish to maintain proximity to or contact with a person. This varies as a function of a variety of factors (for example, age, state of the individual, environmental conditions, etc.);
5. an affectional bond must involve the individual feeling distress at involuntary separation from the person.

The additional criterion which expands an affectional bond to become an attachment bond is that:
6. the infant must seek security and comfort in the relationship with the person.

The seeking of security and comfort in a relationship with a primary caregiver is the defining feature of an attachment bond.

The classification of attachment behaviour between a primary caregiver and a child is essentially derived from the work of Mary Ainsworth. Precise classifications are of academic/research interest and of great value with respect to informing intervention strategies with a parent, as well as for ameliorating dysfunctional patterns of interaction between that parent and a child. While it is advisable to seek a classification determination in a Parenting Capacity Assessment to facilitate any subsequent intervention strategies with respect to addressing attachment problems, it is not crucial to achieve the degree of specificity that is possible in an experimental situation. As the Assessor, it is imperative that you recognize that the Ainsworth categorization of attachment between a parent and a child is essentially accomplished in a well-controlled experimental situation. This is difficult, if not impossible, to replicate during a Parenting Capacity Assessment process. Therefore, from the perspective of this prescribed methodology it is sufficient to identify, first and foremost, the presence or absence of an attachment disorder between the assessed and the child considered to be at risk. This will be a conclusion based on observation, as well as on an understanding of the parent's own attachment disorder and the kind of later-life attachment problems this can create. For a number of reasons, as will be discussed subsequently, given the diminishing confidence in arriving at a differential conclusion, it is probably better to restrict your determination to a broad category, namely identifying whether or not there is an attachment disorder.

The following constitute definitions of Mary Ainsworth's classification of attachment between a primary caregiver and a child as determined by observation of the Strange Situation created under experimental conditions. It is applied primarily to the classification of behavioural patterns between a parent and children two years and younger. According to specialists in this field of investigation, it is likely inappropriate to conceptualize a relationship between a parent and a child older than this as indicative of attachment categories. Rather, with other children it is more appropriate conceptually to view the interaction patterns as indicative of years of daily interactions with the parent and as indicative of the child's evaluation of the parent's capacities. With older children especially, caution should be exercised and conclusions should consider the child's dependency needs, loyalties, possible pressures and what influence living in a foster home or with primary caregivers under a Child Welfare Agency supervision may have on interaction patterns during observation.

In spite of the proliferation of literature on the topic of attachment, or likely as a result of it, there are subtle variations with respect to the labels used to classify observed interactional patterns. It is preferable to use the three categories of attachment as coined and described by Ainsworth in addition to the fourth that was subsequently described some years later after her seminal work. The labels used by Ainsworth are: secure; insecure ambivalent; insecure avoidant; and insecure disorganized/disoriented. Thomas and Chess (1969) use slightly different terminology to describe essentially the same phenomenon. For example, they speak of secure attachment; insecure attachment (anxious/ambivalent); avoidant attachment; and disorganized/disoriented attachment.

It is noteworthy that researchers in this particular, specialized area of investigation have been found to produce reliable classifications with the benefit of minimal training and experience.

The language with which you, as the Assessor, convey a determination regarding the attachment classification you observed should acknowledge that the standard against which your observations are compared were established in a controlled, experimental environment. As such, it is advisable that the definition of your specific or general determination be consistent with the following Ainsworth terms:

Secure Attachment

Observation is consistent with what under experimental conditions would be classified as a securely attached child. This is indicative of a supportive parent/child relationship and is generally considered to be a sign that the parent is "good enough" and conducive to promoting normal development.

In a Strange Situation under this attachment classification, a child is observed to be distressed by the parent's absence but rapidly recovers from distress as evidenced by re-engaging his interests in the environment after the parents return, a return which is invariably greeted with pleasure.

Insecure Avoidant Attachment

Observation is consistent with what under experimental conditions would be classified as insecure avoidant attachment. This is indicative of the caretaker likely to have been preoccupied and/or frequently angry, causing strain on the parent/child relationship and bonding. While not all children go on to develop problems, many such infants tend to remain anxious, clinging and ambivalent in their relationships with their caregivers and others.

In the Strange experimental situation, a child is invariably observed to be less manifestly distressed by the parents' departure. Furthermore, the parents' return will be observed to evoke little or slightly negative responses from the infant.

Insecure Ambivalent Attachment

Observation is consistent with what under experimental conditions would be classified as insecure ambivalent attachment. This suggests that the primary caregiver in all likelihood has been dismissive (neglectful or chronically withdrawn and poorly responsive). While not all children go on to develop problems, many tend to be dismissive and distant in their relationships.

In the Strange experimental situation, a child will be observed to appear "worried" about the parent, even when the parent is present. It will be observed that the child is greatly distressed by the parent's departure and will continue to be distressed upon the parent's return. Under this category of analysis, the child often appears angry with the parent, perhaps even striking the parent or behaving otherwise aggressively.

Insecure Disorganized / Disoriented Attachment

Observation is consistent with what under experimental conditions would be classified as insecure disorganized/disoriented attachment. This is indicative that the caregiver is likely to have many significant unresolved attachment problems. Such issues usually lead to major problems between a parent and a child. Consequently, the child's development is highly likely to be seriously compromised. In a child protection population, this pattern is the one most commonly seen. It is strongly associated with long-lasting and permanent problems in affect, behaviour and relationships.

In the Strange experimental situation, what will be observed is a pattern of interaction between child and parent that is incoherent, confused or inconsistent, especially during reunions.

To aid the analysis of interaction pattern observations between parent and child, there is a sophisticated methodology available with which to systematically describe attachment in young children. While the Attachment Q-Sort (Waters and Day 1983) has not been standardized and still requires your clinical judgment, there may be some merit in using this tool. At least initially you should consider using this tool while you are gaining confidence in your skill in identifying an attachment disorder and while you pursue the development of your ability to reach a higher level of specificity regarding the exact attachment category that applies to a case.

Understanding and classifying the type of attachment that predominates in a parent/child relationship is a complex undertaking, especially insofar as the Strange Situation laboratory experiment does not correlate well with what is observed in the home, office or a supervised visit. Nevertheless, there are fundamental and easily observed behaviour patterns such as if a child consistently shows as much interest in a stranger (for example, the Assessor) even when the caregiver is present. This is reason for serious concerns regarding the attachment between the child and that parent.

The Clinical Task

The onus for successful parent/child relationships relies almost entirely with the parent whose task is to adapt/respond in sensitive ways to the characteristics of that particular infant.

The primary determination, therefore, under this category of analysis is the attachment experiences of the person being assessed. Moreover, it cannot be stressed enough that there are many limitations as to what interpretations can be derived from observations of the behaviour patterns between the assessed person and a child. Nevertheless, while this information is collected under this category of analysis, it is secondary to determining whether or not the assessed person sustained an attachment disorder during their most crucial formative stage of life.

This determination is considered primary insofar as the intergenerational perpetuation of an attachment disorder is inevitable unless a significant intervening variable predicts otherwise. Rarely, some individuals may have recognized this to be a debilitating factor in their personality structure and consequently may be engaged in deliberate, purposeful, remedial strategies to break this cycle of dysfunctionality.

The first task under this category of analysis, therefore, is to test the hypothesis that the case represents an intergenerational perpetuation of an attachment disorder. The self-reported relationship between the person being assessed and his or her primary caregivers, early-life experiences and environmental circumstances are all crucial data sources on which to base a conclusion regarding attachment. Known later-life negative consequences such as academic underachievement, poor employment history, relationship difficulties, promiscuity and substance abuse problems are other indicators of attachment problems and the development of debilitating life-enduring characterological traits.

The ongoing nature of the relationship between the person being assessed and that person's parents are further indicators of early-life attachment problems. This is best exemplified by failed or marginal separation and individuation between the assessed and their parents. Invariably, dysfunctional relationships in adulthood are indicative of unresolved and unmet formative stage needs characterized by chronic dependency and approach avoidance conflicts. If possible, obtaining corroborative information by interviewing significant others will enhance the confidence with which you can formulate conclusions.

It is advisable to use a standardized instrument with which to obtain further information pertaining to the assessed person's attachment experiences as an infant. Insofar as these are self-report instruments which assume that the assessed person will be candid and, more importantly, has the capacity to accurately describe emotional and behavioural experiences, the use of such a tool must be in conjunction with a number of other sources of information. Specifically, a standardized instrument cannot be the sole basis on which a finding of an attachment disorder can be made with significant confidence. To formulate a conclusion with significant confidence requires additional findings as described above. While there are a number of related standardized instruments, the Adult Attachment Interview developed by Main and Solomon (1990) is probably the best for this purpose.

Another standardized instrument of potential benefit to augmenting your clinical formulations regarding whether or not the assessed person sustained an attachment disorder during the formative stage of life is the Attachment Q-Sort (Kobak et al. 1993). This instrument can be used with adolescents also but was primarily designed to explore attachment by systematically examining adults' descriptions of their relationships to important figures in their childhood.

An absence of findings in support of a hypothesis of an attachment disorder based on worrisome behaviours such as substance abuse cannot remain unexplained. Invariably, an exploration for an explanation will reveal positive experiences with alternate caregivers during the person's formative stage in life. As such, the prognosis is likely to be quite optimistic with respect to the person being assessed. In such cases, substance abuse may be situationally determined and the person may well be capable with appropriate assistance of developing what approximates a secure attachment with the identified child at risk. Unfortunately, such a finding is rare, although it is one of the crucial variables that support repatriation between a child and a parent conditional on several requirements being satisfied in a timely manner. In these instances, the provision of appropriate resources as well as significant environmental changes (e.g., associations) will produce marked improvements.

A mandated Parenting Capacity Assessment will unfortunately, in the majority of instances reveal the person being assessed as having sustained an attachment disorder during the most crucial formative stage of life. The next line of investigation should seek to determine the presence of an intergenerational perpetuation of this family legacy as manifested by the relationship the assessed parent has with the child on whose behalf the Parenting Capacity Assessment is being conducted. This type of determination is difficult and must be undertaken cautiously, recognizing that what is observed should be interpreted in the context of the circumstances, such as when the observations are made and who is providing primary care to the child at the time.

The Observation Task

Notwithstanding the limitations inherent in observations long after the family's first contact with a Child Welfare Agency, it is imperative that this be included in the assessment process for a myriad of reasons, not the least of which entails a tenacious protection of your objectivity and a communication of your transparent will to discover as much about the person being assessed as is feasible.

Ideally, a child's interactional pattern with a primary caregiver should be observed and documented immediately when a Child Welfare Agency becomes involved in a case. The task need not be challenging. What is required is precise description of how the parent and child interact. Unfortunately, this seldom occurs in most jurisdictions. Hopefully, the absolute necessity for such baseline data will serve as an impetus to incorporate this information collection into the first contact protocol of all Child Welfare Agencies.

In lieu of having baseline information about the nature of the interaction pattern between a parent and a child, as a Parenting Capacity Assessor, you should spend considerable effort on conducting systematic observations. Ideally, your observations should be corroborated by several workers who have had various degrees of involvement in the case. Case notes can also be extremely beneficial, especially in jurisdictions where behavioural descriptions are required as part of a risk analysis. While the confidence of your conclusions based on the observations of others is less than they would be had you seen the interaction patterns yourself, such corroborative information, nevertheless, can be very important for enhancing the confidence level with which you make formulations and concomitant recommendations.

In terms of a hierarchy of confidence in conclusions based on observations, the greatest is that which is based on observations before a child was apprehended. In cases where there is no apprehension (instead a court-ordered Supervision Order), this does not confound the analyzability of observations and subsequent conclusions.

In instances where a child has been apprehended and your observations occur several months after the event, the confidence with which you can formulate conclusions decreases proportionately. Nevertheless, the behaviour of the parent towards a child can be an invaluable source of data confirming, negating or bringing into question your formulations about the attachment disorder of the person being assessed. A classic example of this is an observation that occurred several months after a child was removed from a parent's care. While the child's response to the mother in this case was not terribly informative, the mother's behaviour toward the child was extremely so. The mother, persistently throughout a two-hour observation period, treated the child as a "sack of potatoes", void of even remotely demonstrative affection. This pattern of behaviour from the mother to the child was confirmed by the visit supervisor as persistent since the agency's involvement with the family. This corroborated observation confirmed and reinforced a conclusion that the mother had sustained an attachment disorder, among other dysfunctionalities, as a consequence of catastrophic early-life experiences. The prospect of this parent establishing a secure attachment with the child was postulated to be remote at best.

On occasions, a child's interaction with a parent during an observation can also reveal, in spite of a parent's best efforts, the presence of an attachment disorder. This is exemplified by a case during which an infant clearly and persistently exhibited aggressive behaviour towards the mother to the extent of engaging in unprovoked hitting. Such clearly evident expressions of anger allow for a specificity of determination insofar as the behaviours are consistent with an insecure ambivalent attachment classification as defined by Mary Ainsworth.

Observations can also produce information on which conclusions can be based concerning the parenting knowledge and skills of the person being assessed.

Knowledge and skills deficits could be a problem, at least in theory, even with securely attached children whose parents could benefit greatly from instructional courses, mentoring, and/or facilitation. While this rarely occurs, as an Assessor acting in the best interest of a child, it is imperative that consideration be given to differentiating between parenting knowledge and skills deficits and an attachment problem. The difference, in fact, is quite fundamental. Knowledge and skills deficits are usually manifested by the disarray of a household, cleanliness and nutritional issues as opposed to worrisome interactional patterns between a parent and a child. This will be discussed in greater detail under the second category of analysis. Suffice it to say at this juncture that a determination is required as to whether or not any observed "disarray" is acute or chronic. In most instances where secure attachment between a child and parent is observed, the disarray will be acute, likely precipitated by some significant situational event such as a relationship break-up.

My preference for conducting observations of interactions between a child and a parent is to be as unobtrusive as possible. When circumstances allow, I prefer to be behind a two-way mirror, letting the parent know that I am there, with the encouragement that the parent carry on normally. It has been my experience, for example, with videotaping group therapy with offenders for research purposes, that within a brief period of time, individuals forget about the cameras, and their peer inmate technicians, and become involved in the dynamics of the interactions in a manner that is indistinguishable from what occurs when videotaping was not being done. My interviews of Access Supervisors has invariably confirmed that the same phenomenon occurs during all access visits. Specific probings with Access Supervisors who are usually present, largely to comply with a court-ordered Supervision Order, almost always reveal that parents conduct themselves similarly regardless of who is observing them. In instances where the parent has made progress, Access Supervisors were able to describe the progressive improvements that occurred over time. Moreover, given the potential legal implications when the welfare of children is concerned, the notes of Access Supervisors have been comprehensive and essentially behaviorally oriented, confirming what was said during interviews with them.

It is imperative that during the observation of interaction between a parent and a child, you make systematic notes. You should mark the time of events or alternatively demarcate every quarter hour of a two-hour observation. A two-hour observation, in fact, is likely the most optimal period of time for obtaining valuable information. In every visit, the beginning phase is short and gives way to the middle phase which invariably constitutes a true representation of interaction patterns. The termination phase is usually abruptly precipitated by the clock and, while brief, usually also reveals much about the attachment between a parent and a child. If at all possible, in addition to corroborating your observations with Access Supervisors or other Child Welfare personnel, there should be at least another two-hour observation within a week or two from your first time seeing a parent with a child at risk. It is recognized that in many instances this is difficult to achieve given time constraints and resource limitations. Furthermore, whatever effort is required to conduct the second observation likely will produce diminishing returns. Subsequent observations after a brief period of time, in the absence of a significant intervening variable, will simply reproduce the same findings. While this further establishes the reliability of your initial observations, reliability can be argued more cost effectively from a theoretical perspective as supported by historical data.

You might find it valuable for organizing your observation of the interaction between a parent and a child to use a standardized method such as the Nims Observation Checklist (2000). This method rates: safety, environment, general behaviour toward the child, teaching, training, control and child-initiated behaviour. The method also neatly summarizes the entire observation. While it is not focused on attachment, it does reveal issues of importance which have attachment implications. I have modified it with considerable success to include observations pertaining to the classification of interaction patterns between a parent and a child. Especially in the event of having to give testimony in court, this tool may be invaluable along with your notes.

Physiological Factors

Inferentially and experientially, it has long been known and observed that attachment problems have progressive and life-enduring negative consequences. These later-life negative consequences, to a large extent, have been associated with "psychosocial" factors such as the individual's personality structure, characterological traits, cognitive developmental perspective, as well as what behaviours are learned and reinforced in the environment to which an individual is drawn. More recently, clearly defined physiological factors have been identified that can explain the "unchangeably" of the harm sustained by a child in a troubled relationship with a parent and a concomitant deleterious environment. The notion of "conservation of neurons" represents a physiological fact that if certain neurological functions are not activated at a critical chronological time, they are lost forever. Furthermore, even if synapses are established, if they are not used sufficiently, these abilities will gradually be lost and remain irretrievable. This certainly applies to the acquisition of language, as evidenced by children who can learn to speak flawlessly any number of dialects to which they are exposed during the first few years of life. Beyond a certain chronological age, while language acquisition does occur, invariably it is never flawless and there will always be a revealing hint of some ethnic/cultural accent. The same principle applies to other functions, including the ability to work co-operatively and collaboratively as an adult.

Neurologically, it is a fact that during the first three years of life the brain undergoes tremendous enlargement. At birth, the brain weighs approximately 300 grams. The brain's growth does not end until the beginning of the third decade when it weighs 1,100 grams. It is crucial to note, however, that most of the growth occurs in the first three years of life. A major feature of this enormous growth during this period is the development of connections (synapses) between nerve cells. It is also during this period that the brain's so-called "hard-wiring" is established. While genetic predispositions play some part in this process, the psychosocial environment has been determined empirically to be primarily responsible for the physical and synaptic developments during what otherwise is known as the most crucial formative stage of life. The impact of the environment through the senses, such as vision, hearing and touch, is dramatic and specific, not merely influencing the general direction of development but actually affecting how the intricate circuitry of the brain is wired. Synapses that are used during the early stages of development are the ones that last; unused synapses disappear or become ineffective (Chugani 1998; Hutten-locher and Dabholkar 1997; Katz and Shatz 1996).

Research on brain development, therefore, has been invaluable with respect to understanding the permanency of characterological traits. That is to say, the lack of maternal nurturing and appropriate stimulations (Spitz and Provence 1967; Cobliner 1966) also profoundly impact on the development of synoptic connections. Therefore, if a child does not experience positive stimuli such as love and affection and is instead neglected or maltreated, parts of the brain are believed never to develop properly. The consequence of this is permanent behavioural and personality propensities that, can at best, with a great deal of concerted and persistent effort, be brought under conscious, deliberate control, but can never be eradicated from the individual's functioning. The best example of this is the development of an addictive characterological personality trait which will be discussed at length under the second category of analysis.

Reflections on the Child

Under the first category of analysis there is a prescribed subcategory that requires clinical formulations regarding the child. Notwithstanding earlier comments that a determination of the child's status is best left to the highly specialized experts in this well-defined field of practice, your observations and conclusions can be valuable with respect to expediting the provision of appropriate resources for a child in need. For instance, in many cases, children remain non-verbal past the formative stage (age three). Insofar as the development of verbal communication is de-termined by physical accessibility and appropriate stimulation by an attachment figure, this finding can be signifi-cant concerning not only enhancing your confidence with respect to the determination of an attachment disorder, but also in identifying the need for special resources to be made immediately available to the child.

Neglected or otherwise abused toddlers invariably have difficulty relating to other children and adults, behave socially isolated, act suspicious of the intentions of others, are observed as hyperactive and unusually alert (at times destructive of property), as well as act aggressively and, in general, socially immature and slow to learn. Such ob-servations can be significant with respect to supporting a conclusion of an attachment disorder and concomitant parenting deficits. Older children who have been maltreated, neglected or otherwise abused as a result of earlier attachment problems have been found to enjoy causing pain to animals, as well as to be unsympathetic to peers who are crying. So called deficit oppositional defiant and conduct disorders also are common among this group.

Older children who manifest negative perceptions of self through their conduct and verbal statements invariably have had negative environmental experiences. For example, Kobak (2001) found that threats of suicide by a desper-ate parent may elicit profound anxiety about parental availability. In addition to the obvious threat to physical ac-cessibility of the parent, the child is also faced with the fear of violence and with the prospect of loss. These threats occur in the context of hostile and conflictual relations which may further create the implication for children that their angry feelings toward a parent may be responsible for that parent's desperation and despair. "You will be the death of me" that follows a child's misbehavior also is likely to confound attachment-related fears with feelings of guilt.

Witnessing violence between parents may also threaten a child's confidence in the parent's availability and be a source of an attachment disorder (Davis and Cumming 1995, 1998). The child's appraisal of marital violence is likely to include the fear that harm may come to one or both of the parents. In addition, parents who are living with constant conflict and fear are likely to have reduced capacities to attend to the child. Therefore, insofar as the goal of attachment is achieved through physical proximity, expectations regarding availability and expectations regarding responsiveness, the experience of significant and/or persistent conflict can create fear in a child that may be readily observed during the prescribed data collection phase under this category of analysis. Parental dysfunctionalities become relevant and worrisome when their manifestations become threats with respect to the availability of that parent and the impact this has on attachment.

Observations and concomitant reflections on the child, under the first category of analysis, are intended to identify both the challenges posed by the child, as well as the parent's capacity, obstructed or enhanced by their own attachment experiences, to respond constructively in a consistently competent manner.

Attachment problems and adverse environmental conditions produce not only later-life negative consequences, but in many cases are immediately evident even to the casual observer, let alone to a Mental Health professional with basic understanding regarding normal human growth and development. One does not need to be a specialist in child development to conclude the presence of a problem when a child hits a parent without being provoked, behaves out of control, or damages material things during a brief observation session when a parent cannot anticipate or bring under control the unacceptable conduct of that child.

Under this subheading the prescribed methodology also requires taking into account any special needs the child has been determined to possess by specialists or is suspected to possess as a result of your observations. It is, therefore, imperative that the special needs of the child be identified (educational, behavioural, physiological, etc.), along with the challenges that these will pose to the parent. More importantly, the issue, of course, is a determination as to the parent's capacity (potential) to predictably, and with competence, respond to the need in a manner that optimally promotes a child's development. This capacity is significantly influenced by the nature of the attachment between the parent and the child.

The preceding discourse regarding the life-enduring, later-life negative consequences of an attachment problem and adverse environmental conditions hopefully has served to establish in no uncertain terms that failing to act in a timely manner, especially with a child in the most crucial formative stage in life, is tantamount to depriving that infant of the life-enduring benefits that are inherent in being parented by competent, developmentally mature and emotionally adjusted caregivers. If the findings under this category of analysis are unfavorable toward the primary caregivers being assessed with respect to their capacity to derive benefits from specialized intervention in a timely manner, such a determination gives serious cause to conclude and recommend intrusive measures with the ultimate goal of placing that infant at risk with adoptive parents.

The Second Category of Analysis:
The Criteria of a Good Parent

*"To be a parent is a right the benefits of which are innumerable.
Such a right comes with an equally onerous responsibility: to do all that is
possible to protect and foster the child's right to develop optimally".*

Alexander T. Polgar, 2001

This category of analysis requires what are the most familiar practice-based knowledge and skills possessed by any Mental Health practitioner. Regardless of discipline, values, theoretical framework or the approach taken to intervention, whatever is done is based on a formulation, formal or informal, explicit or implicit, as to what is the nature of an individual's problem. Always, the definition of the problem determines what goal is pursued, how it is pursued and what outcome is expected from interventions. The practiced ability in this respect is what is required by this category of analysis in the prescribed methodology. The following section is intended to guide you through the special application of your assessment knowledge and skills. Because of the context special application pertains to determining the assessed individual's potential to extenuate personal strengths, to bring under control weaknesses or dysfunctionalities, as well as to learn and apply parenting knowledge and skills in a persistently competent manner.

Findings

Start the findings under this category of analysis with a statement that defines your conclusion and concomitant recommendations as supported by the information you collected and analyzed. It should be easy for the reader to follow. Any redundancy will serve to dispel doubt or reservation with respect to your conclusion. Therefore, instead of, for example, reporting that the findings under all four categories of analysis are the same and support the same conclusion and recommendations, it is far better to delineate in a clear fashion each area of analysis, leaving summary comments to the discussion section of the report. Keep in mind that your report essentially represents an argument that is based on principles of formal logic. Once you have stated your position, the task then is to convince the reader that it is a valid one. To do so, it will be necessary to prioritize in descending order of importance the evidence/premises in support of your conclusion and recommendations. Under this category of analysis, the most important supportive evidence is your clinical formulations subsequently augmented and/or enhanced by your analysis of standardized instruments.

What It Is Not

To define something by what it is not is never good practice and rightfully is frowned upon. To begin this section in such a way, however, cannot be avoided since the propensity of many Mental Health practitioners is influenced by what is commonly referred to as "the medical model approach". The medical model is ideally suited to what physicians do. It is essentially a reactive approach whereby an individual's life or death often is determined by how quickly and how well a problem is defined. This then determines what is taken out of the individual (e.g., the appendix) or put into him or her (e.g., insulin). Presenting problems to a physician especially those which are acute respond well to the reactive interventions provided. These positive experiences are the basis for seeking a medical solution even in instances where there is none.

A Parenting Capacity Assessment is not focused on a child at risk because of a primary caregiver's acute dysfunctional state as a function of some organic process. Individuals in acute non-organic dysfunctional states are also seldom the subjects of a Parenting Capacity Assessment. For example, subsequent to experiencing a profoundly traumatic event, most individuals have access to social support and appropriate expert resources. Moreover, they are inclined to use such resources in a co-operative and compliant manner. Furthermore, while special arrangements may have to be made for the children of individuals in acute states of dysfunctionality, the social support network in these cases is such that children are hardly, if ever, at risk.

I cannot imagine, nor have I seen a case where otherwise functioning individuals in a state of acute crisis had to resort to using the services of a Child Welfare Agency, even temporarily. While I am sure there are exceptions, it is even more difficult to imagine the need for a Parenting Capacity Assessment in these remote instances.

Therefore, a Parenting Capacity Assessment is incompatible with the application of an approach that is based on the "medical model". It is never a mental status examination that requires a rapid and accurate problem formulation (diagnosis) and an equally rapid and appropriate invasive reactive intervention. Tragically, the determination of a child's status based on a parent's capacity is at best ponderous. Applying a medical model using jargon and diagnostic labels, therefore, is not only inappropriate but can hardly be helpful since the report is primarily intended to be used by a non-Mental Health professional, namely a judge, with the socially designated authority to make a timely, decisive disposition of a child's status.

What It Is

A Parenting Capacity Assessment represents a specific application of the psychosocial systems model for assessing and intervening with individuals and their families. To generate a psychosocial profile of suspected deficient/abusive parents it is necessary to understand their functioning within the context in which their behaviours occur, the background from which it was derived, and the existing child-rearing norms that tolerate certain levels of maladaptive interactions especially violence between family members (Wolfe, 1987)

The psychosocial model is particularly relevant insofar as in spite of concerted research efforts no consensus has been forthcoming with respect to a distinctive psychological profile of deficient abusive parents. Instead, there has emerged a consensus that deficient/abusive parenting is a complex interactional event determined by the parents developmental historical experiences and situational variables that elicit characterological personality trait based responses.

The methodology used to conduct a Parenting Capacity Assessment is a unique process designed to produce a series of formulations pertaining to an individual's potential to overcome dysfunctionalities and become a competent primary caregiver to a child. Hence the use of the concept "capacity" as opposed to "ability". Therefore, under this category of analysis, the focus is on defining the obstacles that prevent the person being assessed from doing, in a persistently competent manner, that which is required to promote optimally the development of the child in his or her care.

While the challenge of parenting is to promote optimally the developmental potential of a child, this requirement is not intended to set an unattainable standard for parents. Instead of expecting a parent to be perfect, the required standard is to strive for perfection in promoting the development of a specific child. Why would anyone strive for anything less than this? In this context therefore, the notion of a "good enough" parent at least in theory may differ from case to case due to the individuality of the child in whose best interest the Parenting Capacity Assessment is being conducted. In practice, however, in most cases the differences will be indistinguishable. The obstacles to optimally promoting the development of a child will be the distinguishable differences that require identification.

Sometimes the obstacles may be so-called "chronic psychiatric disorders" identified and labeled previously by physician specialists in psychiatry. Most often the obstacles are personality features and psychosocial factors, which do not respond readily or at all to pharmacological intervention. Consequently, not only is your investigation intended to define the obstacles but also two crucially relevant variables, specifically the availability of appropriate psychosocial intervention resources and time frames in which improvements can be expected of a magnitude and quality required to meet the needs of a child.

The Approach

The following represents that which is defined in the literature as consistent with being a "good enough" parent. The criteria are by no means presented as an exhaustive list. It is, however, prescribed insofar as, from a cost-effective perspective, additional lines of investigation are likely to produce diminishing returns. Nevertheless, from time to time, the unique characteristics of a case may, indeed, require from you additional avenues of investigation. You may also prefer to use additional lines of investigation and analysis because you are comfortable with the approach and because you believe the additional effort will make significant contributions that will be in the best interest of a child on whose behalf the assessment is being conducted.

You may also want to augment your clinical formulations with alternative or additional standardized instruments to what I use with which you are particularly familiar and which you are experienced in using, especially with respect to the analytical benefits a particular tool may have for you. My personal preference is to avoid standardized instruments that are particularly transparent. I also prefer to avoid the use of standardized instruments that tend to confirm the obvious or which are particularly vulnerable to producing false positives. I am specifically referring to instruments designed to "test parenting abilities" by asking questions about parenting practices, expectations of a child and knowledge about developmental phases. My preference is to generate data in which I have confidence with respect to validity and reliability, since this determines the confidence with which I make conclusions and recommendations. Notwithstanding these comments, I have seen creative and informative use of standardized instruments which I would not have included in a typical battery of tools. Therefore, any restrictions on what standardized instruments you use should take into consideration the above cautions and then be limited only by your comfort and expertise administering and interpreting the results of a particular tool.

Cognitive Intelligence

A priority determination made by all Mental Health practitioners pertains to the cognitive intelligence of the person being assessed. Often this is done intuitively, immediately as you engage the person with a view to progressively defining how you interact with that individual. Clinical formulations in this respect are augmented by the background history of the person, including educational and employment experiences.

In addition to informing the manner in which you clinically interact with the person being assessed, a determination pertaining to cognitive intelligent is essential to establish how much parenting knowledge and skills a person can be expected to learn. Moreover, a determination in this respect will provide information with which to explain why a person who has attended parenting courses does not do what is expected. The person may have been incapable of learning the information or alternatively incapable of applying the knowledge and skills as a result of any array of dysfunctionalities.

Clinical determinations regarding cognitive intelligence are intended to inform you with respect to what level of linguistic sophistication the person being assessed possesses, as well as the level of conceptual formulations they are familiar with and can effectively use to interact with you in a meaningful manner. By way of example, abstract, largely conceptual communication styles will largely be incomprehensible to an individual who, as a result of environmental circumstances, has had minimal formal education and is poorly read.

This same example also can be the cause of making a false negative conclusion regarding an individual's innate cognitive intelligence. In fact, while a majority of Parenting Capacity Assessment subjects are profound underachievers, especially academically, I have found them to have significant, albeit unrealized cognitive intellectual potential uncovered through using a non-verbal, culturally unbiased test of intelligence.

I use the Raven's Progressive Matrices to augment my clinical formulations and recommend that you do likewise as a cost-effective, valid and reliable tool with which to determine cognitive intellectual potential, as opposed to ability. Culturally biased tests of intelligence such as the WAIS are useful as psychoeducational assessment tools but, in fact, in Parenting Capacity Assessments, will serve to confirm, at best, that the person being assessed is an underachiever or, at worst, inaccurately define intellectual limitations far beyond that which they actually are.

Interestingly, the Raven's Progressive Matrices non-verbal test of intelligence has revealed the majority of Parenting Capacity Assessment subjects to function within the average range of cognitive intelligence. Moreover, there is a definite normal distribution pattern among the people I have assessed, as well as those assessed by my colleagues.

Incidentally, a statement that an individual likely functions within the average range of intelligence as evidenced by clinical formulations and supported by the Raven's Progressive Matrices results does not constitute a diagnostic label. If, however, you fail to elaborate on the significance of such a finding, this statement will be of little value similar to a diagnostic label, and just as antithetical to the very reason why a Parenting Capacity Assessment is being conducted.

Defining the cognitive intellectual potential of individuals being assessed is predictive of the degree to which they can be expected to learn parenting knowledge and skills. Individuals who fall in the average or above-average range can be predicted to, at least in theory, perform exceptionally well in any instructional program that may or may not have a built-in evaluation component.

For many years, however, I have not been impressed by cognitive intelligence, unrealized or actualized. I have known many clients in the superior and above range of cognitive intelligence, determined by any number of standardized scales, who were profoundly and pathologically dysfunctional. I know socially and collegially the same type of individuals whose lives are tragic patterns of alienation, marginality and concomitant despondence. The universally favorable response to Daniel Goleman's seminal thesis that emotional intelligence matters far more than an individual's cognitive intelligence quotient therefore is not surprising. This notion has been tested by Reuven BarOn with his standardized instrument, the EQ-i, on a variety of samples, including the military, Chief Financial Officers of Fortune 500 companies, as well as the homeless, to name but a few groups all with the same result. Invariably and unequivocally, while cognitive intelligence constitutes a fundamental prerequisite, success defined specifically and generally was better predicted by the person's emotional intelligence.

It is also noteworthy that emotional intelligence as defined and determined by the EQ-i does not identify characterological traits that are life-enduring personality components of an individual's make-up. Instead, emotional intelligence defines that which is amenable to enhancement through focused intervention. This is particularly important insofar as the use of the results of the EQ-i can be particularly informative with respect to recommending particular intervention strategies with which to facilitate and subsequently assess a person's improvements on any or all of the fifteen subscales of this standardized instrument. More of this will be said later.

Notwithstanding the above, determining an individual's cognitive intelligence must be a prerequisite. It can explain, for example, why a person fails to apply parenting knowledge and skills subsequent to a course participation. It may be due to cognitive intellectual limitations. That is to say, the individual never really learned the content material. Subsequent investigations are intended to identify other possible causes not the least of which are negative characterological traits that persistently obstruct an individual's learning experiences, or emotional intelligence deficiencies which obstruct predictable competent application of that which was learned.

Without the timely resolution of obstacles to learning and using parenting knowledge and skills, unfortunately the cognitive intelligence of the person being assessed will be of little, if any, benefit to the child on whose behalf the Parenting Capacity Assessment is being conducted.

However, determining the cognitive intelligence of a biological parent can be of significant benefit insofar as if, there is any truth to inherited genetic propensities, such a finding defines the child as significantly likely to have innate cognitive intellectual potential. In such cases, therefore, it would not be unreasonable to predict that in the "right environment" such potential would be optimally realized. A finding in this regard can not only enhance the prospects of a child's adoption, but also can be used as a strong argument in support of a recommendation that the child's rights to optimal growth and development be a primary consideration in a court-imposed determination. Instead of children simply perpetuating the family legacy into which they are born, an alternative disposition based on, for example, a finding of cognitive intelligence potential will rescue them from a negative destiny and deliver them to become autonomous, independent, adaptive adults.

Clinical Impressions

Your clinical formulations based on the history of the person being assessed, file review, personal presentation and corroborative data from other individuals constitute the most important findings under this category of analysis.

Your clinical formulations are more important than the results of standardized instruments or the diagnostic labels previously applied by other Mental Health professionals without the benefit of this comprehensive Parenting Capacity Assessment methodology.

Your clinical formulations represent the contextualization of findings as it is enhanced by your analysis of the person's history and the relevance of this to the current situation and to the person's capacity to parent a child optimally.

Physical Presentation

While it may be politically incorrect according to some, I prefer to begin my clinical impressions by providing a physical description of the individual. In my estimation, it is not politically incorrect if such a description is elaborated by an explanation of the clinical significance of how a person presents physically Personal hygiene, the appropriateness of the clothes for the occasion, etc., all reveal much about the person's sense of self, the lifestyle to which the person has become normalized and a number of other interpretations that can shed a great deal of light on possible reasons why a child in the person's care is considered to be at risk. Most of us in our early clinical training learned that "eye-balling" an individual can be a significant source of data with which to begin the formulation of hypotheses to be tested by the collection and analysis of subsequent sources of information.

Compliance with appointments is also a noteworthy factor since it says much about not only the habits of the individual but also the importance he or she places on the Parenting Capacity Assessment process.

A clinical formulation about the apparent cognitive intelligence of individuals is necessary in order to convey to the reader of your report the manner in which their presentation likely impacts on how others respond to them. For example, apparently intellectually deficient individuals may have fewer demands placed on them and be treated more leniently. In fact, apparent cognitive intelligence may very well be a tactic used by a person functioning in the average range to avoid responsibility and, more importantly, negative consequences. The converse may also be true. Some individuals can give a false impression of average cognitive intelligence and thereby solicit a great deal of animosity when they are non-compliant, not because of defiance but due to an absence of ability. A clinical formulation with respect to the negative consequences of educational experiences is also crucially important. Invariably, negative educational experiences deprive individuals of actualizing their potential for abstract/conceptual thinking. As a result, they may have significant difficulty relating to court-or Child Welfare Agency-imposed requirements as well as relating to the concerns about their competence as parents. These people justify their situation by very concrete examples such as the availability of food in the house, but are unable to relate to the notion of nutrition.

Family of Origin

The familial experiences of the person being assessed and your analysis of these will establish the etiology of the individual's dysfunctionalities and its chronicity as well as the intergenerational perpetuation of maladaptive behavioural patterns. Most likely, individuals will not understand the negative impact early-life experiences had on their development. In fact, in many instances they will deny the relevance of this with respect to who they are at the time of being assessed. Nevertheless, it is imperative that you collect information with which you can describe how the person came to be in the position of having a child apprehended or to be under close supervision by a Child Welfare Agency. For instance, by understanding as much as possible about the parents of the individual and the environment created by them, it is possible to begin to formulate conclusions about the assessed person's formative stage experiences pertaining to attachment as well as the development of dysfunctional characterological traits. If at all possible, information should also be obtained about the person's grandparents. This can enhance your formulations with respect to the intergenerational perpetuation of dysfunctionalities, including deficient separation and individuation and the continued pathological relationship between children and parents.

Education

The educational experiences of the individual, if troubled, can confirm the negative impact of formative life experiences. A finding of underachievement, especially in light of innate cognitive intellectual potential, is vitally important insofar as environmental influences, as opposed to innate influences, can be concluded to be the greater determinant of the individual's academic achievements. Clinical formulations in this respect also can be significant insofar as they identify the potential of the child at risk in whose benefit the Parenting Capacity Assessment is being conducted.

In this context, identified or possible learning disabilities and/or behavioural problems, while to some degree are innate predispositions, to a far greater degree are universally accepted as environmentally determined. Therefore, the early-life experiences of the individual being assessed are not only crucial with respect to the development of maladaptive characterological personality traits but also establish the potential of intergenerational perpetuation of educational underachievements.

A finding that is significantly different (academic success) than what would be predicted by the early life experiences of the individual being assessed is of equal importance to predictive findings and will require further probing to explain. While this seldom occurs in Parenting Capacity Assessments, incongruent findings can have significant bearing with respect to a determination concerning the capacity of individuals to apply constructively what they have learned.

Employment

The employment history of individuals being assessed and your interpretation of their experiences in this respect will be another later-life manifestation of early-life experiences. An absence of significant work experiences and/or profound employment transience will serve to enhance your clinically logical formulations about the development of individuals, especially when juxtaposed with the work history of their parents and grandparents.

Substance Use

Substance abuse, if at all admitted in a clinical interview, invariably will be presented as a problem in the past but no longer an issue in the present. Unless the person is able to articulate a precipitating significant or accumulative event to achieving abstinence, and unless the person can articulate in-depth involvement in a community-based-twelve-step, self-help program such as Narcotics or Alcoholics Anonymous, the claim is highly suspect. Your clinical formulations with respect to formative-stage experiences are far more important indicators of substance abuse problems. This is especially true if you conclude that the experiences were profoundly negative and, as a result, the person being assessed likely developed an addictive characterological personality trait not unlike the parents and grandparents who will be candidly described by many as having been "alcoholics". While some clinicians will argue that this is essentially a genetic propensity, whether or not it is, for the purpose of a Parenting Capacity Assessment, is quite irrelevant. Moreover, even if such a propensity is genetically determined, environment is still considered to be a far greater determinant as to whether or not this is actualized by the person becoming addicted to one or more mood-altering substances.

Substance use and abuse can have a profound impact on a person's parenting ability. Unless it is brought under control, such a propensity can seriously compromise whatever innate capacities the assessed person may have with respect to rising to the occasion of being a competent parent. Personally, I have great admiration for people who accept the reality of having a characterological addictive personality trait and in a responsible way go about doing that which is required to bring this under predictable control. In my estimation, this achievement ranks amongst some of the greatest, especially in our culture where the use of alcohol and gambling have a persistent presence and are encouraged by a myriad of social conventions.

Relationships

The relationships individuals are capable of, as evidenced by their social network, will also reflect early life experiences. Their relationships are especially indicative of their capacity to trust and their expectations of others. This is determined by what the person being assessed learned to expect from primary caregivers. On many occasions, the assessed person will claim disassociation from troubled individuals from their past and thereby from everyone believing that their isolation is a commendable status, not realizing the dangers isolation pose. Furthermore, the circumstances of friends or acquaintances can reveal much about what is normalized for persons being assessed and the extent to which persons can relate to the concerns about them as competent parents. It is usually during this dialogue that the person being assessed reveals that he/she knows people who are "far worse" parents and wonders why a Child Welfare Agency is not interfering in their lives. This is an inadvertent revelation as to a person's frame of reference and can reveal much about reasons for non-compliance with previous Agency requirements. This also says much about why individuals have neither been compliant nor pursued the acquisition of parenting knowledge and skills and thereby alleviated the concerns of the Child Welfare Agency they so desperately want out of their lives.

The choice of romantic partners or even brief romantic liaisons invariably represents a well-established pattern, the etiology of which is the life experiences of the individual during the most crucial formative stage of life. Many have written extensively on this topic; Hendrix (1990) in particular demonstrating that invariably primary unmet needs are the source of later-life attractions to individuals virtually identical to caregivers who failed to meet the needs of that person as a child. Much to the surprise of individuals who, from time to time, attended counseling with their abusive partners who were on parole, I was able to describe their early-life experiences with considerable accuracy. There is nothing mystical or magical as to why a child of an abusive, alcoholic father would choose one of my parolee clients as a partner in joyful, unconscious anticipation that his initial seductive behaviour was indicative of an ability and will to satisfy her long unmet needs. It is also not surprising that the fervent desire to have these needs satisfied eventually gives way to disappointment, resentment and profound acrimony. When separation eventually does occur, in most cases, single status is brief and is followed by an almost identical repetition of the dysfunctional relationship pattern.

It is disastrous for a child to witness abuse, as well as to experience a parent separating from a number of individuals. Whatever ability a parent may have is invariably compromised by the experience of acrimony and abuse in a relationship. As such, dysfunctional relationships of a parent are not only significant obstacles to parenting, but also serve to normalize dysfunctional relationships. This is the genesis of the child's perpetuation of a family legacy to be also dysfunctional, abusive relationships. Dysfunctional or otherwise abusive relationships also can pose a physical risk to the child in whose best interest the Parenting Capacity Assessment is being conducted. According to Martin Daly and Margo Wilson (1998), "children reared by people other than their natural parents will be more often exploited and be otherwise at risk. Parental investment is a precious resource and selection must favour those parental psyches that do not squander it on non-relatives". They in fact found that a child living in America with a substitute parent was about one hundred times more likely to be fatally abused than a child living with natural parents. In a Canadian city in the 1980s, they found a child two years of age or younger was seventy times more likely to be killed if living with a step-parent and a natural parent than if living with two natural parents. Daly and Wilson, of course, acknowledged that murdered children are a tiny fraction of the children living with step-parents: they acknowledge that the divorce and remarriage of a mother is hardly a child's death warrant. But they certainly identified the more common problem of non-fatal abuse. Children under ten, for example, depending on their age and the particular studied question, were between three and forty times more likely to suffer parental abuse if living with a step-parent and a natural parent than if living with two natural parents.

I once had to do an assessment on an individual employed by a pharmaceutical company. The person stole prescription sleeping tablets to surreptitiously give to his girlfriend's infant so that he could have uninterrupted intercourse with the child's mother. On the first instance, when the child did not respond from a semi-comatose state, a fabricated explanation at the emergency room was believed, but not so on the second occasion. On the second occasion, the boyfriend was criminally charged. The salient issue is that this example represents a classic manifestation of the potential risk to which a parent can expose a child by the inadvertent relationship patterns in which the parent becomes involved.

Your clinical formulations under this category of analysis should be of such quality as to leave no doubt in the reader's mind how the person being evaluated came to be in the circumstance that precipitated the need for a Parenting Capacity Assessment. The person's lifestyle, relationships, procreation, social milieu and so forth should make perfect sense in terms of what is predictable from that person's formative and subsequent stage experiences. Furthermore, your clinical formulations should be able to place the parent along the continuum of what constitutes the literature-defined criteria of a "good parent". As well, the clinical formulations should be able to define the nature of the obstacles which individuals must overcome in order to alleviate concerns with respect to the risks faced by the child in their care and control. Your clinical judgment with respect to resource availability and the timeliness of what can be expected from intervention are also crucial insofar as the luxury of time is not commonly available to a child, especially to one in the most crucial formative stage of life.

The subsequent subheadings under this category of analysis will serve to augment, enhance or otherwise reinforce your clinical formulations which are at the basis of the conclusion and recommendations you declared at the beginning of this section in the report.

Personality Variables

Once the apparent innate cognitive intelligence of the person being assessed is described, the next prescribed requirement is to ascertain the reason for that individual's underachievement status. This determination will likely be required regardless of where that individual falls along the normal curve distribution pertaining to cognitive intelligence. Moreover, this line of investigation is designed to determine the nature of the obstacles to the assessed person's development of emotional intelligence. While the Bar-On scale can define areas that could benefit from enhancement, the scale does not define the obstacles to why any of the fifteen subcategories of emotional intelligence variables were blocked from being acquired. Regardless of how they were obstructed, the issue remains the same. The assessed person has an identified inability to successfully negotiate the obstacles to achieving an optimal quality of life in spite of his/her average range cognitive intelligence.

At this juncture, it is important to reflect on what is meant by personality and the personality structure of an individual. Personality is an abstract concept. As an abstraction and a concept, it really does not exist. The word does not correspond to anything real. It cannot be measured directly and any and all so-called personality tests are really not directly measuring personality. They are measuring, for example, whether a person is hypochondriacal, depressed or hysterical, and so on. I do not believe any standardized instrument is claimed to be all-inclusive, although there is certainly an implication that the various scales (e.g. MMPI-2, 16PF) tap into the major features of an individual's thinking and related behaving.

Therefore, to define the concept of personality, it is first necessary to achieve a shared understanding of how a concept is used in social science. It is rather simple. First, it should be understood that a concept is a made-up word for the purpose of convenience. In other words, as opposed to long-winded descriptions, we use single words, such as "stress". Unfortunately, concepts take on a life of their own and inadvertently we begin to treat them as if they really exist. People are often said to have stress rather than an adverse reaction to a particular situation. Similarly, instead of saying the person manifests a host of behaviours, cognitions and emotions consistent with a category known as schizophrenia, it is often said that the person is schizophrenic as if this is the essence of the individual. In contrast, no one would ever say, "This is my son, the measles". We always say "My son has the measles" since having the measles does not define him in totality.

Once we understand that a concept is really a short form for communicating that is often misused, it is easy to take the next step and recognize that we know a concept by its indicators; indicators that can be observed and measured quantitatively and qualitatively. This, in essence, constitutes an operational definition. Moreover, insofar as there are no "carved in stone" rules, concepts can be defined differentially. This is why it is so important to confirm that we share the same meaning ascribed to a concept. Testing this often produces interesting results.

For our purposes, "personality" represents an infinite myriad of stable and dynamic variables which, in their unique combination, represent in a relatively stable manner who a person is as an individual. Distinguishing between the relatively stable features that define an individual (personality traits) and the dynamic situational])/ determined features (despondency as a result of a loss) is relevant insofar as this has significant implications with respect to formulating a probable therapeutic goal and choosing what interventions are likely to produce a desired outcome.

The timeliness with which the desired effects of intervention can reasonably be expected is the most salient issue, regardless of what personality feature is of concern. The challenge is to identify obstacles, such as denial and concomitant resistance, and to formulate evidence-supported probability statements as to the availability of expert resources, and how much time will be required by the person being assessed to achieve discernable positive results.

It is noteworthy that there is probably an infinite list of personality variables, some more predominant than others and some simply nuances of a major feature in an individual's make-up. This is best exemplified by that which is measured by Catell's 16PF or the Minnesota Multiphasic Personality Inventory-2 standardized instrument. While the initial scales of the MMPI were found to be extremely useful for understanding the thought processes and behaviours of individuals, more recent elaborations and innovations have defined a host of other personality variables with which to even better understand the person being assessed.

It would not be particularly productive to engage in a lengthy and likely futile effort to list personality variables, let alone to try to prioritize them in some hierarchical fashion with respect to how they impact on a person's ability to promote the optimal growth and development of a child. Rather, it is more important to understand that personality traits determine a personality state and that these in turn determine how an individual behaves in any particular situation.

A personality trait is a propensity that is acquired essentially in the most crucial formative stage of life and, to a lesser degree, at subsequent stages, but nevertheless within the first decade of life. Personality traits are life-enduring features of an individual's propensities that directly influence how the person behaves in any particular situation. The best example of this is a characterological addictive trait that in virtually all cases is acquired during the formative stage of life. It cannot be eradicated from an individual's personality make-up and, in fact, will be a life-enduring influence on functioning. Invariably, the addictive characterological personality trait leads to addiction and a myriad of concomitant dysfunctionalities. In spite of the efforts of many and the changing fashions with respect to interventions, a person cannot be "cured" of their addictive characterological trait. That is to say, the trait cannot be eradicated from the personality make-up. The same is true with respect to all the other traits, such as impulsivity, sociability, hostility and so on. Nevertheless, while personality traits are life- enduring defining features of an individual, they can be brought under conscious and deliberate control through the persistent, competent application of override strategies. To use once again the example of the characterological addictive trait, there are many individuals who have and continue to exercise conscious, deliberate control over this propensity by engaging in well-defined strategies. The best known and most effective of all strategies is the community-based, twelve-step Alcoholics Anonymous program. The life-enduring nature of characterological traits is reinforced by the fact that once achieved, abstinence must be maintained through lifelong participation in the a program. Failing to do so regularly results in relapse.

It should be clear then that the relevance of a characterological addictive personality trait on an individual's capacity to parent is that, first and foremost, it must be brought under control and second, and of equal importance, once abstinence is achieved, it must be maintained with predictability through continued commitment and participation in a self-help community-based program, most notably Alcoholics Anonymous. Without such efforts, the innate abilities of the person being assessed will be constantly obstructed from being optimally developed.

A characterological addictive trait actualized therefore is certainly contraindicated to "good enough" parenting and to developing one's capacity as a parent. Under deliberate control through well-defined strategies, an otherwise debilitating trait is no longer an obstacle to parenting. In fact, the control measures, such as working a twelve-step program, can be a source of significant developmental gains and a commendable pursuit of a parent previously considered as worrisome.

In contrast, an acute state of despondence (depression) precipitated by a recent loss can also be contraindicated to "good enough" parenting, especially if it remains unaddressed and becomes a pronounced chronic feature of a person's make-up. This state can be eradicated, however, from an individual's profile and, in fact, is the goal of intervention by competent therapists. As such, the person's despondence negatively affected parenting only temporarily and, once "resolved/cured", it is no longer an issue.

An "aggressive" characterological trait, especially against authority, can be a persistent obstacle to constructively using formal and informal resources through which knowledge and skills can be progressively acquired. Such a characterological trait can be a significant obstacle to academic achievement or skills training, thereby preventing the realization of an individual's innate cognitive intelligence potential. Therefore, not only will such a trait obstruct the academic and employment success of an individual, but also his or her ability to learn parenting knowledge and skills or to constructively use the resources of a Child Welfare Agency.

A characterological trait of impulsivity, often a dominant feature of profoundly underachieving individuals, is not only a significant obstacle to developing optimally innate cognitive intelligence potential but also to applying that which has been learned. The impulsive urges of individuals are so intense as to override/overcome their rationality.

Because of the intensity with which an urge is felt, the person virtually feels compelled to do what they experience. Therefore, while theoretically, as a function of significant innate cognitive intelligence potential, a person can learn knowledge and parenting skills and demonstrate this through some evaluation method, the application of what has been learned is significantly obstructed by the impulsive characterological trait. The classic "marshmallow experiment" of children postponing the gratification of an immediate urge and subsequent studies unequivocally demonstrate that the capacity of individuals to achieve is profoundly influenced by their impulsive propensities.

Under this category of analysis subheading, it is also imperative that you determine how caregivers have or are processing their own abusive history. The degree to which a caregiver has resolved feelings of being abused or deprived will impact directly on that person's ability to parent with consistency, affection and competence. Unresolved issues invariably negatively impact on the individual's capacity to optimally parent and in fact establish the basis of the intergenerational perpetuation of dysfunctionalities. There is minimal evidence that some children are inherently resilient (Sroufe 1997). For example, not all individuals who sustain an attachment disorder develop dysfunctionalities. Likewise, secure attachment is not a guarantee of mental health but rather is viewed by some as a protective factor. Therefore, resilience is a process rather than a trait and should be clearly determined in each case with a view to understanding what impact the assessed persons' early-life experiences have on their current functioning (Pianta, Egeland and Sroufe 1990).

Having obtained a background history makes it possible to begin to build, under this category of analysis, a useful description of the assessed person's personality structure and how the various traits have either been obstacles or have been facilitative to the actualization of innate cognitive intellectual capacities. Obviously, the more salient determinations pertain to defining the obstacles, although positive traits in some instances are more important if they can be channeled into the pursuit of sustainable positive achievements.

It is also important to acknowledge that personality features can all be quantified along a continuum of severity. For example, a positive self-regard when exaggerated becomes an unsubstantiated, irrational and potentially dangerous over-evaluation of one's abilities and capacities. Similarly, a forthright propensity to stand up for one's beliefs and values (to be assertive), when exaggerated becomes manifested as aggressive propensities. Likewise, in children, an extreme form of independence manifests itself in non-responsive progressively and more profoundly withdrawn children. In other words, normal and disordered personalities of the same type are essentially the same in basic make-up (Millon 1999).

It should also be noted that, at least in theory, some individuals with very disturbed personality structures can parent surprisingly well, while other people with no apparent signs of dysfunctionality can be quite destructive as parents. While mostly hypothetical, when such instances occur they likely represent extreme examples as opposed to that which is most commonly found. Therefore, it is necessary to speak specifically to the unique features of each individual case from the generalities defined by empirical studies reported in the literature.

Contextually, it is imperative to consider the personality development of individuals in the context of their social environment. The question that is salient pertains to the degree to which experience and learning have normalized beliefs, lifestyles and specific activities that are contraindicated to promoting optimally the growth and development of a child. Simply put, that to which an individual has been socialized can be a significant obstacle to recognizing knowledge and skills deficits as a parent and to becoming involved and committed to a process with which to enhance areas of weakness.

As can be seen from the above description, invariably the issue in a Parenting Capacity Assessment, regardless of the individual's innate cognitive intellectual potential, is the fact that the person is an underachiever in many aspects of life. The very fact that persons being assessed have not been able to alleviate concerns about themselves as parents, and have not gained the confidence of a Child Welfare Agency, confirms the underachieving propensity mostly attributable to characterological traits. The same can be said with respect to overcoming environmental, social or economical obstacles since not all parents in similar or worse circumstances are the subjects of Parenting Capacity Assessments. By focusing on discovering the obstacles to an individual achieving an optimal quality of life, it becomes possible for you, the Assessor, to speak with greater confidence about what interventions are required and how likely a person is to constructively use them, to make discernable gains from which a child in need could benefit in a timely manner.

Diagnostic Labeling

Without any qualification, the use of diagnostic labels in a Parenting Capacity Assessment cannot possibly be useful, especially since labeling invariably precludes elaboration. Mental Health professionals who are predisposed to use diagnostic labels are also inclined to expect deference on the basis of their credentials. This causes them to be disinclined to explain themselves, expecting the reader to simply accept at face value their conclusion and recommendations. Unfortunately, elitism is alive and well because it is regularly reinforced. The reasons for this are many, none of which is terribly complimentary to professionalism in general and to the judicial process specifically.

The use of diagnostic labels in mental health is an inappropriate application of a physiologically based medical model. It is a flawed extension that is without merit. Consider for example the position of Duncan and Miller (2000) that in medicine a diagnostic label represents a problem and specific intervention. Diabetes ideally illustrates this insofar as the diagnosis prescribes a proper balance of diet, exercise and insulin. In "mental health" labeling a mental disorder is not especially useful in determining what treatment to offer. Most often the client receives the treatment in which the clinician is experienced or entrenched. Moreover, in mental health there is no healthy starting point such as the known range of glucose levels that indicate the presence or absence of diabetes. In mental health the dysfunction is the known factor, while optimal functionality is difficult if not impossible to define (Watzlowich 1976).

The use of DSM diagnostic labels is in fact less scientific than your clinical formulations augmented by the use of standardized instruments such as the MMPI-2. In spite of common beliefs, not unlike the place of the world in the universe at the time of Copernicus, there is nothing particularly scientific about the specific categories (diagnostic labels) used in the DSM manual. One has only to consider the scholarly perspective, and so called heresy, of Kaplan (1995). She has and continues to challenge the unsubstantiated authority of the DSM authors by asking for the evidence that was used to establish diagnostic labels. Her position, and that of many other reasonable scholars, is that diagnostic labels do not convey, accurately and reliably, the nature and etiology of a disorder, let alone a disorder's impact on an individual's functioning, in any capacity. For our purposes this can be expanded to include being a parent.

In the DSM-IV, there are 374 different kinds of mental disorders listed. They are listed under categories, subcategories and sub-subcategories with information for each diagnosis about associated features and disorders; specific age, cultural or gender- related features, prevalence, incidence and risk; course; complications; predisposing factors; familial pattern; and differential diagnosis. Moreover, each category and subcategory is given a multi-digit number including a period which suggests that the manual enables one to make extremely fine distinctions among disorders as between 307.46 and 307.47. Kaplan also points out that each category has a label and a long list of highly specific criteria, as well as a cut-off point. All of these "conventions" invariably give the impression that research was carefully done to determine that, for instance, people regarded as having a "major depressive episode" meet five of the nine criteria listed under that label and that people who meet four or fewer do not suffer from that disorder. In reality, this is not the case. There is little scientific evidence available for some "and none for many", on which to base such fine distinctions.

Paradoxically all this "convention" contradicts the introduction to the DSM-IV manual in which there is instruction to use "one's clinical judgments about the number of criteria the patient needs to meet a classification". Therefore, if one is supposed to use one's clinical judgment in applying these categories, then the pretext of scientific method goes out the window, revealing that it is highly unlikely that everyone defined as having a "major depressive episode" will have the disorder identically.

Criticizing the medical model of diagnostic labeling is not intended by any of the detractors to diminish the deviancy of some behaviours or the distress these cause people who have the problem. The issue is the usefulness of the act especially when conducting a Parenting Capacity Assessment. Furthermore, as an activity it hardly meets the scientific criteria it purports to satisfy. The act of labeling lacks reliability (Williams et al. 1992; Kirk & Kutchins 1992) it lacks validity (Frances, Clarkin and Perry, 1984), and brands and blames the individual (Beutler and Clarkin, 1990: Wright 1992) without contextualizing the individual's circumstance, ignoring almost all other influences but those which could be "treated" with medication.

Kaplan's position, and that of other scholars, is that the DSM-IV handbook, far from being the product of scientific efforts it is purported to be, is actually determined by powerful DSM leaders gate-keeping unscientific decisions about which diagnosis will be allowed and which diagnosis will be kept out of the handbook. To the untrained eye and even to many Mental Health personnel, the DSM-IV appears grounded in science although many features that give this impression turn out on inspection to provide only a veneer of scientific sheen, rather than genuine, carefully supported research.

Where is the harm? Everywhere!

Clinically trained in the early 1970s and characterologically predisposed by personality trait propensities, I am in complete agreement with Kaplan that the act of naming (labeling) is an act of power. To assign a label without reasoned elaboration is not only an abuse of authority but an unacceptable act of creation, redefining an individual by a word that is interpreted as all-encompassing of the person's very essence. This is best evidenced by "He is schizophrenic" or the organization known as "Friends as Schizophrenics". Names shape what we look for (likely differentially since no two clinicians define a label identically) and what we think we see. Moreover, the label "abnormality" in our culture is associated with a vast array of stigma. How different it would be to be told truthfully, especially by someone regarded as an expert, that "at a particular time many people in your position feel as you do" and then to be helped to understand more about why you feel so bad and how to cope with the feelings, perhaps even how to feel better and what you might expect later on. Surely, as Kaplan suggests, this would be a far more constructive approach to helping people in distress. The position is the same in this manual. Diagnostic labels are antithetical to understanding the obstacles to individuals actualizing their potential as parents and, indeed, their potential to achieve an optimal quality of life.

Not only is diagnostic labeling an act of elitist power, it is also motivated by self-interest, fuelled by greed and subject to the dictates of fashion. Diagnoses change as our social tolerances and references change (Beutler and Clarkin 1992). Diagnoses also reflect deviations from what society currently considers morally or socially acceptable (Szasz 1994). For example, homosexuality once was regarded as a mental illness. Finally drug companies are as much in the business of selling psychiatric diagnoses (DSM-IV) as they are selling psychotropic drugs. Obviously one promotes the other (Healy 1997). Healy among many others specifically raises disturbing questions about how much the act of diagnoses is governed by financial interests (Kutchins & Kirk 1997).

Parental Stress

Under this category of analysis subheading and mindful of the problem of labeling, it might be useful to reflect on the notion of parental stress. Rather than treating this concept as something real, an operational definition will quickly reveal that this notion represents knowledge and skills deficits and/or an absence of the aptitude (personality make-up) that is consistent with being a "good enough" parent.

We all know that some of us are better suited to one task than to another and that this is determined by our emotional and behavioural propensities, interests and innate inclination among a myriad of other variables, otherwise known as our personality make-up. Having recognized this has been the impetus for refining selection procedures for a variety of career paths, as for example, air traffic control. Establishing empirically what personality patterns correlate with success as an air traffic controller and training individuals with such patterns optimally has produced unparalleled success in this previously problem-riddled, vitally important function. It's no wonder that a person ill-suited by temperament, and a myriad of other personality traits, to be a parent, deficient in knowledge and skills with respect to meeting the challenges of this onerous responsibility, complains of "stress". Furthermore, it is no wonder that "high parental stress" is commonly identified as a factor in child maltreatment by virtually every researcher and theoretician working in the field of child welfare. Invariably, therefore, while our interests can and do change, if I was ill-suited to work on an assembly line twenty or more years ago, I am just as likely to be ill-suited now for such a daily routine. While I can certainly learn the knowledge and skills required, my aptitude deficit for this task will invariably prevail and be the cause of an escalating subjective experience of negative emotional, physiological and behavioural consequences. Clearly this analogy holds true for parenting as well. Not all of us are ideally suited for the task and while we, to various degrees, can acquire the knowledge and skills necessary for the basic functions, our natural aptitudes will be far greater determinants of our success as parents.

The preceding serves to underscore the need to explain, as opposed to label, and to reiterate that your explanations are more useful than diagnostic labels. In fact, clearly describing and explaining how an individual's potential is obstructed from optimal development is far more constructive and beneficial to reaching a timely determination in the best interest of a child.

My preference is to use Catell's 16PF, a descriptor of normal adult personality and the Minnesota Multiphasic Personality Inventory-2 standardized instrument to augment clinical formulations regarding the personality dynamics of the individual being assessed. While the MMPI-2 is used by many Mental Health practitioners to formulate diagnostic classifications though it was not initially intended for this purpose, it can be an invaluable tool with respect to elaborating your formulations about the personality dynamics of individuals and the extent to which various dysfunctionalities are amenable to benefiting from intervention. There are other personality inventories of equal value available to Mental Health practitioners, some less intimidating to use and interpret. If you are not conversant in the use of personality inventories, I would urge you to select one and to obtain formal training and/or supervision in this respect. There is nothing mystical or magical about any of these standardized instruments, although some require more knowledge and experience to use constructively.

I also use the Rotter Locus of Control Instrument as a means by which to ascertain the personality propensity of individuals to commit themselves to remedial/enhancement experiences. This instrument, in addition to assessing an individual's generalized expectations for internal verses external control of reinforcement, also defines individuals along a continuum of reactivity and pro-activity. Invariably, extremely reactive (external) individuals cannot relate to engaging in effort to bring about improvements or influence their environment insofar as, from their perspective, their life and circumstance is determined by forces outside of their control. The extent to which individuals reveal themselves to subscribe to this perspective greatly influences their capacity to constructively use resources.

Cognitive Developmental Perspective

The over twenty-five year, seminal, longitudinal study of Lawrence Kohlberg (1969) demonstrated through empirically supported evidence that there is a cross-cultural structure to reasoning that occurs in an invariant hierarchical sequence. Progress from one stage to another is a function of cognitive conflict created by the inadequacy at each stage of reasoning. For cognitive conflict to occur, the individual must experience an increasingly broadening range of events characterized by a broadening of situations, people and ideas to which the person is exposed. Through the active construction of meaning, often facilitated by a parent or mentor, the cognitive conflict is resolved until the limitations of the next stage perspective produce the same process. What is significant and relevant about this phenomenon is that at the preconventional level of reasoning, specifically of the instrumental reciprocity kind, emphasis is placed on the satisfaction of immediate needs through the path of least resistance. Unfortunately and tragically, the impoverished environmental conditions that create such developmental stagnation also are the basis of its perpetuation. Early-life negative experiences, academic and employment failures, relationship problems, as well as the social isolation and alienation of individuals, comprise significant obstacles to developing more comprehensive and adaptive interpretations of experiences.

A parent whose primary consideration is to satisfy immediate needs through the path of least resistance, at best focusing on "What can I get away with?" is unable to recognize that the child is a separate and distinct individual with unique needs that are different from the needs of the parent. From the parent's cognitive developmental perspective, the child essentially represents an idealized formulation as to the pleasure the infant is expected to provide through unconditional love and absolute deference to the parent's authority. Moreover, from this cognitive developmental perspective, the child represents to the parent a possession which will be a source of pleasure, similar to material objects that were acquired through some effort. As a parent may be upset by the theft of a television which was purchased, so also a parent fixated at a preconventional level of reasoning will be upset at having a child apprehended. A child is viewed less as a responsibility than as a possession to which the parent is entitled, in the case of a mother by virtue of conception and nine months of gestation. Invariably, this perspective is also revealed by how the parent formulates the issues discussed earlier in this manual. This perspective is also revealed by the adversarial legal stance taken by the parent and supported by the parent's counsel. While understandable, the proprietary perspective is developmentally less comprehensive than the hierarchically advanced principle that encompass the child's inalienable right to optimal growth and development.

The three levels of reasoning, as defined by Lawrence Kohlberg, is described in the Appendix of your report. The description reveals clearly that at the two preconventional stages of reasoning, it is virtually impossible for a parent preoccupied with satisfying immediate needs to communicate to the child that the child is a worthy, separate, distinct and lovable individual (Baumrind 1971; Coopersmith 1967).

A developmentally delayed parent with a preconventional focus will also have neither the ability to convey consistent expectations for behaviour nor the ability for firm but sensitive enforcement of developmentally appropriate standards of behaviour. Cognitive developmentally delayed parents are preoccupied with their own needs, and are unable to encourage independence and individuality. At the preconventional level the parent also cannot recognize that the child has rights, responsibilities and legitimate points of view. The absence of these parenting abilities contributes greatly to the effects that are associated with child maltreatment or abuse. Although cognitive developmentalists emphasize the fact that children are active agents in their own development, including the construction of meaning, those from the symbolic interactionist and attachment perspective unequivocally hold a position that children are also at the mercy of the particular caregiver's hand they have been dealt (Harter 1999).

The relevance of the cognitive developmental perspective of the person being assessed is also that such a determination explains the dynamics of their denial of existing problems, as for example, substance abuse or absence of parenting knowledge or skills. This also explains the resistance to doing that which would produce an alleviation of concerns about their parenting of a child. Denial, in essence, is the creation of fantasy. It is a distortion of reality or a complete fabrication engaged in to create that which is pleasing and to guard against that which is not. Children are exceptionally capable, as a function of their developmental stage, of pretend playing for hours on end. Children are also capable, as a function of their developmental perspective, of quickly sharing their fantasy life and engaging in co-operative pretend play with their peers. Time, influenced by experience and the construction of incrementally adaptive meaning, invariably diminishes a child's capacity to fantasize, daydream or otherwise pretend something is real when it is not. You need only to reflect on your own experiences with respect to how much and how well you daydreamed in your youth and how fleetingly capable you are of this strategy with which to avoid the realities of your adult circumstances. Reality is simply too powerful a force to indulge for any longer than fleeting seconds, in a daydream about winning the lottery or some other pleasing escapism. In fact, even formally structured and supported escapism through movies, as we become increasingly more sophisticated, requires a concomitantly increasing sophistication by filmmakers. This is best evidenced by today's science fiction movies compared to the movies of old, such as "The Blob", starring the late Steve McQueen.

Virtually all individuals, especially those who are coerced into substance abuse programs, reveal themselves to be in profound denial, essentially as a function of their developmental deficits. In spite of several offences related to substance abuse, they can maintain a fantasy about themselves as having no problems in this area. Why would they then strive for abstinence or exert effort and commitment to engage in a relapse prevention strategy through regular attendance and participation in a self-help program such as Alcoholics Anonymous? Similarly, why would a developmentally deficient parent in a profound state of denial engage in any process of self-improvement or improvements in parenting knowledge and skills. As a function of developmental deficits, individuals can engage in elaborate positive fantasies about themselves as to what great parents they are and what unmitigated pleasure they will derive from the child who will unconditionally and perpetually love them and defer to their authority. In most cases, as evidenced by the very fact that a Parenting Capacity Assessment is being done, the probability is profound that this is the cognitive developmental perspective of the person being assessed.

A primary substance abuse intervention strategy employed in residential programs is to address the denial of individuals and their concomitant resistance to doing that which they must in order to achieve abstinence and maintain it. This is accomplished by the implementation of therapeutic communities designed to precipitate cognitive conflict which, when facilitated, is resolved by the participant's creation of a hierarchically more adaptive interpretation of their experiences As the individual's cognitive developmental perspective evolves, his or her capacity to engage in the process of creating fantasy diminishes. The significant factor is that cognitive developmental perspectives do not represent characterological traits. As such, a stage perspective need not be a life- enduring way in which a person interprets events. Therefore, when development does not occur "naturally", it can be facilitated through the purposeful, deliberate exposure of the individual to particular environmental conditions. Unfortunately, to facilitate the development of a more adaptive stage of reasoning requires concerted, protracted effort best accomplished in a residential setting. The availability of such resources is infinitely scarce and usually restricted to felons in custodial dispositions. While mentoring/counseling can be productive in this respect, the intermittent nature of such facilitation dictates that stage progression will be markedly slow and certainly unlikely to occur before it can be of any discernable benefit to a child identified to be at risk.

Notwithstanding these disparaging comments, I have, from time to time, found subjects of Parenting Capacity Assessments to have reached a conventional stage of reasoning. These individuals invariably were able to make constructive use of the results of a Parenting Capacity Assessment report. They were also the ones who received favorable recommendations to be repatriated with their child, conditional on their satisfaction of well-defined criteria. The assessment in these rare cases was extremely beneficial for better structuring/defining the nature of the intervention required by the parents and for identifying the resources through which it could be accessed.

It is possible to ascertain generally the cognitive developmental perspective of individuals by paying clinical attention to how the person views the world and on what the person places emphasis. By understanding what constitutes the three levels that encompass six stages of reasoning, as well as by familiarizing yourself with some of the basic literature in this area, it will be possible for you to speak with considerable confidence as to what internal dynamic maintains and perpetuates the assessed person's denial and resistance to doing that which is necessary. The Defining Issues Test (DIT) developed by Jim Rest (1979), based on the work of Lawrence Kohlberg, has not been widely used for assessment purposes of this kind. The results obtained with this instrument are considered, however, as useful for understanding relationship patterns and the conduct of individuals. The various uses of this instrument have been published in refereed journals and through this have established the DIT as a useful tool in a variety of psychosocial assessments. In my experience, findings in this area of human functioning are particularly useful for explaining the above discussed anomalies in reasoning and behaviour. The DIT can be obtained from, as well as scored by, the Centre for Ethical Studies at the University of Minnesota. Alternatively, a clinical formulation, especially augmented by stage-related behavioural information, will suffice to provide invaluable information.

Social Learning

This subheading under the second category of analysis is significant because it places into context how people learn and how they are socialized. To a large extent, both are a product of repetitive exposure that is accompanied by concomitant conscious or unconscious interpretations. The sequence in which this occurs is irrelevant, although behaviour likely precedes the cognition. Nevertheless, the issue is that we learn about relationships from experience, that is, the environment to which we were exposed. As such, exposure to persistent acrimony models for us that this is what relationships entail and that this is a normal way of being. Similarly, we learn about parenting from how we were parented. What was persistently modeled for us, in our minds, becomes the norm and the accepted way of being.

By way of example, the comments of some participants in my workshops are most salient and best define this very resilient propensity. I have, in fact, lost count of the number of times participants confrontationally expressed their position that they were parented with corporal punishment and that this did them no harm and thereby, in no uncertain terms, communicating that this is an acceptable and desirable parenting strategy to use.

The resilience of a belief system that supports a well-defined type of behaviour is best understood by reflecting on the premise that to learn something new one must give up something old. This requires both the giving up of a certain belief and a concomitant way of doing something. For example, to improve on one's golf game, one must give up certain behaviours and beliefs and incorporate new ones supported by a belief that these will produce better results. The difficulty with which this simple example can be implemented underscores the profound difficulty individuals have giving up well-engrained beliefs that support certain ways of doing things. The complexity of the dynamics are only exacerbated by cognitive developmental perspectives that prevent the individual from relating to a previously unconsidered rationale for giving up something to be replaced by something new.

To illustrate this further, consider that home visits are scheduled well in advance. This gives assessed individuals ample time to create a favorable impression of the domicile in which they are raising, or want to raise, a child. The profoundly objectionable smell, the dirt, the unsafe conditions for a child, the presence of animal feces in and outside of a litterbox, to list only a few unacceptable conditions, all convey that for the person being assessed there is nothing wrong with the home where they intend to raise a child. It is difficult or impossible to imagine an explanation other than that persons being assessed, through repeated exposure, have been socialized to believe that the state of their home is the norm and as such does not require any effort to change in order to create a positive view of who they are. If this is true with respect to the state of the home, one can only wonder how profoundly this also applies to how one treats a child, and the various other environmental conditions to which the infant is exposed.

To elaborate further, consider that even Barbara Coloroso of "Children Are Worth It" and television fame, is likely to admit that she, too, could and should learn more about parenting. Moreover, she likely would be open to such experiences, not unlike those who attend her talks and workshops and those who purchase her books. This reality is the basis of desperate measures undertaken by a Child Welfare Agency and often supported by the courts, requiring parents to attend instructional programs in lieu of knowing what else to do. This is likely the reason why Parenting Capacity Assessments conducted by many mental health professionals include parenting ability evaluations. Instruments that tap into knowledge, skills and expectations of a child are often used, all with the assumption that when deficits are identified and rectified, the acquired knowledge and skills will be applied, at first because the person recognizes these to be better things to do and later because of the positive consequences created by the new parenting strategies. As described earlier, at least in theory, the subjects of Parenting Capacity Assessments are capable of learning knowledge and skills since they mostly function within the average range of cognitive intelligence. Assuming that whatever obstacles in the past prevented them from learning are at least temporarily eradicated, the issue under this subheading is to determine the extent to which individuals simply go through the motions, regurgitating program content, or whether they have really replaced one set of beliefs, values and corresponding behaviours with another. If exposing people to learning experiences produced such positive results, many of the devastating social ills, such as violence and spousal and substance abuse, should be easily eradicated from our culture. Unfortunately, this is not the case, as is evidenced by the less than stellar results of, for example, educational efforts on which many substance abuse treatment programs rely. This is not to say that learning information is not vitally necessary. It is, however, to say that such an intervention strategy is invariably insufficient. To produce sustainable results, educational interventions must take into account and address the profound effects of socialization and the concomitant resistance created by this to abandoning the familiar old and embracing the new.

Reflections on the Child

Under this second category of analysis subheading, a person's capacity to care for a child must be related to that child's temperament and special needs. This consideration warrants a separate section and takes into account, in most cases, the findings and related conclusions of specialists in child development and physician specialists in pediatrics. The parenting capacities of a caregiver must also be related to the parenting demands raised by a particular child at a given time. For example, the physiologically required dietary restrictions of an infant may be beyond the capacity of a parent who subsequently may manage the requirements when the degree of accuracy and specificity is no longer necessary. In the same vein, a parent may find it impossible to understand that an infant cannot relate to him or her on an equal footing, but as the child develops to approximate the cognitive developmental perspective of the parent, their relationship can be expected to vastly improve. To reiterate an earlier point, insofar as there is minimal evidence that children are inherently resilient (Sroufe 1997), invariably the question posed pertains to how much risk is acceptable with respect to what the child is exposed while waiting for that stage in development to which a parent can better relate and respond.

It may be true that some children, regardless of how they are parented, will always be extremely difficult to manage. Accepting this, regardless of how well it is supported empirically, potentially can be devastating as it becomes generalized from a very small to an ever increasingly larger group of infants. Moreover, it can be the basis of parental and societal abdication of responsibility manifested by a "shrug of the shoulders" and an exclamation that this child is part of that very small group of "incorrigibles". Instead, the premise of this Parenting Capacity Assessment is that it is far better and more constructive to recognize that parental pathology likely will permanently harm a child's development and that certain patterns of parental communication and dysfunctionality literally can drive a child insane. Therefore, a child's dysfunctionality may very well be associated with an extreme form of dysfunctional communication patterns within the family (Wynne, Singer, Baitko and Toohey 1977). This view, in fact, reflects the work of communication experts such as Watzlawick, Beavin and Jackson (1967) who, a decade earlier in Paolo Alto, California were researching the impact of communication patterns on relationships, family dynamics and psychopathology.

When interpreting the nature of interactional patterns between a parent and child, beyond attachment considerations, it is important to look for strengths and weaknesses. The intent is to identify areas that could be recommended for enhancement and, more importantly, areas of strength that could possibly be a source of significant encouragement and reinforcement for a parent with a weak sense of self, especially in the role of a caregiver.

It is noteworthy that children's' adaptive behaviours and capacities are not related to social class or, in fact, innate cognitive intellectual capacities inasmuch as they are related to their parental influenced "mental health". Bowlby (1973) identified this in his earlier work and has confirmed these conclusions subsequently. The work of BarOn pertaining to emotional intelligence substantiates these empirical studies, confirming the determining variables to be the environment. For example, adaptive children tend to have had environments that were supportive in specific ways in a manner that was particularly relevant to the developmental tasks they were facing at any given time. Therefore, the capacity to be adaptive develops over time in the context of environmental support. Failures at each developmental stage can serve as an indicator that a child may be on a deviant pathway and at increased risk for further maladaptive behaviours (Egeland, Carlson and Sroufe 1993). In contrast, children with secure histories are more resistant to environmental pressures and are more likely to rebound toward adequate functioning following a period of dysfunctionality (Pianta, Egeland and Sroufe 1990).

Basically, under this category of analysis subheading, your reflections concern the potential harm the child could sustain as a function of the parent's inability to recognize the child's special needs and to respond accordingly. When a child rapidly responds to a positive environment, as for example, in foster care, this is overwhelming evidence in support of parental limitations that begs the question: how amenable are these limitations to positive intervention and how amenable are these limitations to a timely response?

When the child is slow to respond to a positive and nurturing "foster" environment, this need not be indicative that the ascertained developmental deficiencies are the result of conditions for which the parents cannot be held responsible. Even if the delays are due to some physical condition, such as deafness or chronic illness, it is still the responsibility of the parent to identify the need for specialized assistance and to secure these in a timely manner in the best interest of the child. Furthermore, children slow to respond in foster care are often the ones who suffered the greatest and for the longest time and their lack of progress is by no means indicative of unwarranted intervention and apprehension by a Child Welfare Agency.

In doing Parenting Capacity Assessments, about one-quarter to one-third of your cases will be in the interest of a special needs child. The majority of the cases, however, will constitute children who are not unlike their parents. That is to say, they will possess innate cognitive intellectual potential that falls within the average range and they will be at risk to perpetuate their family legacy of underachievement due to environmental conditions created by their primary caregivers.

The Parent's Physical Environment

Under this category of analysis subheading the issue is that the domicile of parents reflects not their taste or budget but essentially their existing ability to attend to that which involves child safety, ranging from whether caustic products are stored out of reach or under lock and key to cleanliness, which usually also involves the management of animal excrement, food waste and, in the case of infants, diapers. Even the poor can be clean and safety conscious. It is, therefore, not politically incorrect for you to formulate conclusions about the functioning of parents based on that which you have noted about their domicile.

The Third Category of Analysis: Social Support Network

*"The Family is in no sense an independent institution; it is part of a
larger context and its functionality is determined by the manner and extent to
which it is connected with the whole."*

Alexander T. Polgar, 2001

This category of analysis pays credence to the adage that "it takes a village to raise a child". While no one would argue with this adage, and there are various references scattered throughout the literature pertaining to the risks faced by children in isolated families, the social network of primary caregivers to date, by and large, has not been comprehensively studied or dealt with in a singular fashion, with very few exceptions. There is one exception, however, where researchers undertook to study and understand the impact of social support networks on the functioning of individuals in a variety of capacities of particular interest to our purpose as parents. This comprehensive initiative was undertaken by the Faculty of Social Work at the University of Toronto between 1977 and 1980. It served to empirically substantiate the experientially known importance of a positive social support network through which individuals receive comfort, encouragement and the benefit of other people's experiences during challenging times in their lives and, through this connection, actualize their own potential. Of particular relevance and importance to assessing parenting capacity is the empirical finding that ultimately a positive social support network produces far greater and more sustainable positive results than time-limited access to the resources of organizations such as Child Welfare Agencies. The university of Toronto Faculty of Social Work initiative also confirmed that risks to children are definably correlated with the degree to which a family unit is alienated or isolated from the mainstream of society, as well as the degree to which there is identification with a similarly marginalized group that normalizes dysfunctionality, an impoverished lifestyle and adverse parenting practices.

The other significant exception is the work of Crockenberg (1981). She studied the relationship between an infant's temperament, maternal behaviour and the adequacy of social supports for the mother. She found social supports for the mother to be the most important prediction of an infant's attachment style, this factor having the greatest impact or irritable babies.

Findings

Consistent with the prescribed format in the organization of your Parenting Capacity Assessment report, the findings under this category of analysis begin with your conclusion as to whether or not the assessed person has or likely could affiliate with a positive social support network. Consistent with the theme of this methodology, the timeliness with which improvements reasonably can be expected is crucial and must be clearly stated. Your introductory comments must also include the implications of the conclusion with respect to the status of the child in whose best interest the assessment is being conducted.

Having clearly stated your conclusion and concomitant recommendations, the next step is to prioritize the findings that support your position. There will be at least two broad spheres of evidence in support of your formulations with respect to whether or not the assessed person is or can be expected to affiliate in a timely manner with a positive social support network. The first sphere of data will be derived from information obtained during assessment interviews, documents and collateral sources concerning the existing social network of the person being assessed. The second sphere of data will be based on your conclusions regarding the assessed person's own attachment experiences and how the person's past experiences impact on current functioning with respect to interpersonal relationships of all sorts and identification with cultural norms and values.

While it is always possible that a person being assessed has a positive social support network with which they are connected, this is a markedly improbable occurrence. It is more probable that to every individual there is a potential positive social support network available but, as a result of a myriad of dysfunctionalities, the assessed person is obstructed from relating to, let alone constructively interacting with, positive others. Therefore, this category of analysis is essentially focused on the assessed person's capacity to overcome or override propensities that are antithetical to constructive affiliation with a positive social support network and to do it in time to benefit the child, especially one in the most crucial formative stage of life.

The primary premise under this category of analysis is that optimal growth occurs in a community environment that fully supports a child's needs and the family's aims. Such support, when sufficiently present, often serves to offset the experiences of "stress" created by insufficient aptitude to be a parent, and parenting knowledge and skills deficits. In the absence of social supports, a child will be at risk to various degrees for neglect, abuse or even sexual abuse, especially when a parent's experience of stress is not ameliorated.

While isolation has been shown to be a risk factor for neglect (Polansky, Chalmers, Buttenwieser and Williams 1979) for abuse (Webster-Stratton 1985) and sexual abuse (Salzinger, Kaplan, and Artemeyeff 1983), Polansky et al. (1981) and George and Main (1979) have stressed that isolation and loneliness also may be self-imposed. The task, therefore, under this category of analysis is to ascertain the extent to which isolation is determined by formative stage experiences or by situational variables, which are more amenable to remediation in a timely manner.

Defining the Existing Social Network

It is highly unlikely that a subject of a Parenting Capacity Assessment will be a total social isolate or a virtual hermit, caring for one or more children. More likely, the person being assessed will be functioning on the margins of a community, alienated from the mainstream but nevertheless in contact with others on a fairly regular basis. It is imperative to ascertain the nature of these relationships in terms of the motivation and benefits that are derived and most importantly how they impact on the child in whose best interest the assessment is being conducted.

Almost all individuals have a need for social contact, motivated by a very basic instinct that defines the nature of the human species. To various degrees, this explains why the indigent homeless, profoundly marginalized individuals, maintain a loose connection with each other in the urban core of many cities, as opposed to living a life of total isolation in a rural area. The significant issue, from this assessment perspective, is the nature of the relationships in these loose connections.

Essentially, cognitive developmentally deficient people are incapable of recognizing or relating to the benefits that could be derived from group affiliation. People whose cognitive developmental perspective is fixated at a preconventional level, at best, associate with others for immediate personal gain derived from actions that are reciprocal in nature. Whatever is exchanged is essentially instrumental and serves to satisfy immediate primary needs. Such interactional patterns are void of features that are identified in the literature as conducive to learning or benefiting from the experiences of others or finding comfort in fellowship. An appreciation of affiliative benefits only comes from a perspective that places greater emphasis on group membership, as opposed to the pursuit of immediate need gratification. In this group of individuals, relationships also are invariably transient in nature.

On occasion an assessed person, as a function of innate cognitive intellectual capacity, instinctively constructs meaning to experiences and, through this process, achieves a beginning conventional form of reasoning. The first stage of conventional reasoning is the reference group orientation. Insofar as circumstance and environment influences which reference group we affiliate with, not surprisingly the propensity is to seek those with who we most readily identify. Identification invariably is predicated more on similarity than dissimilarity. It is, therefore, not unusual to find individuals being assessed to exclaim that none of their friends considers their lifestyle or parenting to be problematic. These same friends will not consider helping a person being assessed clean and tidy a domicile for an assessment visit essentially since they also live similarly and, as such, consider what they do and what their friends do as quite within the norm. The assessed person's reference group is also often in conflict with authority in general and with a Child Welfare Agency in specific.

Individuals whose relationships are predicated on instrumental reciprocity in pursuit of immediate need gratification are far more difficult to facilitate to the next level of reasoning than those individuals who have acquired a reference group orientation, albeit with the "wrong group". With the latter, shifting identification invariably is far easier and less time consuming than promoting one stage growth, especially given the scarcity of expertise and resources that are required to do this.

Shifting group affiliation, to a large extent, is experientially determined. This phenomenon is best exemplified by teenagers who may be reluctant to leave their grade school peers but, within short order, establish a new group of friends in their first year of secondary education. Joining the football team produces similar shifts in reference group affiliations, as do negative experiences such as being cut from a team or failing subjects. Similarly, if a person who is being assessed is found to have achieved a reference group orientation with minimal externally imposed structure and some facilitation, it would not be unreasonable to expect them, in a timely manner, to identify increasingly more with other parents who are earnestly pursuing the development of their parenting knowledge and skills, believing this to be a necessity and something that will ultimately benefit them and their children.

I am specifically reminded of an inner-city project that was designed for single mothers to provide them with parenting knowledge and skills and a positive supportive milieu in which to develop these. Not only was this demonstration project successful, but was also found to have been the impetus for continued friendships, support and sharing of ideas long after the program ended. Reference group oriented people, therefore, are far more likely to make other friends in a timely manner: new friends who are positive and characterized by those attributes defined by the University of Toronto Social Network Study as conducive to positive parenting.

Under this category of analysis subheading, therefore, the requirement is to determine the cognitive developmental perspective of the person being assessed and the implications of this with respect to how quickly the individual can be expected to associate and identify with a positive social support network. Again, the operative term is the timeliness with which this can be expected and the availability of resources required to facilitate a shift in the desired direction. The more profoundly attachment disordered individuals are, the more likely they are to distrust and insulate themselves, engaging with others primarily for purposes of instrumental reciprocity. When needs are not immediate for such individuals their preference is to distance themselves, most notably from the community in which they live, as well as from other marginalized individuals from who they do not have an immediate and pressing need that could be satisfied.

Situational Variables

Consideration should be given to exploring the possibility of self-imposed alienation precipitated by situational variables. While such circumstances are rare, they do occur, especially among immigrant, ethnic or otherwise displaced individuals. This is particularly applicable to those who have had experience with social institutions or agencies in totalitarian states and, as such, have a profound mistrust of them that is generalized to all agencies, including those in their adopted country. When the worrisome behaviour, some attributable to cultural differences, of such individuals raises concerns about the safety of children in their care, their distrust of all social agencies likely will be a significant obstacle to working co-operatively with a Child Welfare Agency or a community based social support network.

Determining the etiology of distrust is crucial insofar as some are much more amenable to amelioration than others, especially among individuals who have attained at least a reference group orientation or better.

There are other situationally or environmentally determined, self-imposed instances of alienation or isolation engaged in by people. Regardless of cause, isolation invariably poses significant risks to children. The more acute the alienation, the more readily it can be alleviated. Unfortunately, in most instances, social alienation and isolation will be a chronic pattern rooted in early attachment problems and progressively manifested in a myriad of relationship difficulties, of an intimate and social nature, which combine to place children at risk.

Later-Life Consequences of an Attachment Disorder

There has been extensive enquiry into whether a secure attachment foreshadows more successful peer relationships and friendships in later life. There is evidence that securely attached infants socialize more competently and are more popular with peers (Vandell, Owen, Wilson and Henderson 1988). In fact, Thompson (1999) has demonstrated that infant/mother relationships likely constitute a prototype for later close relations, at least for a few years if not for a lifetime. One of the most thoughtfully designed intensive longitudinal studies examined the outcomes of secure attachment, producing impressively compelling findings for the predictive validity of such an achievement, especially with respect to subsequent relationship skills (Weinfield, Sroufe, Egeland and Carlson 1999). While there are some doubters of this paradigm, their dissent is essentially ideological and grounded in the preference not to believe in the profoundly determining nature of early-life experiences. Criticisms, regardless of the premise on which they are based, have, however, served to create an impetus for clarifying theoretical formulations and research procedures pertaining to the impact early-life experiences have on the acquisition of social skills, as well as on other social propensities essential for adaptability.

Because infancy is a period of rapidly developing sociability, the legacy of an early attachment relationship includes either enhanced, flexible and positive social skills, which are acquired in the first relationship, or the converse, which entails restricted, inflexible and maladaptive interpersonal patterns of interaction. Thompson and Lamb (1983) report that the acquisition and maintenance of social skills and, more broadly, social predispositions are determined by, or are the direct consequence of, early attachment. This is not surprising insofar as affiliation and general sociability are grounded in a myriad of propensities, such as a positive self-esteem, a curiosity and an interest in others, as well as the capacity to trust. The etiology of each of these propensities is the formative stage relationship experiences of an individual.

The following are some of the abilities that are required for affiliation and constructive use of a positive social support network. The capacities that evolve into abilities are determined, in no uncertain terms, by the assessed person's early-life experiences.

A child learns to trust others when primary caregivers are accessible, responsive and benevolent when afraid or in pain. Children unable to rely on adults to meet their needs and keep them safe, become their own inadequate caregivers and protectors. Attachment deficits subsequently become evident as the child manifests difficulty getting along. A child learns to trust others when primary caregivers are accessible, responsive and benevolent When caregivers are unavailable, unpredictable or abusive, the child does not turn to them for soothing or reassurance with others at home and later in school and in general

A child who achieves a secure attachment, in comparison, is able to form safe, secure and satisfying relationships with others based on intimacy, equality and commitment.

Children learn to express empathy for others when they have received consistent caring and consideration from their primary caregivers. If children do not experience caring, they become predisposed to hurting others without appropriate remorse.

Children, who experience satisfaction and gratification in the daily give and take with primary caregivers will learn to be considerate, playful and fair in their interactions with others. Children who fail to learn such reciprocity from their caregivers may be selfish inconsiderate or coercive in their interactions.

Children who learn to express their real self when they receive encouragement from caregivers and when they develop in an environment where it is safe to be vulnerable will feel confident in being candid about what they think and feel. This propensity is essential for intimacy defined as congruence between emotions, cognitions and behaviour when interacting with others. In the absence of such congruence, the potential of relationships invariably is compromised and unsatisfactory, perpetuating thereby the progressively dysfunctional manner in which that individual approaches others. Moreover, children who have attachment deficits are usually afraid of their own feelings and reluctant to acknowledge or express them to others. They may be willing to tolerate considerable pain rather than risk emotional vulnerability.

Children learn to respect others when they are valued and encouraged by primary caregivers. Children who fail to receive respect from primary caregivers do not learn that they are worthy of respect and are likely to make a habit of disrespecting others.

Social skill deficits and lack of trust have far-reaching and profound consequences, including the development of dysfunctionalities, such as ADHD which, according to Ladneir and Massanari (2000), is likely related to an attachment disorder and subsequent issues. These issues prevent parents from engaging with a supportive positive social support network with which to intervene in a timely and effective manner to mitigate against the potentially devastating consequences the condition can have on the development of a child, Jacobwitz and Hazen (1999) report that because children with disorganized attachment view themselves as helpless and powerless, they see peers (and later others) as potential threats. They do not believe they can master the challenges of engaging with peers (others) and, therefore, lack a strong motivational base for interaction. The peer behaviour of children with disorganized attachment can be expected to shift between extreme social withdrawal and defensively aggressive behaviours, according to these researchers. Insofar as reciprocal communication skills are essential for establishing successful peer relationships, these propensities will mitigate against such achievements. Insecurely attached children will have difficulty with competent reciprocal communications also because they will not perceive a balance of power between themselves and others. Therefore, children with disorganized attachment will know how to play the part of a controlling caregiver or a helpless baby, the victim or the bully, but never as an equal partner in a balanced interaction. It is not surprising, therefore, that the peer interactions of such children are likely characterized by emotional under-control (aggression) or emotional over-control (withdrawal). In some cases, a child may even become immobilized or unable to respond.

Children rejected at home are unlikely to be students capable of soliciting positive reactions from teachers and, later, employers. As such, these children will be persistently frustrated with being underachievers and marginal individuals. The interference is that interference in that individual's life as an adult by a Child Welfare Agency will be perceived as simply a continuation of good reasons to mistrust the system and people in general. Instead of reaching out and benefiting from the services of experts, or the experiences of peers, such individuals become progressively more withdrawn and isolated and thereby place at progressive risk the children in their care.

According to Main et al (1985), adults whose working models reflect insecure attachments generally feel less positive about attachment in all other relationships and tend to deny the influence of attachment experiences on their personality. Furthermore, their interpretation of experiences were objectively perceived to be inconsistent with what they actually described. Therefore, not surprisingly from their perspective, it is perfectly acceptable and, indeed, normal to perpetuate the social isolation, ostracism, mainstream alienation and perverse pattern of distrust and hostility to a broad range of agencies, as well as to those who represent the mainstream of society.

Your determinations under this category of analysis must also factor in the evolving research concerning brain development: specifically, research pertaining to environmental influences on acquiring and maintaining ability-related synaptic connections. The growing body of evidence suggests that a profoundly impoverished early-life environment will fail to stimulate the development of the neurological basis for sociability and subsequently this ability will be lost forever.

While the preceding list is by no means exhaustive, hopefully it conveys adequately and logically that social dysfunctionalities are intergenerational legacies inadvertently perpetuated and likely exacerbated from one generation to the next. To a large extent, the early-life experiences of the person being assessed will explain a myriad of adult dysfunctionalities, including the parent's inability to connect with a positive social support network or, for that fact, to a child protection worker's efforts to be facilitative. Likely, their behaviour is not nearly as petulant or defiant as it may appear to be. Unfortunately, when such individuals are not vindicated by a Parenting Capacity Assessment, the results will serve simply to confirm their distrust and disdain for "the system" and all its representatives. The issue, nevertheless, is the same, namely that they are profoundly obstructed from using resources for connecting with others in a constructive manner. As such, they are left to their own internal devices that are not improved or enhanced upon by the support and experience of others. This is the basis of the identified and verified risk children are exposed to in such circumstances.

Under this category of analysis subheading, therefore, it is essential to provide information with respect to the assessed person's own history of attachment and in regard to the extent to which failures have become actualized as later-life negative consequences in areas that are significantly correlated with sociability.

Standardized Instruments

In addition to information derived from clinical interviews and documentation review pertaining to the assessed person's history, especially early-life experiences, the results of standardized instruments can also be supportive evidence of your conclusions with respect to the assessed person's capacity to affiliate in a timely manner with a positive social support network. As described above, a cognitive developmental perspective determination will be especially useful with respect to informing the timeliness with which positive changes can be expected. The results of various personality assessment instruments, most notably the MMPI-2, can also be extremely useful when issues of trust, empathy, and emotional and social ability are taken into consideration.

The use of standardized social skills inventories, under this category of analysis, is likely to be redundant insofar as it will simply confirm social skills deficits and/or authority conflicts which are the very reason that a Parenting Capacity Assessment is being conducted. It is extremely interesting to find significant social skills competencies (objectively verified with a standardized tool) in a case where there is protracted acrimony and significant differences of opinion about parenting practices between the person being assessed and a Child Welfare Agency. Moreover, it is even more interesting to have such findings when other evidence indicates that the person being assessed is socially alienated and marginalized. While this is rare, when it occurs, it invariably does so among a small group of individuals who are capable of creating an extremely positive first impression but lack profoundly the "substance" with which to sustain the image. Therefore, my personal preference, especially given the realities of resource and financial limitations, is to avoid that which is redundant, and refrain from using transparent instruments with questionable or less than optimal validity and reliability.

The Fourth Category of Analysis: Evidence-Based Expectations for Acquiring and Applying Parenting Capabilities

"We grow neither better nor worse as we get old, but more like ourselves."

May Lamberton Becker Editor and Writer

People become more like themselves with the passage of time. A few, however, as a function of either a profound emotional event or a series of significant emotional events that eventually reach a critical mass, are able to precipitate a significant change in their day-to-day functioning. When such a change does occur, it represents the best and most optimistic example of the human positive potential. The potential for such marked positive changes is the sustaining life force for Mental Health professionals. For us it is especially gratifying to be facilitative agents in the process of individuals bringing about changes in their lives through behavioural strategies, cognitive developmental gains, insights and the relinquishment of defense strategies, such as denial and resistance. We should never lose sight of the fact that to venture from the dysfunctional, albeit familiar, to the functional, unfamiliar ways of thinking and behaving is a significant achievement that can and does occur from time to time. Under this category of analysis, therefore, the objective is to identify variables that will support a conclusion that the individuals being assessed will probably either continue to become more like themselves with the passage of time or with appropriate expert intervention, will bring about improvements in their abilities as parents in a timely manner to be of benefit to the child identified at risk. While Mental Health professionals, are loath to make predictive statements, it is impossible to conduct a Parenting Capacity Assessment without doing so. By its very nature, the concept of capacity requires a predictive statement. The previous three categories of analyses have served to define the assessed person's dysfunctionalities (though in rare cases, the findings may have served to vindicate their claim to be competent parents). The results of your first three categories of investigation have also produced findings with various degrees of predictivity. Defining and applying these predictive features under this last category of analysis should be recognized as at profound odds with popular beliefs. In fact, it is contrary to judicial practices in many jurisdictions where, in spite of the absence of a significant intervening variable, Parenting Capacity Assessments are ordered every two years or subsequent to the apprehension of each new born child. This occurs in spite of the fact that conception occurs almost immediately after the delivery of the previously apprehended infant.

Findings

Start the findings under this category of analysis with a statement that defines your conclusion and concomitant recommendations as supported by the information you collected and analyzed. This statement represents your argument which then must be supported by your findings. The various proofs must be ranked and related to the rationale that justifies the focus of this last category in the methodology.

Tragically, the findings under this last category of analysis can potentially be devastating to the person being assessed. In spite of your knowledgeable and skilled efforts to be compassionate, the best interest of the child must supersede whatever concerns you may have as to how an unfavorable conclusion will impact on the potential primary caregiver. Perhaps to paraphrase the modern lyricist, there are instances where "to be cruel is ultimately to be kind". At worst, faint or false hope will have a progressively devastatingly frustrating negative impact on the person being assessed, let alone the next child who will be ill advisedly conceived. Moreover and tragically, in a win-lose adversarial process focused on procedural matters and the application of rules, the assessed person's legal counsel will use even your faintest optimism, motivated by compassion, as the thin edge of a wedge with which to win a case for a dysfunctional parent and thereby condemn a child to perpetuating that parent's legacy of familial dysfunctionality.

The interconnectedness of the four categories of analyses should be made evident by how you present the supportive evidence for your conclusions. The prescribed format starts with defining the first three years of life as the most crucial and formative in the development of an individual's personality, which directly influences how he or she behaves in a variety of situations. Specifically, under this last category of analysis, it is imperative that the reader (judge) understand the essence of a characterological trait and the life-enduring manner in which the traits determine the personality structure of the person being assessed. The permanence of traits, at least in part, is explained by the most recent research pertaining to the development of the human brain. Specifically, it is not insignificant that physiological research is revealing that neural synapses either fail to develop or are permanently lost as a function of experience. This explains the resilience of personality structures, as well as behavioural patterns. In fact, a synthesis of information in this area of research substantiates the growing consensus among Mental Health and human resource professionals that best practices in hiring procedures incorporate behaviorally based interviews. This underscores the empirical reality that past behaviours predict future behaviour in a deeply significant way. Nevertheless, it is true that individuals can and do gain control over profoundly debilitating characterological traits such as their addictive propensities. While abstinence, for such individuals, does not readily translate to a brighter future for them as parents, in their non-inebriated state they certainly have better prospects of acting in a child's best interest as opposed to pursuing the immediate satisfaction of their addictive needs.

The task under this category of analysis, therefore, is to relate previous conclusions and concomitant recommendations to the vitally important issue of timeliness. Compassion for the assessed must be informed by reason and statistical considerations. Anything is possible: lawyers are fond of trying to trick the Mental Health expert to concede and it is not outside the realm of probability that the person being assessed could bring about marked changes in functionality and thereby parenting knowledge and skills. However, the task under this category of analysis is to make a defensible statement of probability especially with respect to the timeliness in which change can be expected. The challenge is to avoid at all cost creating the impression of faint hope and simultaneously to not devastate a parent by the manner in which you present the empirically supported clinical argument that it is highly improbable the assessed parent can bring about timely discernable changes to be of benefit to a child, especially one in the most crucial formative stage of development.

The Nature of Characterological Traits

The prescribed report format under this category of analysis starts by defining for the reader what is meant by a characterological trait. Unfortunately, the importance of this phenomenon is lost, not only on the general public and the judiciary but also on many Mental Health practitioners. The best example of this is the ill-defined efforts of Mental Health professionals working with "addicts". There is a significantly large group of people who implicitly or explicitly contend that their efforts can bring about a "cure". Similarly, in some jurisdictions, there is a practice that every two years a parent may petition the Court, as mentioned previously, for another Parenting Capacity Assessment on the basis of absolutely no evidence of intervening variables beyond the passage of time. In some cases, the rationale is articulated as parents having "learned their lesson", a claim that is not only incomprehensible but irrelevant without supportive evidence, especially when a child's right to optimal growth and development will be obstructed by an invariably protracted adversarial process.

Any discussion intended to clarify the phenomenon of characterological traits must acknowledge that the challenge of finding an operational definition of the concept is quite formidable. Not even the Minnesota Multiphasic Personality Inventory-2 Manuals adequately define the concept of personality or clearly distinguish which are characterological traits and, as such, permanent defining features of an individual's make-up, and which are other aspects of an individual's make-up that do not necessarily represent life-enduring features of who they are.

This is quite astounding, since surely such, distinction has profound implications with respect to the nature of the intervention with which an individual is provided. Statements about an assessed's poor prognosis, or about his or her falling into a group not amenable to constructively benefiting from intervention, seem often to identify characterological traits. Unfortunately, because of the absence of specificity or clarification, there is no distinction made between dysfunctionalities that can be eradicated and those that can only be brought under control by the persistent life-long application of "over-ride" strategies.

The best I could find with respect to a definition of personality is that it constitutes a synthesis of two concepts identified as character and temperament. Character refers to what is learned as a function of socialization, modeling and the consequences an individual experiences in response to behaviour. Character is very much defined as the nurture component in the dichotomous influences on the development of a human being. Character as a concept seems to refer to the basic ways in which individuals organize their view of who they are, what the world is and what the future holds for them. There are three dimensions into which these various learned cognitive processes can be categorized. The first pertains to self-responsibility. This essentially entails such propensities as initiative and being a self-starter, thereby believing that one's environment can be influenced in a proactive manner. The second dimension pertains to co-operativeness. This entails a perspective that incorporates a belief, that through collaboration, better and more sustainable results can be obtained. The third dimension pertains to self-transcendence. This refers to active, deliberate, purposeful self-actualization of one's potential.

This effort with respect to defining personality is not terribly useful for our purposes. The three dimensions seem to describe cognitive developmental perspectives. For example, self-responsibility is clearly very much a developmental feature as evidenced by the essentially reactive perspective of children. As a function of experience, children become increasingly more proactive until they reach an adaptive, well-balanced ability to distinguish between those elements in their environment over which they have various degrees of control, and those over which they have absolutely no control. Therefore, it is difficult to ascertain which of the various components that make up the three dimensions of character constitute characterological traits and which do not.

The second dimension of personality is said to be temperament. This refers to the innate, genetic and constitutional influences on an individual's make-up. Temperament reflects, therefore, the biological dimensions that impinge on the total make-up of an individual. Cloninger et al. (1993) contend that temperament has four biological dimensions. Without extensively elaborating these dimensions, they are novelty seeking, harm avoidant, reward dependence and persistence. There are others who argue for the addition of other dimensions, most notably Costello (1996), who includes impulsivity and aggressivity as additional dimensions of temperament.

The relevance of distinguishing character and temperament for authors in this field pertains to the nature of the intervention with which patients are provided. For example, insight-oriented psychotherapy is said to be effective in addressing character dimensions, an approach that will have little or no impact on the temperament dimensions. Skill training and the use of psychopharmological medication, on the other hand, are believed to be the most effective strategies when addressing temperament dimensions.

These conceptual efforts approach the vitally important issue of arriving at a differential definition of a dysfunctionality for purposes of defining relevant interventions. Unfortunately, these distinctions do not help us very much with respect to speaking to the issue of time frames in which the subject of a Parenting Capacity Assessment reasonably can be expected to bring about improvements in dysfunctionalities to be of benefit to a child, especially one in the most crucial formative stage of life.

The concept of trait as an enduring difference among people is likely best researched and most familiar in the studies pertaining to anxiety. Spielberger (1972), one of the best noted researchers in this area, distinguished between state and trait anxiety, and developed a standardized instrument to measure these with considerable reliability and validity. According to Spielberger and others (e.g., Thorne 1966, Cattell 1966, Cattell and Scheier 1961, 1963), personality states may be regarded as temporal cross sections in the stream of an individual's life. States are emotional reactions at a given moment in time and at a particular level of intensity. In contrast to the transitory nature of emotional states, personality traits, according to these researchers, can be conceptualized as enduring specifiable tendencies to perceive the world in a certain way and to be disposed to react or behave in a specified manner with predictable regularity. Of particular relevance to conducting a Parenting Capacity Assessment in the best interest of a child is that these dispositional tendencies are uniformly believed to be acquired in childhood. Specifically, formative stage experiences are said to dispose an individual both to view the world in a particular way and to manifest "object consistent" response tendencies. As such, in conducting an assessment, the intent is to determine the nature of the characterological traits possessed by the person being assessed, most notably those that are known to be contraindicated to promoting the optimal development of a child's potential. The intent of the assessment, when so indicated, is to rescue the child from developing an intergenerational family legacy of environmentally acquired dysfunctional characterological traits.

It is noteworthy that the internal, working systems of characterological traits tend to operate outside conscious awareness. This establishes their resilience and resistance to change. While resistance to change is invariably part of any intervention process, including psychotherapy or behaviour modification, some traits produce more resistance than others. The most resilient traits seem to be those that were established during the most crucial formative stage of life. These traits define the internal integrity, coherence and viability of the person. Moreover, given the adaptability of most characterological traits, what may paradoxically appear objectively dysfunctional, subjectively is experienced in a positive manner. This includes the use and abuse of mood-altering substances or cognitive distortions of reality. In spite of negative consequences, through denial or externalization of blame, individuals are invariably reluctant to give up what for them, has been a protective tactic against trauma.

The intimate connection between neurological development and experience cannot be overstated. A child's internal experiences to environmental trauma initially elicit "state" responses. When similar internal and external forces are experienced over time well defined neurological pathways become established. These pathways constitute life enduring characterological "traits" (Perry, Pollard, Blakeley and Baker, 1995). Moreover, the characterological personality traits produced by the traumatic events in a child's life invariably are experienced subjectively as adaptive. This experience and the neurological pathways combine to define the resilience of all traits. At least in theory, however, intervention can create new pathways and through this new or incompatible traits: The time and facilitative expertise required is not only formidable but becomes increasingly more so with each chronological year in an individual's life. More will be said later of the implications this has on the subjects of Parenting Capacity Assessments.

To the best of my knowledge, and in spite of my research efforts, I have not found a comprehensive list of personality traits or even an attempt to arrive at one in print anywhere. Moreover, standardized instruments that purport to objectively define personality not only fail to define operationally the broad concept but also fail to distinguish between a transitory state or a chronic trait. For the sake of expedience, I will resort to the use of labels to illustrate this point and ask you to reflect on the nature of "reactive depression" and the nature of "psychopathy". Clearly, the former is far more responsive to intervention than the latter.

For the purposes of conducting a Parenting Capacity Assessment, such a distinction under this category of analysis is imperative. Moreover, from the perspective of a clinician as opposed to that of a research scientist, my self-admitted bias is that the probability of ameliorating either type of dysfunctionality is far better than what is predicted statistically. This belief system is, however, qualified by the disclaimer that the more resilient dysfunctionalities (e.g., psychopathy) at this time are beyond our knowledge and skill base to effectively influence.

To reiterate, the persistent theme under this category of analysis, the issue, without devastating/decimating the person being assessed, is to offer an evidence-based predictive conclusion with respect to the timeliness and the expertise required so that a dysfunctionality can be ameliorated, by bringing it under control (this applies to traits) or eradicating it as an obstacle to the person becoming a "good enough" parent.

Many "personality features" or types identified by the MMPI-2 are prognosticated to be resistant to treatment. Unfortunately, it is not clearly stated what is meant by treatment. This leaves the standardized instrument user to extrapolate from the data whether the identified personality feature cannot be "cured", or cannot be brought under control, or both. There is also less than adequate clarity provided by this and other standardized personality assessment instruments with respect to the defense mechanism of denial which might support a dysfunctional personality feature and, when ameliorated, allow the actual dysfunctionality to be adequately addressed.

Our understanding of what constitutes a characterological trait may be further enhanced by considering what has been described in the literature as the later-life negative manifestations of an attachment disorder sustained during the most crucial formative stage of life. As such, impulsivity certainly seems to be a characterological trait, as well as that which is involved in attraction to a romantic partner, expectations of a relationship and the extent to which one can commit to nurturing a relationship with a partner or an offspring. Certainly self-soothing propensities appear to be characterological traits that are dysfunctionally manifested through sexual promiscuity and substance abuse. The ability to be co-operative, working with others to achieve an outcome greater than that which could possibly be achieved singularly, also very much appears to be a characterological trait since this, too, can characterize the approach of individuals to collaborative situations throughout their life.

It is beyond the scope of this manual to endeavor to create a list (let alone an exhaustive one) of characterological traits and acute or chronic or situationally determined emotional states. My intent is to identify this as an extremely crucial issue to be taken into consideration under this category of analysis.

Under this category of analysis, the intent is to delineate that something more fundamental than socialization and learning happens during the formative and subsequent stage in life. During this very early phase in the life of individuals an entire system of being is internalized that permeates virtually every aspect of their functioning. Relationship systems, for example, are determined by the early-life experiences of an individual. An abused child learns not only to be the victim but also the role of a victimizer (Sroufe and Fleeson 1986; Minuchin 1974). In the early-life internalization of relationship systems, family roles become interdependent and unhealthy parent/child alliances evolve into role reversals or peer-like relationships (Jacobvitz, Riggs and Johnson 1999; Jacobvitz and Hozen 1999).

Another enduring, fundamental feature of one's personality is the disassociative process with which abused or otherwise maltreated children respond to overwhelming trauma. The adaptive nature of this defense mechanism establishes its resilience as a life-enduring way in which an individual responds to an attachment disorder (Herman 1992; Putnam 1993; Terr 1991; Putnam 1991).

The life-enduring phenomenon of characterological traits, however, need not cast doubt on the enterprise of psychotherapy or other forms of clinical interventions. Instead, the nature of characterological traits serve to better define what outcomes are reasonable objectives and how these may be pursued in a deliberate, well-informed manner. Simply put, while some dysfunctionalities can be eradicated through well-defined interventions, others can only be brought under control through conscious, persistent, life-enduring practices. Still, perhaps there are other trait features that simply disqualify an individual from certain pursuits, and one of them may well be parenting.

Neurobiology

Assuming that there is no underlying neurobiological basis for a personality change as might have occurred from major brain injury, sustained by the person being assessed, research advances in the genetic and biological aspects of personality are beginning to reveal that there is a physiological basis for the stability of personality traits in all individuals. Moreover, traits that have an evolutionary basis have been identified as remarkably consistent over time. Thus, there are reasons to believe that stability in personality is not only likely but quite desirable since there are more well-defined adaptive benefits than there are maladaptive traits in the personality structure of most individuals (Livesley 2001).

In recent years, brain-imaging technologies have enabled researchers to gather new information about the development of a child's brain. Whereas experts once believed that a child's brain was basically inherited and its development determined by his or her unique set of genes, recent findings are revealing that the individual brain is built from a mixture of heredity and experience (Pollack et al. 2000, Shore 1996, Van der Kolk 1994, Zanarini 1997, Jones 2000). While heredity provides some basic parameters for brain potential, experience is increasingly believed to be a far greater determinant of the quality and quantity of the neurobiological circuits that are formed and the way in which the brain is organized to process information. The quality and quantity of stimulating interactions between caregiver and child in the first three years of life is being revealed by these lines of investigation to play the largest role in determining the child's emotional development, learning potential and level of future adult functioning. For example, children who enjoy consistent nurturing interactions with caregivers in their early years become more resilient emotionally and biologically and are better able to tolerate stress in later years (Karen 1994).

The newborn brain is wired only for controlling those functions that are essential for survival (e.g., respiration, heart rate, reflex movement, etc.). At birth, the infant has approximately a hundred billion brain cells that are not yet connected to form the networks that will allow thinking and learning to occur. By the age of three, the child will have formed about a thousand trillion neural connections. This is about twice the number found in the adult brain. The reason for this is that around the age of eleven, a child's brain performs a sort of self-pruning, ridding itself of excess neural connections and retaining the strongest ones. The strongest are invariably those that have been used most often. Moreover, connections that have been repeated most consistently in childhood are most likely to become permanent, whereas a lack of experience is believed to create deficits or complete absences in some neural connections.

A child who is rarely spoken to is believed to develop insufficient neurons for mastering language. Similarly, a child who is rarely played with is not likely to have enough circuits for healthy social attachment or for co-operative play. These invariably are the children who develop into social isolates, or socially awkward people with marginal or altogether absent ability to work co-operatively with others (Blair 2000, Davidson 2000).

The best insurance against emotional and behavioural problems in childhood and subsequently therefore, is the formation of healthy attachment between a child and a consistently available, sensitively responsive, nurturing caregiver (Begley 1977, Perry 1994). This is profoundly significant with respect to timely intervention with the child on whose behalf a Parenting Capacity Assessment is being conducted. Without such timely intervention, children, according to brain development research are destined to a life of dysfunctionality because during their formative stage, as a result of how they were parented, they developed life-enduring, debilitating neurobiologically based characterological personality traits. In the same vein, under this category of analysis, the task is to determine to what extent assessed individuals suffered this fate and, if so, what resources are required to ameliorate their dysfunctionalities. Of equal importance, it is imperative that you ascertain what time frame will be required to bring about discernable desirable results.

This growing body of research concerning brain development also has increased exponentially our understanding of the ways in which trauma affects the neurological and neuro-behavioural functioning of children (de Bellis et al. 1999 and 2000). Evidence is emerging that sustained traumatic experiences, like childhood abuse, neglect or the failure to form a secure attachment in the early years of life, can create a chronic state of hyper-arousal in a child and altered neuro-endocryine activities in the brain, causing the child to become trapped in the "fight or flight or freeze" response (Parry 1994; Van der Kolk 1994). Therefore, when a child's "stress response" system remains activated for an extended period of time, that child's brain will adapt in ways that enable the child to live with the perception of constant threat Tragically, brain adaptation to the environment produce devastating personal and social consequences. In fact the rise in juvenile violence and crime over the last decade is being reported as having a strong correlation particularly with findings pertaining to brain development. There is a pronounced consensus that the nature and quality of caregiver interaction in the first three years of life significantly influences the way in which the brain develops. Changes in the neurology of the child's brain result in cognitive, emotional and behavioural propensities. Parry (1995) lists the following as neuro-behavioural problems likely to be identified in traumatized, hyper-aroused children:

Hypersensitivity and over-reaction to neutral stimuli;
Autonomic hyper-arousal and motor hyperactivity;
Increased startle response;
Profound sleep disturbance;
Problems controlling emotions;
Cognitive deficits and distortions;
Impaired social functioning; and
Impulsivity and aggression.

While by no means an exhaustive list, it certainly serves to underscore not only that from which the child must be rescued, but also the intergenerational perpetuation of dysfunctionalities by parents who likely endured early childhood trauma and inadvertently pass on their family legacy. It is crucially important to convey the extent to which characterological trait propensities are resilient and the extent to which the traits are perceived subjectively as adaptive. This essentially prevents individuals from understanding the nature of their dysfunctionalities, let alone learning to apply persistently, with competence, control strategies while at the same time learning appropriate parenting knowledge and skills and applying these also with predictably consistent competence.

A failure to provide a consistent, nurturing and stimulating environment, therefore, has a dire consequence for a child's brain development (Pickle 2000). In fact, many believe that not only is the first year of life extremely important, but also the prenatal period which combine to form the environmental influences on the child's development. Under this category of analysis, the focus, therefore, is on the early-life experiences of individuals and the impact these have subsequently had on their capacity to learn parenting skills and, of equal importance, apply them (Sperry 1999).

Personality Predictors

Having identified the profound importance of distinguishing between characterological personality traits and the dynamic dimensions of an individual's make-up, the next step under this category of analysis is to identify the predictive qualities of salient personality features. While the malleability of personality is at the very heart of "clinical intervention" and while personality tends to be conceptualized as a dynamic phenomenon, in reality, this is far less the case. The reason for this is that counselors from all disciplines must believe in the dynamic aspects of personality and invariably consider that almost all dysfunctionalities are amenable to being ameliorated, although many counselors also acknowledge that the knowledge and skills required has not yet been developed for specific conditions. This is both a functional and adaptive belief system capable of sustaining the curiosity and commitment of clinicians to positively impact on the human condition.

While adaptive for counselors, a belief system that "anything is possible" must be tempered considerably by the realities of statistical probability when a child's right to optimal growth and development is at risk. Much can be accomplished by "counseling" and invariably more good than harm comes out of almost all interventions. If in pursuit of this, however, one gambles with an infant's future, this constitutes wanton callousness, at worst, and at best, a profoundly uninformed view of personality.

The question, therefore, is how resilient/resistant to change are the dysfunctionalities that compromise the personality of the person being assessed. While the range of personality variables can be broad, in most cases they will cluster around that which was described as representative of deficient/abusive parents under the second category of analysis.

To begin to factor in considerations pertaining to resilience and timeliness when a child's welfare is at stake, it is necessary to take into account that there are two kinds of pressures that impinge on the make-up of an individual. There are pressures from the environment and there are pressures from within the organism. Because of the constant interaction between what are otherwise known as "nature and nurture", the combined effects of these is immense.

At this stage in the assessment process, you will have much information about the assessed person's formative stage experiences and subsequent family dynamics. This will be the information on which you formulate a conclusion as to how these have impacted on the development of the person. If the environment in which the individual spent the first decade plus some years of life remained relatively similar over time, whatever family pressures led to the development of the person being assessed to take the pathway that person is on at the time of assessment are likely to persist (Peck and Havighurst 1960). This is why attempts to change a child's functioning by means of individual intervention without simultaneously intervening to change the family environment by means of family therapy and other interventions tend to be useless. Therefore, if there is no history of such intervention measures, especially during the first decade in the assessed individual's life, the probability is considerable that not only are dysfunctional characterological personality traits of the person well established but, all other aspects of that person's personality make-up are as well.

Environmental pressures as well as the structural physiological features of personality tend to maintain development on a particular pathway. In combination, there is a profound self-regulatory process that works to maintain the particular direction of an individual's development.

Cognitive and behavioural structures determine what is perceived and what is ignored, how a new situation is interpreted and what plan of action is likely to be constructed to deal with it. Current structures determine what sort of person and situation are sought after and what sort are shunned. In this, an individual comes to influence the selection of the environment that is preferred and thereby establishes a self-perpetuating process (Bowlby 1973).

Because these strong self-regulative processes are present in every individual, interventions aimed at changing the environment without attempts to simultaneously influence the personality structure of the individual tend to be futile. Under this category of analysis subheading, the task, therefore, is to synthesize the findings and conclusions under the first three categories, informed by the reality that no variable has a more far-reaching effect on personality development than the experiences of individuals in their family during the first decade of life, especially the first three years. Based on early-life experiences, the individual will subsequently have demonstrated through their personal history what working models had been constructed with respect to how the world works and how the assessed person responds and/or makes things happen. By recognizing that individuals base all their expectations on these models and, thereby, plan for the rest of their lives, it will be possible to form conclusions with considerable confidence pertaining to the prospects of individuals for realizing, in a timely manner, whatever potential they have as parents.

Many subjects of Parenting Capacity Assessments have histories of profoundly negative experiences that predict with marked probability specific dysfunctionalities being manifested in the assessed person's role as a parent.

For example, the probability of physical abuse being perpetrated by the person being assessed is predicted by that person's experiences of abuse, both physical and emotional, as well as exposure to family violence. The potential for neglect is predicted by extreme poverty, depression and, most notably, isolation from support. The potential for sexual abuse is also predicted by social isolation, as well as by a family constellation that is comprised of a mother who has been abused and/or who distances the child and is living with a non-biologically related caretaker who also has a history characterised by maltreatment.

It is important to assess how caregivers have, or are, processing their own abusive history, whether it is through denial, forgiveness, reconciliation or resolution. The degree to which a caregiver has resolved feelings of being abused or deprived will impact directly on that person's ability to parent with consistency, effectiveness and competence. Most often, the subjects of Parenting Capacity Assessments are those who either idealize their own relationship with parents, or who admit that they were abusive or neglectful, but deny that this has in any way negatively impacted on them. Moreover, some subjects of a Parenting Capacity Assessment who remain preoccupied with feelings of rage and deprivation are more likely to have difficulty meeting the emotional needs of their children and providing the sensitive attunement and sustained involvement that their infants will need in order to form a secure attachment.

Of equal importance to defining better what intervention strategies are likely to produce timely, favorable results are the dynamics that support the stability of an assessed individual's personality. While the neurobiological variables are clearly important, environmental variables are also important, if for no other reason than that they are more readily capable of being altered. For example, while empathy, the ability to understand the perspective of another, may be developed incrementally as a function of directed learning experiences, impulsivity, in contrast, may simply be brought under control by the application of well-defined strategies.

To bring about any improvements, the absolute prerequisite is that individuals recognize and accept that their various dysfunctionalities must be addressed and that from doing so, positive/desirable outcomes can be realized. Individuals socialized to be defiant toward authority and through experience to view their circumstance as "normal" are hardly likely to be inclined to commit energy and personal effort over a protracted period of time to bringing about changes in how they think, interpret experiences and behave.

A most paradoxical intervention conundrum involves a person who uses the defense mechanism of denial based on and sustained by profound developmental deficits. In the pleasing fantasy created by the developmentally deficient perspective, individuals are highly unlikely to begin, let alone sustain a process through which cognitive growth and development can occur. Therefore, while cognitive developmental perspectives do change/improve over time, they do so essentially as a function of ever-broadening life experiences. As individuals move from the insular, familiar environment to one that is increasingly complex, greater exposure invariably precipitates cognitive conflict that requires the persistent active construction of meaning. Adults who are developmentally deficient, unless physically coerced, as for example by incarceration, to participate in programs designed to promote cognitive development, invariably remain fixated at perspectives that maintain indefinitely their defense mechanism of denial.

Under this last category of analysis, a significant challenge for an assessor is to remain cognizant of the potential confounding influences of transference. While tenaciously guarding objectivity, the assessor must recognize that in spite of whatever optimism may be harbored regarding the human capacity to change, these must be tempered by considerations of probability, especially with respect to the timeliness with which discernable improvements can be realistically expected. Moreover, it must be remembered and reported that the more profound the dysfunctionality, the more resistant it is to change and the more resilient it is to external influence.

Behavioural Predictors

"Past behaviour predicts future behaviour", is no longer a colloquialism. Instead, it is becoming increasingly recognized as an empirically validated reality of the human condition as a function of the previously described environmental and biological factors. In fact, organizations ranging from the smallest to the largest, are increasingly using behaviorally based hiring practices whereby selection interviews focus on the past behaviours of candidates. The premise is that these predict how the candidates will conduct themselves in the future. With respect to conducting a Parenting Capacity Assessment, there are two broad categories of behavioural predictors. The first pertains to the assessed person's past experiences parenting a child. It is, therefore, imperative to determine whether or not this has occurred, even with a twenty-year-old who may have already had a child apprehended. That child may have been apprehended at birth or shortly thereafter. The child's status at the time of being apprehended, therefore, can be a significant source of information with respect to how that parent behaved in the past. Without a significant intervening variable, there is absolutely no reason to believe that the assessed person's behaviour will be any different than it was in the past. In fact, there is good reason to believe that all aspects of the person's functioning will become increasingly more pronounced as the person becomes more like himself or herself with the passage of time.

The claim of having "learned their lesson" is simply semantic nonsense, especially if it is argued without supportive evidence. While, undoubtedly, individuals may be well intentioned, and truly believe "things" will be different with the child in question, such sentiments without concerted verifiable effort do not produce positive results. People with activated good intentions seldom, if ever, are the subject of Parenting Capacity Assessments.

The predictive strength of past behaviours is probably most pertinent with respect to the role of grandparents of a child at risk. It is simply amazing that alternative caregivers to a dysfunctional parent are often decided to be that parent's own primary caregivers. That is to say, the child's grandparents. Moreover, in such cases, seldom, if ever, is a Parenting Capacity Assessment seen by a Child Welfare Agency or the court as necessary. Insofar as there is little disagreement with the axiom that all human beings are the sum total of their past experiences, and that the most significant determinants of who we are, are the experiences of our most crucial formative stage of life, it is lost on most people that the dysfunctional parent is the product of the parenting that was provided by the child's grandparents. There is absolutely no reason to believe that the grandparents will parent the child at risk any differently than they did the parent in whose care the child is considered to be at risk. Moreover, there is every reason to believe that the grandparents have been becoming "more like themselves with the passage of time", not unlike the parent being assessed. Unless indicated otherwise by reliable and valid information, grandparents are not viable alternative caregivers and, if any decision is made in this respect, it should also be well informed by a Parenting Capacity Assessment.

There are two specific instances that exemplify the above two considerations. The first was a mother who gave birth to a child under the most adverse conditions and in a most dysfunctional relationship just prior to the start of menopause. Her child was apprehended and a Parenting Capacity Assessment was ordered. It was discovered that the mother had two older children, one who had refused to have contact with her for the past ten years and another who was living on social assistance, unskilled and unemployable, in and out of jail. These findings and a clear, progressive deterioration in the assessed person's functioning and circumstances were concluded to be powerful predictors of how she would raise the infant on whose behalf the Parenting Capacity Assessment was being conducted. The overwhelming evidence in support of clinical conclusions and recommendations served to produce one of the most timely determinations of a child's disposition and concomitant placement for adoption where the child's optimal growth and development had an infinitely greater prospect of being realized.

The second example pertains to an extremely dysfunctional parent driven by out-of-control intense impulses exacerbated by an addictive characterological trait. By default, the grandparents were the primary caregivers of the child with the belief that, at any time, the parent would "come to her senses" and become the "good mother" the grandparents idealized her capacity to be. A Parenting Capacity Assessment found the parent to be highly unlikely to rise to the demands of parenting in the foreseeable future, with or without the provision of resources. A recommendation that the child be placed for adoption was met with a unified family response that the grandparents would assume parenting responsibility. Insofar as the child was considered not to be at imminent physical risk in the care of the grandparents, whereas he was in the care of the parent, this arrangement was acceptable and implemented without the potentially significant, informative benefits that could have been derived from assessing the parenting capacity of the grandparents. How and why these individuals were considered by child protection workers, or for that fact by the Court, as suitable alternatives, beyond the fact that they did not pose imminent physical risk to the child, is simply incomprehensible. It is condemning the infant to an almost certain fate, not unlike that of his mother.

The second category of behavioural predictors is the assessed person's history of benefiting from the constructive use of available resources. One significant behavioural indicator is the academic and/or skill training successes of the person being assessed. If there is a history of underachievement, this is indicative of obstacles that block the person's self-actualization. The assessed person's track record of working with community or Child Welfare resources also is a profoundly robust indicator of how that person will actualize good intentions articulated during a Parenting Capacity Assessment process. At times, your investigations will be able to explain past failures on the basis of incompetent and/or inappropriate intervention being provided, from which the person instinctively disengaged because it served no purpose and was of no benefit. If a Parenting Capacity Assessment can shed light on what would constitute more appropriate intervention, timeliness with which a positive response can be anticipated remains an issue, especially for a child in the most crucial formative stage of life.

Most often, the past use of resources by markedly maladaptive individuals will have been intermittent, inconsistent and of brief duration. In response to extreme pressure, there may have been brief instances of compliance. As soon as the crisis passed, a predictable pattern of disengagement invariably characterizes the behaviour of parents in whose care a child is considered to be at risk. Non-compliant behaviour can be understood and explained in many instances by the dynamics of denial. Normalization of lifestyle and parenting practices that are objectively judged to be dysfunctional but subjectively constitute the person's total frame of reference, are also powerful forces that mitigate against the constructive use of resources. Why should someone engage in a long and difficult change process when that change is not perceived, in any shape or form, to be necessary?

Routinely, and very much as a function of the dysfunctionality of individuals, they mistakenly pursue their version of the path of least resistance (e.g., embroilment in the adversarial system) instead of taking the avenue that is most likely to produce results and, paradoxically, is the path of least resistance. The adversarial process is perceived to be the path to vindication of individuals as competent parents, while actually it is more likely the path to confirmation of their dysfunctionality. Tragically, the issue of timeliness is lost on the adversarial judicial process, resulting in an exacerbation of the trauma already sustained by a child. Research completed during the last five years provides the basis on which to designate this delay as an unconscionable occurrence and, in essence, to constitute institutionalized brutalization of a vulnerable child in need.

Unfortunately, given the protracted nature of a judicially determined process, many parents are indirectly vindicated insofar as the status quo of their lives remains. Such incidents become the basis of much urban folklore, shared and distorted in a community, each and every version fuelling the adversarial perspective of parents whose childcare abilities and capacities are in doubt.

Under this category of analysis subheading, the issue is seldom the motivation or the good intentions of individuals being assessed. The issue is the ability of individuals to follow through with that which they intend. Cognitive developmental perspectives and characterological personality traits can be formidable obstacles to the actualization of their potential to learn and apply parenting knowledge and skills. In the same way, these same obstacles prevented them from achieving the academic potential of which they are capable, as well as developing concomitant behaviours that could have led to gainful employment and achievement of autonomous, independent, adaptive functioning in the community.

At this stage in the Parenting Capacity Assessment process, there may be evidence in support of a recommendation that the positive potential consequences of modified or new intervention strategies be evaluated over a specific, well-defined period of time. Most often, however, the Parenting Capacity Assessment process will have served to move from the impressionistic, experientially based concerns of child protection workers to empirically validated reasons for decisive action in a child's best interest. This is far from "rubber-stamping" the views of child protection workers and is equally far from the redundancy that some child protection workers consider Parenting Capacity Assessments to entail.

Standardized Predictive Indicators

Standardized instruments with predictive components fall within two groups. Most notably, the MMPI-2 profiles incorporate predictive statements with respect to how an individual can be expected to approach counseling and the extent to which certain personality anomalies can be positively influenced by the provision of resources. The challenge is to interpret profile configurations as to whether they identify a characterological personality trait as opposed to, for example, a situationally based temporal dysfunctionality that can be "cured" with proper intervention. Poor prognosis, for example, in MMPI-2 profiles likely depict characterological traits as unlikely to be eradicated, as opposed to predicting the probability of bringing the dysfunctionality under control. Nevertheless, while not sufficiently differentiated or specified, predictive statements pertaining to patterns of results on standardized instruments can be extremely useful for the purposes of supporting your conclusions and recommendations under this last category of analysis.

The second group of standardized instruments is made up of those that measure elements in an individual's make-up that can be changed or improved. The best example of this is the Bar On Emotional Quotient, which specifically articulates that each variable measured can be improved upon by the introduction of specific strategies. While the results of this and other instruments can be encouraging, in essence the only difference is with respect to what objective is set and through what intervention it can be achieved. With a characterological trait, the goal is to override the propensity whereas with depression, for example, the objective is to eradicate the dysfunctionality by freeing the anger that is suppressed through specific intervention strategies.

Under this category of analysis, the salient issues remain the same. They are of equal importance and pertain to the availability of expert resources and the timeliness with which desirable outcomes can be expected.

What Can Be Expected from Program Participation and Treatment

Counsel representing a parent will often resort to appealing for compassion from the Court on the basis of faint hope. By the time a trial will take place some parents will be reported to have made significant improvements in their compliance with counseling appointments and program attendance. It is advisable to anticipate this in all cases and to speak to the issue of faint hope in an authoritative as well as compassionate manner.

The first premise for a faint hope argument invariably is parenting program attendance. Improved or total compliance especially with a requirement often imposed by a Child Welfare Agency can be a formidable argument when made out of the context of your findings. In context, this argument has little merit beyond confirming findings that the assessed have within their behavioural repertoire desirable behaviours which they are able to enact for brief periods of time especially when structured to do so by significant external forces such as an impending trial. There will be other examples of such short lived positive behaviours as for example a home that exceeds standards of safety, cleanliness and orderliness. Tragically, while the assessed individuals know the differences between right and wrong their dysfunctionalities as described under the second category of analysis prevents them from doing that which is adaptive in a predictably consistent manner. Moreover, while their cognitive intelligence in the average range provides them with the ability to learn parenting knowledge and skills the issue in almost all cases is the application of that which is known.

It is imperative that under this category of analysis it is made explicitly clear that while cognitive intelligence is important, emotional intelligence is a better predictor of success in all endeavors especially parenting.

The second premise for a faint hope argument is participation in counseling. This to can be a formidable argument, since it is also often required by a Child Welfare Agency and there is much mysticism about what reasonably can be expected from the process. Moreover insofar as most assessors also engage in providing some form of intervention your adaptive optimism as a therapist must be tempered by the science of probabilities applied in conducting a Parenting Capacity Assessment.

Your eternal optimism as a therapist must also be tempered by the basic tenets of empirical practice as well as the realities concerning the availability and access to competent expert counselors.

In most jurisdictions, certainly in Canada where we have universal access to medical care, physician specialists in psychiatry are the resources most often used. As physicians their intervention essentially is pharmacological. Medication in most cases will have very little impact on improving an assessed's capacity to parent. Expertise in specific modalities of counseling is not only difficult to find but even more difficult to access. Furthermore, when such expertise is available and can be accessed, discernable positive results take time. Time is however of an essence, especially for a child in the most crucial formative stage of development.

Consider the following treatment issues under the first three categories of analyses:

ATTACHMENT

An attachment disorder sustained by the assessed individual during the formative stage of development can be addressed specifically by mental health professionals who specialize in this area of practice. Research in this vitally important are of human development has been invaluable with respect to informing practitioners' intervention plans based on case specific understanding of the attachment dynamic (Cramer, 1986; Stern, 1995). Unfortunately, the recognized need for expertise in this area is painfully slow to emerge. This impacts on both the identification and access to such experts. Of equal importance is the assessed individual's resistance to this type of intervention. Resistance is grounded in denial and perpetuated by a myriad of factors including persistently ambivalent relationships with primary caregivers. Furthermore, even in an ideal situation the pursuit of building new neurological pathways incompatible with those that obstruct the development of secure attachment is time consuming. The general principle is that two to three months of intervention is required for every year in an individual's life. For a twenty year old mother this means forty (40) months of intervention. These and other complex issues mitigate against the realization of timely positive outcomes to be of benefit to a child in need of establishing a secure attachment which then can develop into a true positive psychological relationship with a parent.

CRITERIA OF A GOOD PARENT

Under this category of analysis there are two broad areas of finding which compromise an individual's capacity to parent and which in turn may be focused on in counseling. The first area of findings pertains to the unusual features that define the uniqueness of individuals. The second area of findings pertains to that which is relatively constant to most cases. These themes in Parenting Capacity Assessments also mirror what is reported in the literature as characteristic of deficient/abusive parents. Self esteem issues and aggressive propensities are common findings and represent areas of dysfunctionality routinely addressed in counseling.

Discernable and sustainable improvement in self-esteem among many requirements most importantly is determined by real, meaningful positive achievements. A positive sense of self cannot develop without concomitant sustainable accomplishments. These simultaneous processes take time. While the efforts of a parent involved in such a process is commendable the issue nevertheless remains the same. Will sufficient gains be made in time to benefit the child, especially one in the most crucial stage of development.

Involvement in anger management focused intervention is commonly required of a parent being assessed and in most communities it is relatively available. To have a realistic expectation of such involvement requires an understanding of the dynamic which must be articulated under this category of analysis. It is first and foremost a characterological trait. It cannot be eradicated from the personality structure of an individual. Moreover, an aggressive personality trait is the second most stable feature of an individual's makeup after cognitive intelligence. Once established during the formative stage of development and reinforced subsequently by environmental factors in childhood, this propensity continues in adulthood even after many interventions to stop it. Most violent adults were aggressive and troublesome children (Robins 1991). While there are many individuals who have achieved and maintain control over their aggressive propensities as those who have done likewise with their addictive propensities this level of success does not come easily. Success of significant degrees certainly does not come from "attendance at a few sessions". Rather success comes with persistent support and effort over a protracted period of time, relapse always looming with the abandonment of the various strategies with which control was achieved in the first place. Invariable, the time required is contraindicated to the best interest of a child especially one in the most crucial formative stage of development. A significant exception is defined by verifiable, long-standing program participation and control over a characterological trait propensity such as aggression or addiction.

Overcoming the pleasing and efficient fantasies (denial) of individuals, promoting their cognitive developmental perspective or their dysfunctional romantic attractions, to name but a few more common worrisome issues, while probable achievements to pursue, take time and access to expert facilitative resources. It is incumbent on you as the assessor to convey these realities in the Parenting Capacity Assessment report and thereby dispel any illusions that a hasty compliance with program and/or counseling requirements a few months before a trial even remotely approximates grounds for a faint hope argument.

SOCIAL SUPPORT NETWORK

Social isolation and alienation is a function of many variables most notably the inability to trust. Past relationship failures, disappointments of joyful expectations and emotional pain to name but a few precipitating factors all combine to make the individual profoundly uncomfortable in most social situations. Even if positive affiliative opportunities were available these would be so outside the individual's comfort zone as to elicit an instant and instinctive avoidance of such encounters. These debilitating propensities are amenable to intervention that is dual focused. Of equal importance the person has to experience a systematic desensitization to aversive (phobic) social situations; incremental acquisition of appropriate interpersonal skills; and a developing ability to reflect on experiences and through this achieve sociability that characterize the norm. This is a formidable undertaking from which improvement is probable, albeit time and expert resource consuming. Moreover, it is an absolute prerequisite that impulsivity, substance abuse and other characterological personality trait obstacles are addressed before this initiative is undertaken. A child in the most crucial formative stage of development does not have the luxury of time to wait for a parent to achieve the positive outcomes.

Parenting Capacity Assessments are ordered most often after considerable efforts have been made to assist a parent or family in trouble. Less worrisome and thereby less dysfunctional parents constructively utilize the resources with which they are provided and in short order alleviate the concern that precipitated the Child Welfare Agency's involvement. Non-compliance with imposed requirements, outlined in minutes of settlement and continued decompensation by parents speaks to their degree of dysfunctionality as well as the profound obstacles they must overcome to alleviate concerns about their ability to parent responsibly with competence. Eleventh hour compliance a few short months before a trial and their unrealistic expectations as to how their actions will be viewed also speaks to their dysfunctionality. Notwithstanding these frequent occurrences, it is imperative that you convey in your report under this category of analysis a clear distinction between genuine effort with a concomitant probable timely positive outcome, and last-minute, desperate measures, which like previous brief surges of positive conduct will also be short-lived.

CHAPTER 4
Pulling It Altogether

"While reductionism aids in the study and understanding of complex relationships among finite or infinite elements, their true nature can only be known by understanding the whole that they constitute."

Ludwig von Bertalanffy 1968 On General Systems Theory

"Whatever else personality may be it has the properties of a system."

G.W. Allport 1961

This chapter will serve to emphasize the need to reconstitute that which was segmented for the purpose of achieving clarity. For the very reason that it is necessary to engage in reductionism it will never be possible to do justice to representing the complex system that defines an individual. Nor will it be possible to adequately convey all that which infringe on an individual's functioning and thereby the degree to which they cannot be blamed for their dysfunctionalities. Nevertheless, it is imperative that attention be drawn to this reality of the human condition and the compassionate dignity to which the assessed is entitled regardless of the reasons which support the recommendations elaborated and reiterated in this section of a Parenting Capacity Assessment report.

Discussion

The discussion section is not intended to be a summary, but instead a representation of a complex system with many parts that impinge on one another in the context of simultaneous external and internal forces. This system can change, yet remains the same, as a function of the interplay of conscious and unconscious forces that drive the organism to be responsive and adaptive, while also maintaining its essential integrity.

In the discussion section, the intent is to convey to the reader the complexity of the individual being assessed and thereby the equally complex and expert interventions required to change any part of the whole which will also impact, to various degrees, all other aspects of the system, and thereby the totality of the individual. In other words, the pursuit of simple solutions can produce unintended complex results profoundly different from what was intended. For example, a well-intentioned requirement that a parent attend a certain program, a singular experience from which only good can come, may well precipitate a series of alternative reactions with devastating consequences. Consequences, such as a parent's inability to comply, may precipitate an intense negative self-evaluation with which the person attempts to cope by externalizing blame, which in turn will be interpreted as defiance or petulance and as indicative of an absence of true commitment to a child.

Notwithstanding the complexities of the human personality, by this time the reader of your report will be able to understand better the nature of the person being assessed. Moreover, the preceding sections of your report will make it easier for you to integrate the various components to put forth a plausible argument.

For example it may be that a synthesis of your findings warrants the introduction of well-defined interventions that have a marked probability of producing timely, positive results. As such, under the discussion section in the report, your task is to argue for additional time during which the assessed, is predicted to acquire parenting knowledge and skills, and with equal probability to resolve obstacles to applying these in a manner that will be of benefit to a child.

Alternatively, a synthesis of your findings may warrant an argument that, while the potential for positive change, to various degrees, is a reality, desirable and discernable results cannot be expected in the case, certainly not in time to be of benefit to a child, either in the most crucial formative stage of life or subsequently.

The discussion section of your report is also intended to resolve instances where conclusions and concomitant recommendations under the four categories of analyses are not uniformly consistent or indeed are contradictory to each other. While this will be a rare occurrence, it does happen from time to time. These rare instances will pose the greatest challenge to your clinical analytic skills. How you resolve the inconsistencies will impact on the timeliness with which a determination is made regarding the status of the child in question and requires, therefore, a clearly evident rational approach. This is best accomplished by presenting a defensible weighting of the four conclusions under the categories of analyses in reference to the child's developmental stage. On the basis of this it will be possible for you to be definitive in spite of inconsistencies and thereby maintain the focus of your work in the best interest of the child.

By reconstituting what was artificially disassembled to once again constitute a complex whole, the intent of this section is to convey in no uncertain terms the futility of simple solutions and disjointed efforts, especially when they are compared to the enormous contravening forces with which they are invariably met.

In brief, this section of the report is intended to convey that the problems that place a child at risk are not simple and cannot be simply addressed or solved. While assessed individuals can and should be extended a great deal of compassion for the circumstance of their life, the same compassion must also be extended to the child's inalienable right to optimal growth and development. To resolve justly the competing claims for compassion, the discussion is ultimately intended to bridge the body of your report with the following specific recommendations.

Recommendations

In spite of having declared previously, under the four categories of analyses, your conclusions and concomitant recommendations, supporting your position by various findings, it is not at all redundant to restate and elaborate the recommendations. This is especially important in the rare instances when the evidence under each of the four categories of analysis did not support the same conclusion or the same recommendations. Under the first category of analysis, your conclusion and recommendation may have been that the child be placed for adoption whereas, under another category of analysis, the findings may not support such a conclusion. Indeed, the findings may support an alternative disposition.

In this section of the prescribed report format, your challenge is to arrive at a definitive recommendation with respect to what would be in the best interest of the child. As such, a recommendation with respect to a child's disposition will not be a redundant statement but rather a decision that is carefully weighed and rationalized by all that you articulated previously, including what you wrote in the discussion part of the report.

You can never reiterate too often the need for timely action, especially since it is a point that seems to be lost, particularly on the judicial aspects of a Child Welfare System. If for no other reason, in the future some operational audit or inquest may find it useful to notice how often timeliness was emphasized in a Parenting Capacity Assessment and employ this data as an argument to implement systems with which to expedite what is done in the best interest of children. In my view (one shared by many others), the worst fate of a child is to be in a state of protracted limbo. Second to judicial delays are unjustified efforts to give a parent another chance to comply with yet another myriad of requirements. This, in most cases, simply postpones the inevitable and robs the infant of an opportunity for optimal self-actualization. It is imperative, therefore, that your recommendation in this respect be supported very clearly, thereby maintaining the focus of your report on being a solution rather than an exacerbation of a problem.

Another sphere of recommendations, useful in some instances, pertains to intervention strategies which, when successful, can justify repatriation of the assessed person with the child. Alternatively, the recommended intervention may simply serve to improve the functioning of individuals, and thereby also the quality of their life, but not necessarily their parenting. In some instances, the recommended interventions may justify less than intrusive measures undertaken by a Child Welfare Agency the next time the person being assessed finds herself in yet another pregnancy.

This comprehensive Parenting Capacity Assessment methodology will provide a profound advantage, usually unavailable to service providers, with respect to optimally defining the nature of a problem and, through this, becoming better informed with respect to what intervention will produce the most timely and beneficial results. It is, therefore, incumbent on you to take advantage of this opportunity and expedite the intervention efforts of expert resources if warranted, although it is possible that their interpretation of your findings may differ. Nevertheless, insofar as the efficacy of intervention is largely determined by how well a problem is defined, there is great potential for the assessed person to benefit personally from what would otherwise be a potentially devastating assessment experience.

Another sphere of recommendations constitutes the explicit acknowledgement of the right of individuals to be treated with dignity and compassion, regardless of how abhorrent their dysfunctionality may be.

I believe that at every opportunity it behooves us to convey that as Mental Health professionals, our assessments are not condemnations of people, insofar as we subscribe to the perspective that people are neither good nor bad, evil or saintly. They simply are. In the same manner as we tenaciously refrain from calling a child "bad", we should refrain with equal tenacity from calling an adult a "bad" person. As with children, so also with the adults, the evaluation is of what they do, as evidenced by their behaviour, that is influenced by their thinking, emotions and cognitive perspective. Therefore, even an individual with the most despicable dysfunctionalities is entitled to compassion. This compassion might be expressed through assistance in working through the meaning and content of the Parenting Capacity Assessment, or the permission to grieve the loss of the child through a final time-limited visit.

While it is highly unlikely that you will, I feel compelled to say that you do yourself and all mental health professionals a disservice if you resort to a recommendation prefaced by "in my opinion" without substantiating/proving with evidence what you state. Statements of "in my opinion" constitute the worst form of elitism or arrogance and are rarely, if ever, valued by reasonable, learned or otherwise competent individuals. By now, hopefully, I have been successful in convincing you that, in every respect, it is infinitely more functional or adaptive to articulate your views as an argument supported by evidence. In other words, as it will be persistently evident in the second part of this manual, the prescribed format requires from you conclusions and recommendations that are prefaced with "the findings under this category of analyses support". I trust that, on reflection and with some soul searching, you will abandon, in all aspects of your work, the phrase "in my opinion" and strive towards evidence-based formulations that are readily apparent to all who are interested.

In the same spirit, conclude your report by acknowledging that, in spite of your best efforts, there may be a need for further clarification, which you will be more than prepared to provide in writing and, if necessary, in person, not instead of the written elaboration but in addition to it.

CHAPTER 5
Appendices and References

The prescribed format requires a section in a Parenting Capacity Assessment that is atypical from the traditional way of writing a report. This section is intended to protect the well defined integrity of the methodology while addressing specific albeit sometimes ill conceived Terms of Reference posed most often by the legal counsel of a Child Welfare Agency. Moreover, instead of cluttering the body of the report, in this section all the documentations reviewed are listed as well as elaborations of for example stages of cognitive development. In the interest of precipitating a timely determination in the best interest of a child at risk the intent is to provide as much informative detail as possible instead of leaving this level of elaboration to occur in testimony at a trial.

Appendix A: Terms of Reference Posed by a Referring Child Welfare Agency and Concise Answers

This will be the most frustrating part of your report. It will challenge your patience and professional tenacity. You will be tempted to ignore the Terms of Reference but you cannot. You cannot ignore the Terms of Reference simply because you agreed to conduct the Parenting Capacity Assessment and part of this agreement entails doing what is asked of you by the legal counsel in the employ of the referring Child Welfare Agency and, in some instances, the legal counsel in the employ of the person being assessed.

Invariably, the Terms of Reference of a particular Child Welfare Agency pose virtually the same questions for every case. (Occasionally they do not even remember to change the names.) Furthermore, the very nature of that which is asked reveals profoundly limited knowledge about the fundamental issues involved in conducting a Parenting Capacity Assessment. What the questions do reveal is that the judicial focus is markedly different from the mental health approach to determining an individual's capacity to parent a child identified to be at risk as a function of a parent's dysfunctionalities.

The prescribed strategy in this manual is to identify the existence of Terms of Reference in the body of the report, list them in an Appendix, and provide precise and concise answers orienting the reader that they are best understood in the context of the Parenting Capacity Assessment report in its entirety. Hopefully, the practice of abdicating responsibility for formulating Terms of Reference to legal counsel will be abandoned by Child Welfare Agencies and will be replaced by a vastly more informed approach utilizing the most current thinking and research which, in essence, reflects the approach prescribed in this manual. Hopefully, Child Welfare Agencies will also come to formulate Terms of Reference that will require the contextualization of information obtained under the four categories of analyses used in this prescribed methodology.

There will always be extraordinary or atypical circumstances that will require additional questions and concise responses. Moreover, from time to time, legal counsel for the person being assessed will pose specific questions that may or may not be relevant or informed, but nevertheless will require a response. Therefore, as an Assessor, it is in your best interest to acquire some knowledge, skill and patience in responding to any and all kinds of questions. As demonstrated in Part Two of this manual, it is preferable to strive for precision and conciseness, in responding to Terms of Reference, referring the reader to specific sections in the body of your report for purposes of elaboration.

Appendix B: Sources of Documented Information

This Appendix is added here (as opposed to in the body of the report) simply as a stylistic decisions insofar as the documents reviewed can be extremely numerous. It is imperative that they be listed, largely as a preventative measure against a claim that a Child Welfare Agency purposefully withheld information in order to bias the conclusions and concomitant recommendations reached by a Parenting Capacity Assessment process. Furthermore, while documentations will be far less relevant sources of information than envisioned by the lawyers involved in a case, much time and energy can be saved by acknowledging what you read and that you focused on the relevance of information to your task of conducting a Parenting Capacity Assessment.

While potentially extremely tedious to complete accurately, especially in light of the fact that sometimes documentation is not clearly dated and labeled, the potential negative consequences of being less than precise warrant the energy required to complete this section in the report accurately. Even if you delegate the task, which is essentially clerical, it is still vitally important that you verify what is listed in your report as having been reviewed.

Appendix C: Stages of Cognitive Development

There is a general failure to appreciate the fact that cognitive development in humans occurs in an invariant hierarchical sequence and that the structure of this development is the same across different cultures, albeit that the content through which this structure is revealed will differ significantly in many instances. Insofar as this is a significant consideration in formulating conclusions and recommendations in the report, it is necessary to inform readers about this aspect of human functioning with which they may not be familiar. The decision to provide a brief outline pertaining to the three levels and six stages of reasoning in the Appendix is essentially a stylistic, pragmatic one, intended to achieve optimal balance in the body of the report between informing the reader to the relevance of your investigations and of the results obtained.

While the practice among most Mental Health professionals is to reserve such elaborations to cross examination in court, one premise of this prescribed methodology is that this practice may exacerbate the already protracted process and contribute to the practitioner's co-option to being part of the problem as opposed to being part of the solution. Therefore, it behooves you to do all that you can to enhance the process, promote a timely resolution or otherwise expedite matters in the best interest of a child. Providing such information in an appendix also allows the reader the discretion as to when and if it will be consulted.

Descriptions of each level and the six stages of reasoning are provided in the appendices of Part Two in this manual.

APPENDICES FOR PART ONE

APPENDIX A

Principles of Critical Thinking

The ability to think critically is a fundamental prerequisite to undertaking the complex task of conducting Parenting Capacity Assessments, especially given the potentially profound consequences of your findings, conclusions and concomitant recommendations. It is important, therefore, to briefly review the basic tenets of logic.

The ability to understand and apply rules of logic and to critically evaluate and synthesize the information available to you is the overriding expertise you bring to the task of conducting a Parenting Capacity Assessment. Without this ability, the synthesis of various sources of information will be seriously compromised. Without this ability, placing into context what you find also will be seriously compromised. Most importantly, without this ability, communicating to a non-Mental Health professional (a judge) will also be seriously compromised. It would be advisable, therefore, to review a basic introductory text on logic. If you did not take a philosophy course on logic, there are many publications readily available in university or college bookstores that you should review and have as a reference in your personal library. It will suffice, however, to briefly review what constitutes critical thinking. The rationale behind Watson and Glasser's Critical Thinking Appraisal (recommended as an assessment tool in the methodology), is ideally suited for this task.

Watson and Glasser view critical thinking as a composite of "attitudes, knowledge and skills". Operationally defined, the concept of attitudes pertains to an inquisitive propensity associated with the ability to recognize the existence of problems and an acceptance of the general need for evidence in support of what is asserted to be true.

Operationally defined the concept of knowledge pertains to understanding the nature of valid inferences, abstractions and generalizations. This is a prerequisite to weighting the evidence with which you support an argument or a conclusion.

Operationally defined, the concept of skill pertains to the competence with which you apply the attitudes and knowledge required for critical thinking.

Inference

An inference is a conclusion drawn from certain observed or supposed facts. In fact, the conclusions that you draw from all the various sources of information collected and analyzed in the process of conducting a Parenting Capacity Assessment constitute inferences. The confidence with which you can make an inference is determined by the confidence you have in the information (observations, descriptions provided by others, standardized instrument results, interviews, collateral information) on which it is based. It is imperative, therefore, that you qualify and, when possible, quantify the inferences (conclusions) you make. For example, if the lights are on in a house and music can be heard coming from the house, you might infer that someone is home. This inference may or may not be correct. The people in the house may not have turned the lights and the radio off when they left the house. Therefore, the inference should be qualified by a statement such as "assuming that the people turn the lights and the radio off when they leave the house" the information supports a conclusion that they are home.

More specific to our task, you may infer (conclude) from admitted promiscuity, relationship problems and substance abuse that an individual being assessed sustained an attachment disorder during the most crucial formative stage of life and unless addressed with success this will have profound and broad implications on the person's parenting capacity. While self-reported dysfunctionalities do have a potentially significant impact on a person's parenting capacity, the inference (conclusion) about the presence of an attachment disorder may or may not be true. The dysfunctionalities may have been precipitated by an unresolved adult trauma that precipitated out-of-character anomalous behaviours. Specific or collateral information about the individual's early history will significantly increase the confidence with which you can make an inference (conclusion) that the person sustained an attachment disorder.

Assumption

An assumption is an unsupported premise. It is taking for granted that a certain premise applies while acknowledging that there is no real tested/examined evidence in support of it. For example, when you say, "I will complete this Parenting Capacity Assessment by the end of next month", you assume that you will be alive to do the work and that what you produce will be perceived by others as the assessment report you intended it to be.

More specific to our task, to take for granted that a referral to conduct a Parenting Capacity Assessment by its very occurrence defines the existence of a dysfunctional parent constitutes an assumption that could potentially also lead to methodological errors, as well as unsupported inferences.

Deduction

A deduction constitutes another order of conclusions made on the basis of evidence. As such it is a particular type of argument. Whereas an inference may or may not be true, a deduction by definition represents a logical process that must produce a true conclusion. Therefore, to make a deduction requires that all the premises support the conclusion or argument being made. For example;

> Every mammal has a heart.
> All horses are mammals.
> Therefore, every horse has a heart.

Such rigor is seldom, if ever, possible in the determination of parenting capacity. It is imperative therefore to be vigilant about whether or not a conclusion is a qualified inference and that even conclusions made with the greatest of confidence do not venture into the realm of a deduction.

A deductive argument, therefore, is either entirely true or entirely untrue. There are no degrees of truthfulness (conclusiveness). If a deduced argument is logically correct, the premises support the conclusion completely and are true; the conclusion cannot be wrong. If a deductive argument is logically incorrect, the premises do not support the argument at all.

The point is that all your statements/conclusions/arguments are formulations of probability. In some you will have greater confidence than in others. Even when you make a conclusion with the greatest of confidence it likely can never be a deduction and to present it as such, inadvertently reveals a logical deficit which will compromise your credibility as an expert.

Interpretation

Interpretation constitutes a decision whether or not a conclusion "logically" follows from the information available. "Jumping to a conclusion" occurs when there is not enough supportive information or the information is not relevant to the conclusion being made. Given the profound potential consequences of the recommendations derived from your conclusions, it is imperative that you do not jump to conclusions.

There are no hard and fast rules as to what type or amount of information is enough to make a conclusion. The number of instances that constitute sufficient statistics varies from case to case, from one category of analysis to another. Sometimes two or three pieces of supportive evidence may be conclusion. The number of instances that constitute sufficient statistics varies from case to case, from one category of analysis to another. Sometimes two or three pieces of supportive evidence may be enough; sometimes many more will be required. Such determinations will be based on your practice wisdom and the confidence you have in the findings. The relevance of the information you rely on as evidence in support of your conclusions is similarly determined by your practice wisdom.

In conclusion, it is important to have realistic expectations about the logical approach to conducting a Parenting Capacity Assessment. Logic deals with justification of your conclusions, not with the discovery of facts. Nevertheless logic provides the tools for evaluating the arguments/conclusions you make; as such it is indispensable to intelligent expression and understanding.

The goal of this prescribed methodology is to guide this discovery process of facts and the inferences that can be made from them. Logic provides the critical tools with which to evaluate the soundness of inferences. That is to say, once an inference is made, it can be transformed into an argument and logic can be applied to determine whether it is correct or not. Therefore, while logic does not really tell us how to make inferences it does tell us which ones we ought to accept.

APPENDIX B

Standardized Assessment Tools

Many standardized instruments specifically designed to be used in the assessment of Parenting Capacity as opposed to ability assume respondents will be candid and, more importantly, have the ability to accurately describe their emotional and behavioural experiences. This is a significant assumption that is difficult, if not impossible, to accept at face value especially when the opposite is most often true. Moreover, if indeed individuals were willing and able to be candid and forthright, they would likely not be the subject of Parenting Capacity Assessments. Instead, they would be pursuing, with commitment and tenacity, endeavors with which to realize their potential as parents. By this very action, a Child Welfare Agency's concerns would not achieve the threshold that precipitates a need for a Parenting Capacity Assessment.

It is, therefore, extremely crucial that whatever standardized instruments you employ, do not assume candor or co-operation and have validity indicators that will disqualify results when certain criteria are reached. As well, self-report standardized instruments should be balanced by instruments that ascertain either innate potential, such as the **Raven's Progressive Matrices**, or actual ability to learn and apply problem-solving lessons, such as the **Watson-Glasser Critical Thinking Appraisal**. It is also preferable to use self-report standardized instruments that do not readily convey what response patterns produce optimally desirable results. For example, the **Rotter Locus of Control** instrument defines the adaptive perspective for most applications as that which is neither too reactive (external) nor too proactive (internal) but falls within the middle range, otherwise described as the norm.

Never lose sight of the fact that questions on a standardized instrument represent a series of verbal stimuli and the responses are scored in terms of their empirically established behavioural correlates. A scoring system that is based on some external criteria is otherwise known as empirical criteria keying. In empirical criterion keying, the responses are treated as indicative of certain behaviours with which they were found to be associated. Therefore, an empirically criterion-based inventory is not based on the assumption of accuracy on the part of the tested with respect to observations of self. Whether a response is valid in some absolute sense is not the issue. The issue is that the person responded in a particular way. The outstanding example of criterion keying in personality test construction is the **Minnesota Multiphasic Personality Inventory-2**.

As such, conclusions and recommendations cannot be solely based on the results of standardized instruments. They must be based on a synthesis of other pertinent information about the individual. Conclusions and recommendations also must be informed by the science of personality theories and human behaviour.

It should be kept in mind that all self-report inventories are especially subject to faking in a positive or negative way, depending on the agenda of the individual being evaluated. Many items on such inventories have answers that are recognizable, as socially more desirable or acceptable than the others. Respondents may be motivated to "fake good" or choose answers that create a favorable impression. Alternatively, respondents may be motivated to "fake bad" thus making themselves appear more disturbed than they are (Anastasi, 1988). Therefore, it is imperative that whatever instrument or tool is employed also incorporates relatively "subtle" or socially neutral items as verification keys that detect faking or response sets.

Finally, any test you may choose to use must be interpreted in light of a myriad of additional factors, not the least of which should be the consistence of test results with logically coherent clinical formulations, situational variables, including age, gender, education, socio-economic status, ethnic influences and geographic milieu.

Mindful of these reservations, you may wish to review and consider also using instruments specifically designed to be used in assessing a parent's ability (as opposed to capacity) to keep safe or otherwise protect a child while promoting a child's optimal growth and development. The following list is by no means exhaustive and are provided simply for purposes of orientation.

Child Abuse Potential Inventory;

Milner and Ayoub, 1980

This instrument evaluates rigidity, distress, unhappiness, loneliness, problems with family and others, negative concept of the child and self, and child with problems.

The Michigan Screening Profile of Parenting:

Heifer, Hoffmeister and Schneider, 1978

This is a fifty-item questionnaire that taps into the emotional needs met by a child, the assessed individual's relationship with parents, the assessed individual's interaction with others, expectations of the child, and general coping capabilities.

Adult Attachment Interview:

Main and Goldwyn, 1998

This instrument is designed to ascertain, from the perspective of individuals being assessed, the nature of their relationship with primary caregivers in their youth. Insofar as perception is more important than reality, according to the designers of this instrument, the instrument is believed to be capable of augmenting clinical formulations as to whether or not the person sustained an attachment disorder and thereby is likely to inadvertently perpetuate the intergenerational occurrence of likely progressive dysfunctionalities.

Adult/Adolescent Parenting Inventory:

Bavolek, 1984

This instrument was normed on populations of known abused and known non-abused adolescents. The known abused adolescents were considered to be at risk for parenting their children. The instrument claims to significantly discriminate between known abusers and non-abusers. For example, it taps into inappropriate parental expectations, parental endorsement of physical punishment, role reversal and lack of empathy towards a child's needs.

The Objective Parenting Profile:

Oldershaw, Walter and Hall, 1989

This instrument measures parenting ability and is said to be capable of successfully distinguishing maltreaters from non-maltreaters. It is a three dimensional analysis of a parent-child relationship designed to determined whether or not a child is at risk as a result of what a parent and child do, their style of interaction and how one perceives the other.

Emotional Quotient:

Reuven BarOn, 1997

Including a determination of an individual's emotional quotient serves to enhance the prescribed curiosity and objectivity of the methodology advanced by this manual. This analysis is also consistent with the principle of least intrusive measures ensured by legislation in most jurisdictions. While the standardized instrument developed by BarOn (1997) has not yet been used to determine parenting capacity, it is an ideal tool for defining those features in a person's current functioning capable of being improved upon by focused and well-defined intervention.

The fifteen variables grouped under five categories not only represent what BarOn has determined empirically to constitute emotional intelligence but also likely what constitute many of the obstacles to the development of an assessed person's innate potential. The results obtained from the use of this instrument can also serve to better inform what type of intervention is required by a parent, establish clear outcomes and determine when optimal results have been achieved.

Insofar as the EQ-i has predictive properties for specific functions it would not be unreasonable to expect that in short order the use of this tool will reveal which of the fifteen variables correlate with parents successfully alleviating the concerns of a Child Welfare Agency.

The focus on emotional quotient under the second category of analysis is experimental. While I have used this instrument with significant success for hiring purposes, I have not yet used it in a Parenting Capacity Assessment. Since it is readily available, easy to use with some orientation and is relatively inexpensive, I strongly recommend due consideration be given to incorporating this focus in the assessment process.

Unfortunately, as is the case in many other instances in life, intervention to rectify a defined problem is not readily available. That which is readily available is costly, likely beyond the means of many who will be the subjects of a Parenting Capacity Assessment and require access to a computer for on-line learning. Nevertheless, given the potential benefits to a parent, and satisfying the legislative criteria of least intrusive measure, it warrants the effort required to explore the usefulness of including this determination regarding an individual's capacity to become a "good enough" parent.

A Word About The Invoice

In Part Two, after the references, there is an example of an invoice. The hourly rate is yours to determine. In some jurisdictions the rate may be defined by the professional organization with which you are affiliated. Keep in mind that such fee schedules are almost always just recommendations and that your rate should be commensurate with the experience and expertise you bring to the task. Refrain from undervaluing your services because unfortunately this inadvertently also can lead to undervaluing your practice wisdom and skills by others.

As can be seen from examining the invoice, we have decided to follow certain billing practices simply out of practical necessity. Billing for interview hours is a relatively simple function. Travel time and expenses is similarly uncomplicated. We also manage administrative time in the same manner.

The more difficult task in preparing an invoice for your professional services is accounting for documentation review, and report preparation time. One solution has been to apply a type of a flat rate schedule. While we unanimously believe that the flat rate schedule is extremely conservative, we have agreed on the numbers because we believe that the law of averages in the long run will bring us closer to the actual time we spend on these difficult to track tasks.

In conducting a file review many pages can be scanned and some will need more than the three minute flat rate that is invoiced per page. We are extremely careful never to charge for duplications in a file sent for review as well as for court related forms, which can also be found duplicated in several places within a file. On the average, three minutes per page is a fair accounting.

Accounting for your professional time in preparing a report is the most difficult task. Some pages are as easy to compose. Some pages are extremely difficult and time consuming. Billing at half an hour a page in our collective experience is an understatement of our time. Most of us calculate forty five minutes per page of report preparation and some of us believe that on the average it is closer to sixty minutes. Our rationalization for the half hour flat rate is that the generic sections of our reports make up for the discrepancies.

Ultimately you have to be comfortable with how you decide on the billing rate for these two tasks. The operative term is your comfort (ethics), not what the market will bear.

The decision to invoice at an hourly rate for editing a draft report is based on the tremendous variance in time with which this is accomplished. Determined by many factors, the editing time required can be very brief or lengthy. Experience most often has nothing to do with it. The difficulty of the case and your frame of mind during the report preparation significantly influence the subsequent editing time. Therefore when we edit, the challenge is not only to attend to the task but also to keep track of our time. Most often we do this considerably well, and when we don't we opt to be conservative in the time we bill.

Finally, and much more will be said of this in a separate but related publication, remember your invoice represents the value you place on your professional time. The invoice is not rendered for your opinion. This is never for sale under any circumstance.

Concluding Remarks to Part One

The first part of this manual was designed to convey the reasoning and procedures that go into conducting a Parenting Capacity Assessment, as well as the manner in which your findings are reported to a judge who will take into consideration the report along with other variables in making a determination with respect to the status of a child.

The next section represents an actual report. It is a composite of many cases selected to demonstrate what the report should ideally look like, how it should be organized and how it should read. Any similarity with actual cases is coincidental and represents the commonality of themes found in the majority of instances.

For purposes of clarity, the material you should use verbatim in your report is presented in a different font from the composite case example that is provided. Even the composite case example can initially be of significant value with respect to acquiring and becoming comfortable with the method of presenting results. Feel free, therefore, to copy that which is useful for this purpose also. Ultimately, however, with practice will come confidence in the use of language that will optimally communicate the evidence that supports your conclusions and recommendations.

If you are a novice in this field of practice, the above comments are also intended to liberate you from whatever standards you may have set for yourself to be original or creative. As noted earlier, there is ample opportunity for you to demonstrate your expertise and autonomy with respect your analysis and interpretation of findings pertaining to each category of analysis.

For the seasoned practitioner, the above comments are intended similarly. Even if you are comfortable with your own style, procedures and methodology, and even if these have produced satisfactory results, hopefully as a function of your practice wisdom, you will see the profound benefits of striving towards standardization. Therefore, while you may be inclined to make modifications that improve on the prose and the articulation of rationales, you will be inclined equally to maintain the integrity of the format so that the pursuit of standardization is not compromised.

Part One of this manual concludes with two Appendices. The first one contains a very brief review of principles of logical thinking. The second constitutes a brief annotated list of possible tools that you may wish to investigate with the very clear understanding that the list is by no means exhaustive of what is available. Insofar as it has been my practice to use some tools and then, for a variety of reasons, elect to discontinue their use, hopefully this also will be a constantly dynamic variable in your practice. It is desirable and appropriate to replace one tool with a better one as it becomes available or known to you. We do this in our kitchens and workshops and in virtually every aspect of our lives, why would we not do likewise in our professional endeavors.

REFERENCES TO PART ONE

Providing references for research or scholarly works cited in the body of your report, while atypical, is not an unusual practice in as much as Mental Health professionals also are trained social scientists. At the end of the actual Case Example in Part Two of this manual there is a list of all the references which were cited in the Preamble to every category of analysis. Doing this serves two vitally important functions. First and foremost, the practice of providing a comprehensive list of references forces you to ensure that you have a thorough understanding of what is in the literature and to convey this in a reliably accurate manner. That is to say that your interpretations of the cited materials should be able to be confirmed as accurate as opposed to representing conscious or unconscious distortions, in order to support a particular perspective that you are advancing. Many counsel for the "unhappy/dissatisfied" person being assessed will, in fact, review some (if not most) of the references to ensure that this did not occur. Secondly, it is optimal professional practice to be comprehensive and to fully disclose what is relevant and pertinent to how you conducted the assessment. Withholding information or selectively providing information is not only unprofessional but certainly places into doubt your objectivity and your unbiased role as expert providing information to facilitate a timely determination of a child's status.

It is also scholarly to demonstrate the breadth and depth of your approach and the degree to which your formulations are consistent with how other competent professionals reach conclusions. A Parenting Capacity Assessment with its profoundly broad and long-term implications warrants professional competence that is informed not only by practice wisdom but also by scholarly works.

Note that the references at the end of Part One in this manual differ from those which appear at the end of Part Two. The references in Part Two should be in your actual report, whereas the first list is intended for your purposes.

Finally, consistent with the fact that Mental Health professionals are also social scientists, the citing of references follows the scientific rule, as does the manner in which the list of references is provided.

Ainsworth, M.D.S. Attachment beyond infancy. **American Psychologist**, 44,709-716, 1989.

Anastasi, Anne. **Psychological testing: Sixth Edition**. New York: MacMillan Publishing Company, 1988.

Andrews, D., & Bonta, J. **L-SIR: The level of service inventory: revised.** Toronto, Canada: Multi-Health Systems, 1995.

Armstrong, Louise. **And they call it help: The psychiatric policing of America's children**. Reading Massachusetts: Addison-Wesley, 1993.

Baumrind, D. Current patterns of parental authority. **Developmental Psychology Monographs**, 4, 1-102,1971.

Bavolek, S. **Handbook for the adult-adolescent parenting inventory.** Schamberg, DC: Family Development Associates, 1984.

Begley, S. **How to build a baby's brain**. (Special Addition), Newsweek, Spring/Summer, 1997.

Bowlby, J. **Attachment and loss: Vol 1. Attachment.** New York: Basic Books 1969/1982.

Bowlby, J. **Maternal care and mental health**. (World Health Organization Monograph No. 2), Geneva: World Health Organization, 1951.

Bowlby, J. **Forty juvenile thieves: Their character and home life**. London: Hogarth, 1946.

Bretherton, I. Young children and stressful situations: The supporting role of attachment figures and unfamiliar caregivers. In G.V. Coelho & P.I. Ahmed (Eds.), **Uprooting and development**. New York: Plenum Press, 1980.

Bretherton, I. Open communication and internal working models: Their role in the development of attachment relationships. R.A. Thompson (Ed.), **Nebraska Symposium on Motivation,** Vol 36, Lincoln: University of Nebraska Press, 59-113, 1990.

Caplan, Paula J. **They say you're crazy: How the worlds most powerful psychiatrists decide who's normal.** Reading, Massachusetts: Persus Books, 1995.

Cattell, R.B. Patterns of change: Measurement in relation to state dimension, trait change, liability and process concepts. **Handbook of multivariate experimental psychology**. Chicago: Rand McNally & Co., 1966.

Cattell, R.B., & Scheier, I.H. **The meaning and measurement of neuroticism and anxiety.** New York: Ronald press, 1961.

BarOn, R. **BarOn emotional quotient inventory: Technical manual.** Toronto: Multi-Health Systems Inc., 1997 (1-800-268-6011). In the United States, New York: North Tonawanda (1-800-456-3003) International +1-416-492-2627.

Beutler, L., & Clarkin, J. **Systematic treatment selection: Toward targeted therapeutic interventions**. New York: Brunner/Mazel, 1990.

Chugani, H.T. A critical period in brain development. **Preventive Medicine**, 27, 184-190, 1998.

Cloninger, R., Svrabic, D., & Prybeck. T. A psychobiological model of temperament and character. **Archives of General Psychiatry**, 50, 975-990, 1993.

Coopersmith, S. **The antecedents of self-esteem**. San Francisco: Freeman, 1967.

Costello, C. (Ed.), **Personality characteristics of the personality disordered**. New York: Wiley, 1996.

Cramer, B. Assessment of parent-infant relationships. In T.B. Brazelton & M.Y. Yogman (Eds.) **Affective development in infancy**. Norwood, NJ: Ablex, pp 27-38,1986.

Crokenberg, S. Infant irritability, mother responsiveness, and social support influences on the security of infant-mother attachment. **Child Development**, 52, 857-865,1981

Daly, M., & Wilson, M. **Homicide**. Hawthorne, N.Y.: Aldine de Gruyter, 1988.

Davis, P.T., & Cumming, E.M. Marital conflict and child adjustment: An emotional security hypotheses. **Psychological Bulletin**, 116,387-411,1995.

Davis, P.T., & Cumming, E.M. Exploring children's emotional security as a mediator of the link between marital relations and child adjustment. **Child Development**, 69, 124-139, 1998.

De Lozier, P. Attachment theory and child abuse. In CM. Parkes & J. Stevenson-Hindu (Eds.), **The place of attachment in human behaviour**. New York: Basic Books, 1982.

Duncan, B.L., and Miller S.D. **The heroic client**. San Francisco: Jossey-Bass, 2000.

Egeland, B., Carlson, E., & Sroufe, L.A. Resilience in process. **Developmental Psychology**, 5,517-528,1993.

Erikson, E.H. **Identity and the life cycle**. New York: W.W. Norton, 1980.

Fanshel, D., & Shinn, E.B. **Children in foster care: A longitudinal investigation**. New York: Columbia University Press, 1978.

Fox, R.A. **Parent behaviour checklist test manual**. Brandon, VT: Clinical Psychology, 1994.

Frances, A., Clarkin, J., & Perry, S. **Differential therapeutics in psychiatry.** New York: Brunner / Mazel, 1984.

Freud, S. **General psychological theory**. New York: MacMillan Publishing, 1963.

Garbarino, J., & Bronfenbrenner, U. The socialization of moral judgment and behaviour in cross-cultural perspective. In T. Lickona (Ed.), **Moral development and behaviour**. New York: Holt, Pvinchart and Winston, 1976.

George, C, & Main, M. Social interactions of young abused children: Approach avoidance and aggression. **Child Development**, 50,306-318,1979.

Harter, S. **The construction of the self: A developmental perspective**. New York: The Guildford Press, 1999.

Healy, D. **The anti-depressant era**. Cambridge, M.A.: Harvard University Press, 1997.

Heifer, R.J., Hoffmeister, J., & Schneider, C. **A manual for use of the Michigan Screening Profile of Parenting**. Boulder, Co: Test Analysis and Development Corporation, 1978.

Herman, J. **Trauma and recovery**. New York; Basic Books, 1992.

Hollis, James. **The middle passage: From misery to meaning in midlife**. Toronto: Inner City Books, 1993.

Huttenlocher, P.R., & Dabholkar, A.S. Regional differences in synaptogenesis in human cerebral cortex. **Journal of Comparative Neurology,** 387, 167-175, 1997.

Jacobvitz. D., Riggs, S., & Johnson. E.M. Cross-sex and same-sex family alliances: Immediate and long-term effects on daughters and sons. In N.D. Chase (Ed.), **Parentified children: Theory, research and treatment.** Thousand Oaks, CA: Sage, 1999.

Jacobvitz, D., & Hazen, N. Developmental pathways from infant disorganization to childhood peer relationships. In J. Solomon & C. George (Eds.), **Attachment disorganization**. London: The Guildford Press, 1999.

Karen, J. **Becoming attached**. New York: Warner Books, 1994.

Katz, L.C., & Shatz, A. Synaptic activity and the construction of cortical circuits. **Science**, 247,1133-1135,1996.

Kirk, S.A., & Kutchins, H. **The selling of DSM: The rhetoric of science in psychiatry**. New York: Aldine, 1992.

Kobak, Roger The emotional dynamics of disruptions in attachment relationships. In J. Cassidy and PR. Shaver (Eds)., **Handbook of Attachment**, New York: The Guildford Press, 1999.

Kobak, R., Cole, H., & Irenz-Gillis, R. Attachment and emotion regulation during mother-teen problem solving: A control theory analysis. **Child Development**, 64, 231-245, 1993.

Kohlberg, L. Stage and sequence: The cognitive-developmental approach to socialization. In David A. Goslin (Ed.), **Handbook of socialization theory and research**. Chicago: Rand McNally, 347-480, 1969.

Kutchins, H., & Kirk, S.A. **Making us crazy: DSM: The psychiatric bible and the creation of mental disorders**. New York: Free Press, 1997.

Ladnier, R.D., & Massanari, A.E. Treating ADHD as attachment deficit hyperactivity disorder. In T.M.

Levy (Ed.), **Handbook of attachment interventions**. Toronto: Academic Press 2000.

Livesley, J.W. (Ed.) **Handbook of personality disorders: Theory, research and treatment.** New York: MacMillan Publishing, 2001.

Mahler, M.S., Pine E, and Bergman A. **The psychological birth of the human infant**. New York: Basic Books, 1975.

Main, M., & Goldwyn, R. **Adult attachment scoring and classification system**. Unpublished manuscript, University of California at Berkely 1998.

Main, M., Kaplan, N., & Cassidy, J. Security in infancy, childhood and adulthood: A move to the level of representation. In I. Bretherton & E. Waters (Eds.), **Growing points of attachment theory and research. Monographs of the Society for Research in Child Development**, 5 (1-2, Serial No. 209) 66-106, 1985.

Main, M., & Solomon, J. Procedures for identifying infants as disorganized/disoriented during the Ainsworth Strange Situation. In M. Greenberg, D. Cicchetti, & E.M. Cummings (Eds.) **Attachment in the preschool years: Theory, research and intervention**. Chicago: University of Chicago Press, 1990.

Mead, G.H. **Mind, self and society**. Chicago: University of Chicago Press, 1934.

Mead, G.H. Social consciousness and the consciousness of meaning. **Psychological Bulletin**, 7, 397-405,1910.

Mead, G.H., The social self. **Journal of Philosophy, Psychology and Scientific Methods**, 10,374-380, 1913.

Miller, J., Williams, K, English D., & Olmstead, J. **Risk assessment in child protection: A review of the literature**. Washington, D.C.: Association of Public Welfare Administrators, 1988.

Millon, J. **Introduction to: Essentials of Millon inventories assessment**. New York: MacMillan Publishing, 1999.

Milner, J., & Ayoub, C. Evaluation of "at risk" parents using the Child Abuse Potential Inventory. **Journal of Clinical Psychology**, 36,945-948, 1980.

Minuchin, S. **Families and family therapy**. Cambridge, MA: Harvard University Press, 1974.

Nims, J.P. **Observation Checklist**, Toronto, Ontario: Multi-Health Systems Inc., 2000.

Oldershaw, L., Walters, G.C., & Hall, D.K. A behavioural approach to the classification of different types of physically abusive mothers. **Merrill-Palmer Quarterly**, 35, 255-279, 1989.

Peck, R.R, & Havighurst, R.S. **The psychology of character development**. New York: Wiley, 1960.

Perry, B.D. Neurobiological sequelae of childhood trauma. In M. Murbery (Ed.), **Catecholamine function in post traumatic stress disorder**. Washington, D.C.: American Psychiatric Press, 1994.

Perry, B.D. Incubated in terror: Neurodevelopment factors in the cycle of violence. In J.D. Osofsky (Ed.), **Children, youth and violence**. New York: Guilford Press, 45-63, 1995.

Piaget, J. **The moral judgment of the child**. New York: Harcourt, Brace and World, 1932.

Pionta, R., Egeland, B., & Sroufe, L.A. Maternal stress in children's development: Predictions of school outcomes and identification of predictive factors. In J.E. Rolf, A. Masten, D. Ciechetti, K. Neuchterlen, & S. Weintraub (Eds.), **Risk and protective factors in the development of psychopathology**. New York: Cambridge University Press, 215-235,1990.

Perry, B.D., Pollard, R.A., Blakley, T.L., Baker, W.L.Childhood trauma, the neurobiology of adaptation, and "use-dependent" development of the brain: How "states" become "traits". **Infant Mental Health Journal**, 15.271-291,1995.

Pickle, P. Community-focused attachment services. In T.M. Levy (Ed), **Handbook of attachment interventions**. Toronto: Academic Press, 2000.

Polansky, N., Chalmers, M., Buttenweiser, E., & Williams, D. The isolation of the neglectful family. **American Journal of Orthopsychiatry**, 49, 149-152, 1979.

Provence, S. **Infants in institutions: A comparison of their development during the first year of life with family reared children**. New York: International Universities Press, 1967.

Putnam, F.W. Dissociation and disturbance of the self. In D. Cicchetti & S. Toth (Eds.), **Rochester symposium on developmental psychopathology: Disorders and dysfunctionalities of the self**. Vol 5, pp 251-266. Rochester, N.Y.: University of Rochester Press, 1993.

Putnam, EW. Recent research on multiple personality disorder. **Psychiatric Clinics of North America**, 14,489-502.1991.

Rest, J.R. **The defining issues test: Manual**. Minneapolis: University of Minnesota Moral Research Projects, 1979.

Robins, L.N. Conduct disorder. **Journal of Child Psychology and Psychiatry**, 32(1): 193-212, 1991.

Salzinger, S., Kaplon, S., & Artemeyeff, C. Mother's personal social networks and child maltreatment. **Journal of Abnormal Psychology**, 92, 68-76,1983.

Schneider-Rosen, K., & Cicchetti, D. The relationship between affect and cognition in maltreated infants: Quality of attachment and the development of visual self recognition. **Child Development**, 35,648-658, 1984.

Sperry, L. **Cognitive behaviour therapy of DSM-IV personality disorders: Highly effective intervention for the most common personality disorders**. Philadelphia, PA: Brunner/Mazel, 1999.

Spielberger, CD. Anxiety as an emotional state. In CD. Spielberger (Ed.), **Anxiety: Current trends in theory and research** (Vol. 1), New York: Academic press, 1972.

Spinetta, J., & Rigler, D. The child abusing parent: A psychological review. **Psychological Bulletin**, 77,296-304, 1972.

Spitz, R., & Obliner, G.W. **First year of life: A psychoanalytic study of normal and deviant development of object relations**. New York: International Universities Press, 1966.

Stern, D.N. Self/other differentiation in the domain of intimate socioaffective interactions: Some considerations. In P. Rochat (Ed.). **The self in infancy: Theory and research**. Amsterdam: Elservier, pp 419-430, 1995.

Sroufe, L.A. & Fleeson, J. Attachment and the construction of relationships. In W. Hartup & Z. Rubin (Eds.), **Relationships and development**. Hillsdale, N.J.: Erlbaum, 1986.

Sroufe, L.A. Psychopathology as outcome of development. **Development and Psychopathology**. 9, 251-268,1997.

Sroufe, L.A. Relationships, self and individual adaptation. In AJ. Someroff & R.N. Emde (Eds.), **Relationship disturbances in early childhood**. New York: Basic Books, 1989.

Steinhauer, P.D. Assessing for parenting capacity. **American Journal of Orthopsychiatry**, 53,468-481,1983.

Steinhauer, P.D. Adoption. In B.D. Garfinkel, G.A. Carlson & E. B. Weller (Eds.), **Psychiatric disorders in children and adolescents**. Philadelphia: W.B. Saunders, 1990.

Szasz, T. Diagnoses are not diseases. **Skeptic**, 2, 86, 1994.

Takahashi, K. Are the key assumptions of the "Strange situation" procedure universal? **Human Development**, 33,23-30, 1990.

Terr, L. Childhood traumas: An outline and overview. **American Journal of Psychiatry**, 148, 10-20, 1991.

Thomas, A., Chess, S., & Birch, H.G. **Temperament and behaviour disorders in children**. New York: University Press, 1968.

Thompson, R.A. Early attachment and later development. In J. Cassidy & P.R. Shaver (Eds.), **Handbook of attachment: Theory, research and clinical applications**. New York: The Guilford Press, 265-286,1999.

Thompson, R.A., & Lamb, M.E. Security of attachment and stranger sociability in infancy. **Developmental Psychology**, 19,184-191,1983.

Thorne, EC. Theory of the psychological state. **Journal of Clinical Psychology**, 22-127-135, 1966.

Tizard, B., & Rees. J. A comparison of the effects of adoption, restoration to the natural mother, and continued institutionalization on the cognitive development of four year old children. **Child Development**, 45,92-99,1974.

University of Toronto, Faculty of Social Work, **Symposium papers: Helping networks and the welfare state**, May, 1980.

Vandell, D.L., Owen, M.T., Wilson, K.S., & Henderson V.K. Social development in infant twins: Peer and mother-child relationships. **Child Development**, 59, 168-177,1988.

Van der Kolk, B.A. The body keeps the score: Memory and the evolving psychology of PTSD. **Harvard Review of Psychiatry**, 1, 253-265, 1994.

Wald, M.S., & Woolverton, M. Risk assessment: The emperors new clothes. **Child Welfare**, 69,483-511,1990.

Waters, E., & Deane K. Defining and assessing individual differences in attachment relations: Q-methodology and the organization of behaviour in infancy and early childhood. In I. Bretherton & E. Waters (Eds.), **Growing point in attachment theory and research**. Chicago: University of Chicago Press, 1985.

Watson, G. & Glasser, E.M. **Watson-Glasser Critical Thinking Appraisal**. TU Psychological Corporation, 1980.

Watzlawick, P., Beavin, J.H., & Jackson, D.D. **Pragmatics of human communication**. New York: W.W. Norton & Company, 1967.

Watzlawick, P. **How real is real?** New York: Vintage 1976.

Webster-Stratton, C. Comparisons of abusive and non-abusive families with conduct-disordered children. **American Journal of Orthopsychiatry**, 55,59-69,1985.

Weinfield, N.S., Sroufe, L.A., Egeland, B., & Carlson E.A. The nature of individual differences in infant-caregiver attachment. In J. Cassidy & P.R. Shaver (Eds.), **Handbook of Attachment: Theory, research and clinical applications**. New York: the Guilford press, 68-88, 1999.

Williams, J., Gibbon, M., First, M., Spitzer, R., Davies, M., Boru, J., Howes, M, Kane, J., Pope, H.. Runsaville, B., & Wittchen, H. The structured clinical interview for DSM IIIR (SCID)II: Multi-site test - retest reliability. **Archives of General Psychiatry**, 1992.

Wolfe, D.A. **Child abuse: Implications for child development and psychopathology**. Beverly Hill, California: Sage Publications, 1987.

Wright, R. Labeling: The need for greater person - environment individuation. In C.R. Synder & D.R. Forsyth (Eds.), **Handbook of social and clinical psychology: The health perspective**. New York: Pergamon, 469-487,1992.

Wynne, L., Singer, M., Bartakko, J., & Toohey, M. Schizophrenics and their families: Recent research in parental communication. In J. Tanner (Ed.), **Development in psychiatric research**. London: Hodden & Stoughton, 254-286,1977.

PART TWO

The Prescribed Report Format:
A Composite Case Example

This section in the manual constitutes an example of a report, in its entirety. The example is fictional although based on a composite of several cases. Identifying variables have been significantly changed to protect the confidentiality of the people who were assessed, as well as the agencies who made the referrals. Any factual similarities with real cases are unintentional and sadly reflect common variables in the histories and circumstances of individuals who are the subjects of Parenting Capacity Assessments. For purposes of clarity, there are two fonts used to distinguish between the standard template prescribed to be used in each and every report, and the case-specific conclusions and recommendations supported by the various findings produced by the prescribed Parenting Capacity Assessment methodology.

A.T. Polgar Associates Inc

CONSULTANTS IN ORGANIZATIONAL AND INDIVIDUAL BEHAVIOUR

678 Main Street East
Hamilton, Ontario
L8N 1M4
905-545-8944

Alexander T. Polgar, Ph.D.
Director

Parenting Capacity Assessment Conducted in the Best Interest of:
Amanda Jones   **d.o.b. 05 September, 1999**

PREPARED AT THE REQUEST OF:

Child Welfare Agency of Brown County,
300 King Street,
Mainway, Ontario
K2C 2M9

WITH THE CONSENT OF:

All Parties

COUNSEL FOR THE SOCIETY:

Mr. Tom Phillips,
300 King Street, Mainway, Ontario

OTHER COUNSEL:

Mr. David White
Black and Gray,
Barristers and Solicitors,
234 Hunter Ave., Mainway, Ontario
(for the mother, Susan Jones),

SOCIAL WORKERS :

Ms. Felicity Clinton, Family Service Worker
Ms. Shannon Whittaker, B.A., M.S.W.
Family Service Supervisor

REPORT DATED :

June 26, 2001

115

PRÉCIS

The findings of this Parenting Capacity Assessment support a conclusion and recommendation that it is contra-indicated to the best interest of the child to be in the care and control of her profoundly dysfunctional mother, Susan Jones. In the best interest of the child who likely has considerable innate cognitive intellectual potential, in order to optimally realize her capacities, Crown Wardship is recommended for the explicit purpose of placing her for adoption in a timely manner. Insofar as the child is in the most crucial formative stage of life, it is imperative that every effort be made to arrive at a definitive determination in a timely manner. This case represents a classic example of an innately cognitively intelligent parent who, in spite of this capacity, is profoundly dysfunctional in a manner and intensity that is extremely difficult, if not impossible, to mitigate let alone in time to be of discernable benefit to the child. Under the first of four categories of analysis used as part of the methodology for conducting this Parenting Capacity Assessment, the etiology of the mother's dysfunctionalities was found to be attributable to a severe attachment disorder. Under the second category of analysis, the mother was found to reveal classic later-life negative manifestations of her attachment disorder that characterize her according to literature-defined criteria as "a deficient/abusive" parent. Under the third category of analysis, as a function of the mother's personality structure and developmental deficits, she the use of denial. Through this defense mechanism, she resists interventions and fails to constructively use resources which could ameliorate her dysfunctionalities and thereby her circumstance. The extent of her denial was found to be so well ingrained and profound as to produce an extremely worrisome prognosis. The significant confidence in the conclusions and concomitant recommendations cited above is established by the clinically logical coherence of all the findings.

Caveat

Invariably, Parenting Capacity Assessments are conducted as a result of a myriad of concerns identified by a Children's Aid Society. It is a given that there are presenting problems. Judgments as to the extent and depth of the problems and the amenability to change are critical considerations in deciding on the physical and developmental risks to a child and the amount and type of intervention which will be required. Furthermore, a salient question pertaining to intervention concerns the timeliness with which such measures can be expected to produce discernable improvements that would be of benefit to a child, especially in the most crucial formative stage of development.

It is also a given that when a parent is facing the possible loss of a child, that parent likely will mask, will unconsciously distort or frankly lie about events, feelings and behaviours. In most instances, however, the parent firmly believes what he or she is reporting. Such a belief is essentially a function of the defense mechanism of denial. Denial, in essence, is the creation of a pleasing fantasy by a cognitive developmentally deficient individual. Part of creating a pleasing fantasy can entail a minimization of personal responsibility for the negative consequences of past decisions and behaviours, as well as an idealization of the future. In denial, a cognitive developmentally deficient individual invariably is unable to comprehend the onerous responsibility of parenting and expects the mere fact of being a parent to reward him or her

117

with the child's unconditional love. The task of a Parenting Capacity Assessment is to go beyond the defenses and look at the capacities of the individuals being assessed. The determination pertains to the person's capacity to form meaningful and nurturing relationships; a determination of the individuals capacity to acquire parenting knowledge and skills and, more importantly, apply them in a predictably competent manner. There is a further determination required with respect to the person's capacity to affiliate with an optimally supportive social network. The last determination pertains to the probability that positive and supportive interventions will result in timely meaningful change or compensate for identified inadequacies.

It is because of these complex realities that Parenting Capacity Assessments are based on a myriad of data sources. These include the verbal statements of individuals. The relevance of verbal statements, however, is determined by their logical consistency with other sources of information and that which is known about personality structures.

Reasons for the Referral

The nature of the referral requesting this Parenting Capacity Assessment and a review of the extensive file materials provided are indicative of a rather typical Child Welfare case whereby unaddressed challenges posed by the mother as a child progressively escalated, culminating in her child being considered at risk, physically and developmentally. The concerns climaxed in the child's apprehension. In spite of the financial resources of the mother's parent, in spite of the maternal grandmother's post-secondary education, and in spite of her professional career, she has been at a loss as how to manage her daughter's behaviour. She has also been at a loss with respect to identifying and securing appropriate Mental Health resources for her. While the maternal grandmother's past actions have been commendable with respect to ensuring that her daughter was engaged in constructive pursuits through a myriad of activities, clearly these tactics were insufficient to mitigate the development of negative characterological trait concomitant behaviours. The traits progressively compromised the mother's functioning prior to having her child and continue to do so subsequently. Involvement by the Society was precipitated by a police investigation which found the mother in a semi- unconscious state of intoxication and her infant daughter in potentially critical danger of falling out an open second storey window. Subsequently, the Society's concerns were confirmed by the child's maternal grandmother who expressed the belief that her granddaughter is at physical, emotional, and developmental risk in the care of the child's mother who, in spite of expressed good intentions, promises and intermittent efforts, was spiraling out of control. Moreover, the mother's judgment and behaviour, already marginal, was described as being further compromised by her out-of-control substance abuse. Especially when inebriated, the mother's behaviour was described as incrementally and indiscriminately aggressive, placing the child in an unacceptable climate of unpredictable episodic outbursts of violence.

It is noteworthy that the mother's substance abuse propensities and concomitant violent outbursts have served to have a profoundly negative impact on her relationship with the child's father. He, in fact, is described as having abandoned all effort to assist the mother. In the recent past, any contact between them was described as markedly acrimonious. While the child has contact with her father, at this time he is not in the position to put forth a plan for her care and reportedly is not contesting the possibility that the child may be placed for adoption. As such, he is not party to the proceedings and is not a subject of this Parenting Capacity Assessment process.

After a period of resistance to participating in the Parenting Capacity Assessment, a consent was reached between the mother and the Society and a Court order was made in February 2000 for a Parenting Capacity Assessment to be performed. In the context of conducting the assessment, the Society requested that six specific questions be addressed. These are listed in Appendix A along with concise answers which will be best understood in the context of the body of this report.

Rationale For The Method

A Parenting Capacity Assessment by definition focuses on a parent, parents, or other individuals who put forth a plan to become primary caregivers to an infant. While a Parenting Capacity Assessment is done in the context of "Child Welfare", the focus is primarily on the adults. Considerations of a child's development become relevant in instances when apprehension has occurred and the child's condition becomes an additional indicator of a primary caregiver's ability to promote growth and development, physically and emotionally in an environment of safety. The nature and extent of harm sustained by the child in such instances is relevant with respect to, first and foremost, defining the type of remedial intervention that is required for the child and secondly, with respect to defining the extent to which a primary caregiver was negligent and/or abusive while a child was in his or her care.

The approach, therefore, to conducting a Parenting Capacity Assessment is based on the premise that children require for their optimal cognitive, emotional and behavioural development, a nurturing relationship with emotionally well adjusted, knowledgeable and competent primary caregivers. Moreover, a Parenting Capacity Assessment is based on the premise that it is through such nurturing relationships that children develop into adaptive individuals and thus optimize their true potential.

The method for conducting the Parenting Capacity Assessment is based on a synthesis of three theoretical models. The first draws on personality theory in order to distinguish between variables which can be eradicated from the make-up of an individual and variables which can only be brought under control through the application of persistent strategies. The assessed individual's own attachment history is a significant determinant of personality development and functioning. Securely attached and attachment troubled individuals both invariably repeat their respective legacies. The second pertains to cognitive development that impact not only on a primary caregiver's definable ways of viewing experience and perception of the world but also on concomitant behaviours. Deficits in this respect, while potentially detrimental to promoting the optimal growth and development of a child, can be resolved with appropriate intervention. The question is within what timeframe to be of benefit to the child in question. The third theoretical framework concerns social learning and is intended to ascertain less what an individual has learned to do and more what that individual has the potential to learn and, more importantly, apply in a persistently competent manner.

To elaborate further, cognitive developmental principles are integral considerations with respect to conducting a Parenting Capacity Assessment, essentially because cross-cultural and longitudinal studies empirically demonstrate that the nature and the impact of primary caregivers on the development of a child are determined by how the adult interprets experiences and views the world. Primary caregivers who are "well-adjusted" and mature in thought and behaviour are considered to be predisposed through a variety of resources to be optimally effective as parents. "Well-adjusted, mature" primary caregivers are also considered to be cognizant of the numerous responsibilities related to parenting and to take these to be of such importance as to arrange their personal lives, as much as possible, to respond to the needs of a child, especially during the child's formative years and early adolescence. "Well-adjusted, mature" primary caregivers also recognize their personal knowledge and skills limitations with respect to meeting the onerous challenges of parenting and actively pursue improving their abilities in this regard. Less "well-adjusted, immature" or intellectually limited individuals, as a consequence of any number of dysfunctionalities, especially developmental deficits, often instinctively use the defense mechanism of denial to create a favorable fantasy about themselves and their parenting and, through this, fail to experience any motivation to bring about improvements in themselves or in their knowledge and skills with respect to meeting the challenges of raising a child. While less "well-adjusted, immature" or intellectually limited individuals often can recognize desired responses to parenting questions or act appropriately with a child for brief periods of time, invariably they are less than consistent with respect to the actual application of parenting principles. As suck on optimal Parenting Capacity Assessment is based on determinations of cognitive intellectual potential, emotional intelligence, cognitive developmental perspectives, personality factors and the socialization experiences of individuals. Clinically these considerations are better predictors of persistent proactive positive conduct, specifically the motivation to actualize potential by learning and applying effective parenting techniques.

Given these premises, a prerequisite to conducting a Parenting Capacity Assessment, is knowledge with respect to environmental conditions empirically known to promote optimal development in a child and clinical knowledge and skills in determining a caregiver's capacity to approximate the ideally "well adjusted, mature" individual who can create the environmental conditions required for optimal development

The profound potential consequences of conducting a Parenting Capacity Assessment, therefore, require that the rationale and basis on which conclusions are made be well defined and substantiated with empirically determined findings. Moreover, to assist the Court, it is considered equally important that the findings be related to that which is reported in the literature, in refereed journals as well as scholarly publications.

Given the theoretical basis which underlies the methodology for conducting this Parenting Capacity Assessment, the use of diagnostic labels is considered as antithetical and of little, if any value to Social Service personnel and/or community-based Mental Health counselors who invariably are the primary resources to parents in difficulties. Moreover the presence of a mental illness does not automatically disqualify a parent as a primary caregiver, although the exact nature and treatment (pharmacologically) of the illness is the purview of physician specialists in psychiatry. Such intervention, therefore if not initiated prior to the commencement of a Parenting Capacity Assessment is expected to be done so upon referral, with a view to ascertaining the benefits of pharmacological intervention, initiated and monitored by a physician specialist. In these instances, without knowing the outcome of pharmacological interventions, it is advisable to delay the completion of a Parenting Capacity Assessment.

The complexity of the issues requires a presentation format that will produce optimal comprehensiveness and clarity. With this in mind, the body of the following report is organized under four headings that can answer any Terms of Reference, posed by a Child Welfare Agency which reflect relevant legislation. While the four categories of analyses are presented separately for the purposes of clarity, in reality they are interrelated to form a complex system that impinges on the growth and development of a child. The four categories are based on what is reported in the literature. As such, they are considered to be capable of producing predictive probability conclusions with respect to an individual's capacity to create conditions under which a child's optimal growth and development can occur. The four categories of analyses pertain to:

a. Attachment;
b. Criteria of a good parent;
c. Social support network;
d. Evidence-based expectations for acquiring and applying parenting capabilities.

Under each heading, a literature review is provided which establishes the relevance of the issues. This literature review is then followed by the specific conclusion pertaining to the issues being examined and a delineation of the findings that support the conclusions and recommendations. In essence, the findings constitute the variance between the theoretical ideal and the actual individual putting forth a plan to be the primary caregiver to an infant on whose behalf the assessment is being conducted.

Sources of Information

The following report is based on;

1. A review of documentation provided by the Society, as itemized in Appendix B;
2. Four assessment interviews conducted with the mother, Susan Jones;
3. Interview conducted with the mother's Family Service Worker;
4. Interview conducted with the Children's Services Worker;
5. An observation of the child in interaction with the mother during a Supervised Access Visit;
6. Interview conducted with the maternal grandmother and;
7. Interpretation of five standardized instruments administered under supervision to the mother.

The standardized instruments administered to the mother were chosen specifically to obtain corroborative data to enhance and support clinical formulations. The mother was administered the Raven's Progressive Matrices. This instrument measures cognitive intelligence in a culturally unbiased manner. The Raven's can also define unrealized cognitive intellectual potential. The mother was also administered the Minnesota Multiphasic Personality Inventory-2 to identify dysfunctionalities and the extent to which their manifestations have the potential to compromise the actualization of her potential to acquire and apply abilities to competently parent the child. The Rotter Locus of Control Instrument was also completed by the mother to determine the extent to which she is capable of recognizing that there is a connection between her actions and consequences as opposed to viewing her circumstance as a series of random events over which she has little or no control. The mother also completed the Watson-Glasser Critical Thinking Inventory. This instrument evaluates her existing and thereby her potential problem-solving skill, which is a necessary ability in dealing with the complex tasks of realizing her parenting potential. The mother also completed the Defining Issues Test standardized instrument, which is designed to categorize cognitive developmental perspectives. This, in part, also reveals an individual's existing ability to accept responsibility for the broad and long-term implications of actions, in contrast to using the immature mechanism of denial with which to avoid emotionally painful experiences. While the standardized instruments reveal existing functioning and abilities in so doing the results also reveal the magnitude of improvement required and the timelines with which such gains reasonably can be expected.

Documentation Review-Findings

It is understood that Affidavits and other documentation in part entail descriptions of what was observed and to various degrees the observers' attributions as to the meaning of the behaviours being described. Sometimes the information is obtained first hand by a Child Welfare professional and, on other occasions, it is second-hand information, although invariably there is supportive documentation, as for example behaviour logs in a residential facility. Insofar as certain knowledge and skills are required to make systematic observations and even more knowledge and skills are required to formulate a conclusion based on that which was observed, Affidavits are therefore subject to scrutiny and cross examination, a process designed to ensure that a Trier of Fact is presented with information that is valid and reliable and thereby useful with respect to informing the determination process.

It is not within the purview of a Parenting Capacity Assessment to scrutinize Affidavit materials in this manner. Affidavit materials, however, invariably serve as a source of information with respect to the nature of the differences between a Society's perspective and the perspective of the primary caregivers being assessed. Affidavit materials also invariably establish reasons, at least in part, for conducting a Parenting Capacity Assessment.

More importantly, the descriptions of behaviours in Affidavit materials are particularly relevant insofar as this information allows a broader view of an individual being assessed beyond that person's conduct with assessors. While the descriptions of behaviours are assumed to be invariably less than complete, the descriptions are, nevertheless, assumed to be truthful. That is to say, while it is possible that a reported observation is fabricated, the probability of this being so is taken as highly unlikely to be the case. If a parent is described as using profanity with an infant, this report is accepted at face value although the interpretation of such behaviour may be quite different from that which was formulated by the person reporting the event. A Parenting Capacity Assessment, therefore, addresses the extent to which there is a correlation between what is clinically and objectively found and what is described in Affidavits and other documentation.

The Affidavits of individuals being assessed, unless clearly indicated otherwise, are assumed to be documents essentially crafted by their legal counsel. Nevertheless, these too can be important information about the cognitive perspectives of individuals since at least in theory they contribute and consent to the content of the document.

The intent of this section in the report is not to reiterate that which is documented. The purpose is to acknowledge that the conclusions of this report were informed by additional information, although not necessarily by the interpretations concerning the reported observations. Moreover, the purpose of this section is to offer clinical interpretations of the written materials with a view to placing into context the need for a determination that is ultimately in the best interest of the child by protecting the child's right for optimal growth and development and determining the capacity of the assessed individuals to meet obligations to competently promote this.

By way of a summary statement, the clinical and empirical findings of this report support in no uncertain terms the Society's concerns as they are documented about the mother and justify equally in no uncertain terms the need for a Parenting Capacity Assessment to be conducted with the view to bringing about a timely determination with respect to the status of the child.

A reading of the materials produced an overwhelming impression of a profoundly dysfunctional individual progressively conducting herself in self-defeating ways and at significant risk of deliberately or inadvertently hurting herself, as well as the child, especially when inebriated. The documentation also reveals a classic example of the disservice produced by the use of a DSM-IV diagnostic label without elaboration or explanation as to the etiology of the disorder, a definition of the disorder, or the implications the dynamics of the disorder have on the mother's ability to parent, as well as on her capacity to acquire knowledge and skills and to apply these in a predictably competent manner. Moreover, the DSM-IV diagnostic label provides no clue as to how amenable the disorder is to intervention and in what time frames discernable improvements can be predicted. To non-Mental Health professionals, the diagnostic label is virtually meaningless. It is likely also meaningless to the Child Welfare professionals concerned with what implications the label has with respect to the mother's existing ability and timely realization of whatever potential she has as a parent.

Notwithstanding the lack of utility in using and reporting only diagnostic labels, the mother's documented behaviour over the years is certainly consistent with the clinical formulations of this Assessment about her condition. Moreover, the mother's efforts through her Affidavit materials, instead of advancing her claims of bringing about significant improvement in her circumstances, accomplish the exact opposite outcome. Inadvertently, through her Affidavit statements, she confirms the consistent clinical formulations of Mental Health professionals who had contact with her previously. With the passage of time, her actions as described in the reports establish greater confidence in the formulations concerning the nature of her dysfunctionalities.

It is noteworthy that the mother's presentation and statements during the clinical assessment interview conducted for the purpose of this Parenting Capacity Assessment denied the existence of worrisome information on her file. In fact, when she was asked what the documentation will reveal about her, she minimized past events. She made no reference to numerous police and psychiatric involvement, the prescription of psychotropic medication, incidents of violent outbursts, altercations with many people, including the child's maternal grandmother, paternal grandparents and the child's father, and documented profound substance abuse she engaged in over several months preceding the commencement of this assessment process. Moreover, in her assessment interview presentation , it was as if she had either forgotten the fact that she produced an Affidavit in which she acknowledged past transgressions and claimed vast improvements or truly believed that her controlled demeanor and concerted effort to "perform well" during the assessment process would cancel out her well-documented and corroborated history of dysfunctionality.

From a clinical perspective, that which is reported pertaining to the mother fits a well-defined albeit complex clinical profile. She was consistently found by various physician specialists in psychiatry, to manifest a variety of disorders including antisocial, borderline and paranoid personality features. The elaboration, explanation and relevance of these classifications of the mother's dysfunctionalities will be discussed in detail under the second category of analysis in this report. Suffice it to say that such classifications are representative of the gravest later-life negative manifestations of an attachment disorder sustained by an individual during the most crucial formative stage of life. Sexual promiscuity, substance use and abuse, violent outbursts and relationship difficulties of all sorts, are all also classic negative manifestations of progressive dysfunctionalities associated with early life experiences which fail to meet the special needs of an individual.

In spite of brief episodic acknowledgement of difficulties by the mother, as documented in her Affidavits, reports about her behaviour are consistent with a clinical formulation that she uses denial to defend herself against the unpleasant realities of her circumstances. As a function of this defense mechanism, the mother is revealed through the documentation not to have pursued with any consistency a course of action to bring about some stability in her life and, more importantly, bring under control elements in her personality that are a source of great concern about her as a parent. Instead, she uses what appear to be quite formidable intellectual capacities to externalize her problems, blaming everyone else for her difficulties. At best, she is occasionally depicted as paying some lip service to the need for support or assistance.

It is interesting to note from the documentation reviewed that depression has also been identified, along with anxiety and anger management issues. The implications are that her depression likely represents suppressed anger which, from time to time, bursts to the surface, especially when she is disinhibited while under the influence of some mood-altering substance. Given the turbulent nature of her circumstances, it is not surprising that she is documented as manifesting anxiety which, in essence, represents a foreboding fear of the unknown.

The documented efforts to provide the mother with anger management training produced virtually no discernable positive results. Furthermore, the mother was less than compliant with what was required by the program she intermittently attended. Requiring the mother to attend this program likely constituted an act of desperation by the Society, motivated by a need to do something in lieu of doing nothing to respond to what otherwise is a rather immobilizing, complex array of difficulties.

The same could be said with respect to other program involvements offered by the mother as proof of her intent to meet the responsibilities of being a parent. Given her apparent innate intellectual potential even if she were able to apply herself to learning parenting knowledge and skills, it is highly unlikely that this would have resulted in predictably consistent and competent application of course materials. This conclusion is based on documentation that depicts the mother as profoundly driven by her immediate emotional state, a propensity that is consistent with the classification of her dysfunctionality by Mental Health professionals who have seen her in various states of incapacitation.

A reading of the documentation also suggests that there is a profound lack of understanding about the mother's dysfunctionalities by those people who have direct, ongoing contact with her. The child's maternal grandmother as well as Society workers, seem to single out her episodic bouts with depression as the focus of their attention, likely because this is an easier disorder to understand and, when addressed properly, it tends to respond favorably to intervention. Moreover, the documentation clearly reveals that the child's maternal grandmother harbors unsubstantiated, unwarranted, and most of all, unrealistic expectations that if only appropriate psychiatric care could be found for her daughter, this would resolve all her problems and she could assume full responsibility as a competent parent for the child. It is important to note that the maternal grandmother's perspective is quite different from the perspective revealed by the mother. The mother, in fact, denied in interviews the various reported events in the materials reviewed, insisting instead that everyone has been fabricating "stories" about her behaviour.

Notwithstanding the mother's claim with respect to the "fabrication of stories", she is documented as having admitted to being treated for depression by her family physician, as well as attending relationship counseling. Corroborative information revealed, this not to be the case, certainly not to the extent claimed by the mother. When asked during a clinical interview to respond to this, the mother simply reiterated that these were malicious fabrications. Fortunately, while corroborative data is difficult to obtain in most cases, in this instance there are letters from counselors with respect to the mother attending one session only or attending an assessment but no follow-up session.

Contrary to the mother's efforts to minimize that which is documented about her history, or for that fact, deny past problems pertaining to cognitive and emotional issues, there are corroborative findings by Mental Health professionals that document worrisome information. The mother has been found to reveal symptoms consistent with major depression and to have a mood disorder problem. These formulations were made by Mental Health professionals during periods of "crisis" in the mother's life. When the circumstances subsided, so also did her resolve to address issues. The reports of Mental Health professionals document the mother revealing behaviour consistent with the classification of borderline personality disorder, along with episodes of uncontrollable rage. The mother's propensities in this respect were described in the reports as exacerbated by her abuse of alcohol, which she persistently is noted to deny. In fact, one Mental Health professional considered the mother to be a "pathological liar" with a "severe antisocial personality disorder".

There is a constant theme of alcohol abuse in the documentation. Furthermore, the descriptions of the mother's behaviour suggest a formulation that she loses touch with reality when she is intoxicated. Such occurrences are usually indicative of significant substance abuse usually found among much older individuals with a severe addictive characterological personality disorder. In this case, as evidenced by the numerous police reports reviewed, there is no doubt that the mother has a profoundly debilitating propensity to abuse alcohol. More importantly, in the absence of a significant intervening variable, there is absolutely no reason to believe that this propensity does not persist or, in fact, that it is not escalating.

What is troublesome, especially with respect to the possible risk the mother poses to her child is that the reports reveal her to be particularly belligerent when intoxicated. She is depicted as particularly belligerent to her immediate family members, as well as toward the father of her daughter. Moreover, the mother reportedly has exposed the child to her rage and violent outbursts. This is absolutely contraindicated to her daughter's welfare. In fact, such exposures are associated with the emergence of progressive violent behaviours in children who are the products of such environments. This is well documented in the literature pertaining to the development of antisocial aggressive behaviours in children (Shamsie, Nicholl & Madson 1999). Without addressing these propensities in the mother, the documentation suggests that there is a profound probability that eventually she will also act out her rage against the child. Furthermore, it would not be unreasonable to speculate that the mother has acted out aggressively in violent manners at other times in addition to those known to the police and in addition to that which is documented. This hypothesis is supported by information provided in an interview with the maternal grandmother.

The documentation reveals the maternal grandmother suffers from depression for which she is being treated with medication by her family physician. Given the persistent turmoil and acrimony in her life, the maternal grandmother's mental status is very much a predictable reaction to an impossible situation. What is surprising is that the maternal grandmother somehow manages to focus on the welfare of the child while also desperately seeking "psychiatric help" for her daughter.

The Society's documented concerns with respect to the mother's abilities are several. The most important concerns pertain to the child being exposed to potential harm as a result of the mother's neglect during episodes of irrationality, as well the child being exposed to the mother's outbursts of rage and violence. Both are contraindicated to the optimal development of a child and certainly give rise to serious concerns about the child's welfare should she be returned to the mother's care and control.

A review of the Society's case notes do not reveal any inconsistencies in the Affidavits of Child Welfare workers or the reports of Mental Health professionals. There is nothing in the written records that would give rise to harboring a more favorable and optimistic view of the mother's dysfunctionalities. Consequently, it is difficult to ascertain the reason for not taking more definitive action earlier. The written case notes reveal that the primary caregiver to the child essentially has been the maternal grandmother and on occasion her father. This is consistent with the nature of the mother's dysfunctionalities, insofar as in spite of her obvious innate intellectual potential, her labile and intense emotional state prevents her from focusing on any task or endeavor that could produce sustainable long-term benefits. A dysfunctionality of this type is contraindicated to the complex, demanding task of responding appropriately to the developmental needs of a child, especially during the formative and subsequent stage of life.

The most recent case notes reveal a pattern of inconsistent access visits by the mother with the child, according to the mother, due to conflicts with her work schedule. Regardless of any reason for the inconsistency of contact, from a clinical perspective, this is not in the best interest of a child. In fact, the entire accommodating arrangement and the effort to facilitate contact between the child and the mother when it suits her is contraindicated to the best interest of the infant. This is especially so insofar as the mother's well-defined pattern of dysfunctionalities gives no reason to believe that anything other than a precisely structured Access Schedule is required.

The case notes also reveal several instances during which, in no uncertain terms, it was brought to the mother's attention that it would be in her best interest to seek and co-operatively use counseling and other Mental Health services. There is no evidence of the mother consistently acting on this encouragement, although there are references in the case notes to the mother excusing her failures in this respect because she lacked the funds to pay for a service or could not attend due to work schedules, access visits and other "interfering demands" made on her.

The mother's Affidavit, which is intended to attest to the substantial changes in her life during a three- month period, is especially noteworthy in its counterproductive nature. More importantly, this Affidavit very much confirms the nature of her dysfunctionalities and the dismal prognosis as to bringing these under timely control to be of any discernable benefit to her child.

A marked indicator of extremely worrisome dysfunctionality is the mother's belief that a mere three months represents significantly more than a beginning acceptance of a problem and tentative efforts to bring it under control. Consistent with the mother's dysfunctionality, in her Affidavit she minimizes the profoundly debilitating nature of her problems and, in no uncertain terms, seeks to convince the Court that they were of such a minor nature as to be easily controlled, indeed, resolved in a brief period of time. Furthermore, the Affidavit conveys that resolution was brought about by her own efforts, unaided by professionals and without persistent involvement in a community-based self-help program such as Alcoholics Anonymous to address her alcohol abuse propensities.

The mother claims in her Affidavit to have attended a drug and alcohol abuse assessment and that the findings revealed no issues to be addressed. She concluded that "I wasn't required to attend counseling for substance abuse". In reality, however, the mother never attended the follow-up session with the assessor and therefore did not discuss the findings or the implications of what was determined. Therefore, it was not the assessor who concluded that she was not in need of intervention, it was the mother. This interpretation is confirmed by the assessment report in which it is noted that "given that Susan says she has not had a drink in over seven months, she does not feel the need for counseling and/or treatment at this time". This is hardly consistent with the mother's Affidavit claim that the assessment found her not to be in need of intervention.

It is interesting to note that the mother's Affidavit carefully states that she did not consume any alcohol or drugs while in the presence of her daughter but does not speak to this practice otherwise. Certainly since this Affidavit was written and submitted, there is documented evidence of alcohol consumption by the mother. This is consistent with the nature of her dysfunctionality and especially consistent with the absence of any concerted, well-defined effort on her part to achieve and maintain sobriety.

The mother's Affidavit description of her "renewed relationship with my mother" and "stable relationship with the father of my child " not only confirms he inability to understand the nature of her difficulties, but also her unfounded, unrealistic, largely irrational evaluation of her circumstance. Moreover, her statements confirm the dismal prognosis insofar as soon after the filing of this Affidavit, her relationship with her mother deteriorated once again, as did the relationship with the father of her daughter.

In summary, the extensive documentation that was reviewed for the purposes of this Parenting Capacity Assessment, including the mother's own Affidavit, provides a clinically coherent, logically consistent picture of a well-defined, complex dysfunctionality which is extremely difficult to bring under control for well-motivated individuals, let alone someone like the mother whose basic, unconscious defense strategy is to minimize the gravity of her circumstances and to create a pleasing fantasy about herself. These dynamics are otherwise known as being in a state of denial. This unconscious defense mechanism, in fact, is central to the nature of the mother's dysfunctionality which will be discussed at length in the body of this report. Suffice it to say that her state of denial is the very reason why, in spite of the availability of potentially beneficial resources, the success rate with individuals such as the mother is extremely low and requires extensive time and facilitative expertise.

Circumstances Pertaining to the Commencement of this Parenting Capacity Assessment

On the 10th of May, 2000, the mother was contacted by telephone and an appointment was arranged for the 7th of June for her to attend a full day at our offices to be interviewed, as well as to complete a number of standardized instruments. During the telephone conversation, she presented as eager for the assessment process to commence, expressing an understanding that it was imperative for her to be there on the appointed date and time. The day before her appointment, she left a telephone message confirming the arrangements. She subsequently left a message that same night stating that she would be in attendance the next morning, although she sounded unclear as to how she was going to get to the appointment from her residence in the country. The following day, the mother failed to attend as scheduled. Subsequently, that same morning, the mother telephoned, explaining that her friend who was going to drive her did not show up. What followed was a number of incoherent statements that she had had only three hours sleep the night before, that her friend did not wake her and that she was coming home from work and needed a shower but her friend would not wait, acknowledging that she worked until 2:00 a.m. and her pick-up time was 9:00 a.m. In the same conversation, the mother stated that the Society required too many things for her to do and that this conflicted with the requirements of her employer. Furthermore, she said that she had had to take her dog for a walk when she came home from her job and that this prevented her from going to bed.

These events elaborate further the mother's dysfunctionalities as revealed by the documentation that was reviewed. Clearly, in spite of her best intentions and ability to recognize the importance of compliance with an appointment set in advance and agreed upon, her behaviours were driven by some emotional, situationally determined state. As documented by the Affidavit materials, the emotional drive of the mother is invariably more powerful than her reasoning abilities and at least while in theory she should know better, she invariably engages in self-defeating behaviours in spite of her best intentions. It is important to note that the mother was indeed able to do that which was required of her to attend the next appointment. She got a good night's sleep and was ready to be transported by her friend at the agreed-upon time. These events reveal in a very concrete way that the mother can be profoundly obstructed by her dysfunctionalities from acting on her good intentions, which in turn is contraindicated to her being the custodial parent of her child.

Background Information

To better understand the results of a Parenting Capacity Assessment, the findings pertaining to the individual being assessed should be considered in the context of that individual's personal background. The intent of this section is not to provide a detailed chronological history of events in an individual's life but to highlight the salient aspects of the person's early-life experiences, which invariably are determinants of current functioning.

This section is significantly corroborated by information provided by the maternal grandmother. The mother's self-report of her background while confirmed to some degree by her the maternal grandmother, also reveals her to have a profoundly different interpretation of her early-life experiences and how she was parented.

The mother declared vehemently at the onset of the Assessment interview that "my mother hates me" and thinks that "I am stupid". Paradoxically, the mother described herself as being treated as a "spoiled princess", always dressed for school in a special way, provided with horseback riding lessons from the age of three, as well as a myriad of other unusual experiences including extended summer holidays at European destinations. Nevertheless, she characterized her mother as emotionally abusive throughout her life. In contrast, the maternal grandmother described the mother as a challenging child from the beginning. She was described as having a high energy level and a strong personality characterized by a precocious effort to be independent. This was said to have often taken the form of defiance of the structures and limits placed on her. In an effort to constructively challenge the mother's energies as a youth, the maternal grandmother confirmed that she enrolled her in a variety of activities.

The maternal grandmother's information reveals that she recognized immediately that her child had special needs. Moreover, she also recognized her considerable intellectual potential. To a lesser degree, the maternal grandmother revealed understanding that the mother was obstructed from realizing this as a result of her special needs.

While the maternal grandmother recognized that her child had special needs and while her efforts are commendable, she were clearly less than optimally informed about the challenges she was facing and the additional resources she required to mitigate against the development of dysfunctionalities. This is best exemplified by the fact that the maternal grandmother recognized very early that the mother had relationship difficulties. She was said to have not liked her classmates and considered the neighbours to be "snobs". Moreover, the maternal grandmother recognized that the mother dealt with her relationship problems in maladaptive ways. For example, her reaction to a part-time employer she did not like was to always be late for work. Her indirect expression of aggression culminated in her dismissal. Being aware of the existence of a problem was however, insufficient, especially since the maternal grandmother was unaware of its potential gravity, as well as unaware of a need to obtain the services of an expert resource.

The progression of the mother's dysfunctionalities can be ascertained by the astute and comprehensive recollection of the maternal grandmother. For the first six months of her life, the mother was said to have had colic so severe as to require constant medical intervention. At the age of three, she reportedly started to have "wild tantrums". At daycare, she was described to be an aggressive, defiant child. For example, she refused constantly to follow any of the children's' play was structured. She was also described as whining and constantly demanding attention. It was acknowledged that the maternal grandmother, during the first three years of the mother's life, was treated for depression. Furthermore, it was acknowledged that the maternal grandfather was extremely ill, leaving the maternal grandmother alone, more often than not, to cope with an "extremely difficult" child.

Reluctantly, the maternal grandmother acknowledged that her granddaughter exhibits the same innate propensities as her mother. Moreover, while reluctant to admit it, the maternal grandmother revealed that the chronology and the nature of her granddaughter's challenging behaviours are virtually the same as those of the mother. The maternal grandmother also acknowledge that her optimism with respect to the child is more indicative of her hopeful thinking than it is of what she knows to be the case.

The maternal grandmother, in spite of all that she experienced with her daughter, revealed, at the very end of the interview, an element of denial or perhaps unrealistic hopeful thinking about the nature of her daughter's dysfunctionalities. In spite of having read literature pertaining to the dynamics of personality disorders, in spite of the corroborated classification of her daughter's disorder by Mental Health professionals, and in spite of her first-hand traumatic experiences with her inebriated aggressive state, the maternal grandmother admitted to hoping that this assessment would find her daughter to be easily treatable, attributing all her problems to alcohol abuse alone, as opposed to the other causes manifested long before she started her substance abuse pattern.

The maternal grandmother, acknowledged that her daughter has for a long time felt herself to be unloved and that this is likely to be indicative of what she knows to be an attachment disorder. She presented as reluctantly accepting having failed the special needs of her daughter but not blaming herself insofar as she considers herself as having done everything she possibly could. She was in agreement that her daughter would have challenged any parent, including even professionals with expertise in child development, parenting knowledge and skills.

The maternal grandmother, age sixty-one, is a business manager of a thriving multidisciplinary medical practice in a large urban setting. She has held this position for the past thirty years. The mother described the maternal grandmother as someone who can be difficult and unreasonably demanding. The maternal grandmother also was described as someone who can be very obsessive about some things and not about other things.

The maternal grandfather died after a prolonged illness shortly after the mother's birth. He was a production manager of a multinational corporation. In this capacity, he was required often to be away from home for protracted periods of time. The mother said that she knows him to had been a "drinker", but has no personal recollection of him.

Consistent with the clinical formulations as to the mother having considerable innate intellectual potential, she described herself as a markedly above-average student in elementary school. This was confirmed by the maternal grandmother who said it was easy for her daughter to earn grades in the high eighties and nineties without any effort on her part. In a high school that focused on developing the athletic talents of students, the mother said she enjoyed a successful first year. The second year, however, proved to be progressively problematic and she dropped out within the first semester. At the same time as when she dropped out from high school, the mother also left the home and community where she was raised. She began a virtual street existence, at times working in an illegal massage parlor, as well as engaging in other criminal activities. She was convicted of several offences, served a period of incarceration and was placed on probation. Consistent with the mother's dysfunctionalities, over a seven-year span, she had no history of gainful employment. Approximately sixteen months prior to the commencement of this Parenting Capacity Assessment, the mother reportedly started to work in the physical fitness industry, most notably in an attendant capacity. She, in fact, reported that she likes this lifestyle, enjoying the high level of activity, ambient music and the lively interaction with people.

The mother described her social network as entailing a broad group of acquaintances. She said that her preference was to always be "loosely connected", enjoying the freedom that comes from this. As such, she did not describe having one best friend or a long-term relationship with any one person, including someone with whom she may have attended school or shared an interest.

Given the mother's early-life experiences, her romantic attraction patterns appear to be based on an unconscious drive to satisfy unmet primary needs. As such, she appears to be inadvertently attracted to individuals who unconsciously remind her of her own primary caregiver. She described the first phase in all her relationships as being characterized by an initial joyful anticipation that the person will satisfy her long unmet cravings. Based on her description, it would seem that for the very reason that she is attracted romantically to an individual, her joyful anticipations are invariably disappointed. Her disappointments was described as rapidly escalating to resentment which she said turns to acrimony. Some of her relationships reportedly persist, while others quickly end, only to be replaced by another. The mother's pattern of romantic relationships is significant insofar as it is closely associated with early negative life experiences, most notably an attachment disorder.

The mother inadvertently revealed that the child has been exposed to the acrimony between herself and the child's father during their brief and turbulent relationship. Unfortunately, the child has also been exposed to several other acrimonious relationships that mother has had. This too is most certainly contraindicated to her best interest.

As evidenced by her Affidavit material, in subsequent interviews the mother was eventually willing to acknowledge past substance use and abuse. She, however, denied any current propensities in this respect. She admitted only to the very occasional "social glass of beer", claiming to focus her energies on her work and her place of residence. These claims, however, were found to be inconsistent with reports by Society workers and the maternal grandmother. Independently, both sources confirmed episodic intoxications, concomitant acts of aggression, non-compliance with scheduled access visits and non compliance with other requirements imposed by the Society as a means by which the mother could demonstrate her ability to do that which is in the best interest of her child.

During the clinical interview, the mother did not acknowledge any problems she was working on, stating it was months since she had seen a counselor.

In summary, the mother's history is consistent with the progressive emergence of considerable dysfunctionalities that culminated in the Society's involvement in her life and the progressively escalating concerns about her capacity to become a competent parent. From a clinical perspective, the mother's background information is consistent with conditions that precipitate the various dysfunctionalities described in the documentation reviewed and the dysfunctionalities which were found in this Parenting Capacity Assessment.

Salient Issues

Delineating the salient issues from the perspective of a potential caregiver can reveal much about the character, as well as the views of that individual, especially pertaining to parenting. This section in the report is intended to describe concisely the mother's perspectives as to why her child has been apprehended. More importantly, this section is intended to ascertain her ability to accept responsibility for events insofar as this determines the extent to which she can commit herself to exert effort to bring about meaningful changes that could produce improvements in her abilities as an individual and as a parent. In fact, the extent to which she can accept responsibility for events, to a large extent, constitutes a determination of her capacities to bring about improvements that will alleviate the Society's concerns about her as a parent.

The salient issue from the mother's perspective is to be vindicated by this Parenting Capacity Assessment. She articulated a belief that the Assessment will confirm the malice of the maternal grandmother and others and thereby reveal concerns regarding her consumption of alcohol, her "depression" and isolated lifestyle to be unfounded. Moreover, the mother expressed the belief that she expects the Assessment to vindicate her position that she has never abandoned the child and in fact asked for brief assistance from the maternal grandmother only until she found suitable accommodations. In the mother's view, the concerns of the maternal grandmother and the Society are unwarranted and their actions harmful to her and her child.

From a clinical perspective, the mother's formulation as to the pertinent issues, that is, reasons for the Society's involvement and the reason for conducting a Parenting Capacity Assessment, exemplify her approach to the entire process. She approached the assessment essentially as an academic test in which she wanted to do well. She reportedly said that she "aced" the interviews, as well as the standardized instruments she completed. Unfortunately, as will be discussed at length under the second category of analysis, the mother's dysfunctionalities prohibit her from optimally utilizing her innate cognitive intellectual potential. Instead of acknowledging difficulties and accepting responsibility for ameliorating them, her primary effort was to externalize blame and minimize the severity of her problems. Thereby she inadvertently revealed the same self-defeating propensities in the assessment, process as she has throughout most of her post-pubescent life. This tactic is extremely worrisome and does not bode well for her prospects for timely change. While experience even with the most difficult of cases dictates that change is possible, this case, more than most exemplifies the question of probability being the most salient issue. Therefore, an operational definition of the mother's dysfunctionalities must include above all a determination as to the probability of her making discernable improvements in a timely manner to be of benefit to the child, especially during this most crucial formative stage of her life.

CATEGORIES OF ANALYSES

A) ATTACHMENT

Lowery (1984) found that considerations with respect to "goodness of a parent" or "which parent is a better adult" are less important criteria than the quality of the relationship between a child and a parent Her findings and subsequent related research have shown that the quality of the parent-child relationship has a greater impact on the child's wellbeing than the qualities of the parent as an individual The welfare of the child is described by her as inextricably imbedded in the combined parent-child interaction. Furthermore, Lowery defines the quality of the relationship as related to the personality structure of the parent.

Rohman, Sales and Louie (1987) reported that "the child's need for interpersonal stability and continuity may be more important to his or her wellbeing than a stable physical environment". Chess and Thomas (1987), in describing their "goodness of fit" concept, delineated the vitally important nature of the emotional attachment between a mother and her child. The quality of the relationship was described as determined by the parent's ability to recognize the unique needs and characteristics of the child at different developmental stages, an awareness of different possible approaches to handling children's behaviours, and the parent's ability to structure demands and expectations according to the child's ability and temperament while accurately interpreting the child's behaviour.

Not too long ago, grief at separation was considered as quite transient for an infant and children in general. More recently, however, not considering the child's emotional relationships, especially in infancy, has come to be recognized as discounting children as persons with emotional vulnerabilities and viewing them as merely possessions. This view has evolved significantly as a function of empirical studies to the extent that expert clinicians cite the parent-child emotional relationship as being the one that influences them most in recommending a custody disposition. Goldstien, Freud and Solnit (1973) elaborate on this issue by stating that:

> *"For the child, the physical realities of his conception and birth are not the direct cause of his emotional attachment. This attachment results from day-to-day attention to his needs for physical care, nourishment, comfort, affection and stimulation. Only a parent who provides for these needs will be able to build a psychological relationship with the child on the basis of the biological one and will become his 'psychological parent' in whose care the child can feel valued and wanted."*

The quality of a child's attachment to a parent is a reflection of the child's sense of his or her value in the parent's eyes. This, in turn, is related to the quality of the parent's attachment to the child. While some argue that even a negative parental relationship is preferable to no relationship with that parent, there is, however, a consensus among clinicians that denial of access in protection cases or wardship is appropriate at one stage in the child's life, between the ages of birth and five or six years but not at later stages, such as past the formative years (Parry et al 1986).

The salient issue under this category of analysis, therefore, is that personality development is determined by the quality of attachment between child and caregiver. More importantly, this is essentially a formative years' phenomenon and, as such, takes place from birth through the first few years in a child's life. There is some debate in the literature as to the length of this time frame. The best informed empirically based consensus is that by the age of three, much of the characterological traits of an individual are established and become lifelong defining features of that person (Bowlby 1980). Consequently, there are profound later effects of early attachment issues. For example, empirical findings have demonstrated that early experiences become the basis for the person's conceptualization of what to expect in relations with other people throughout life. Furthermore, the effects of attachment patterns pass from one generation to another by shaping the caregiver-infant relationship (Sroufen & Fleeson 1986).

Although poor early attachment and disturbance may not produce immediate negative symptoms, it does express itself during later developmental periods. An attachment disorder is particularly likely to resurface in adolescence when it can present as deficits in morality, empathy, caring and commitment Fonagy and his co-workers (1995) described how impaired morality, disruptive behaviour and borderline personality disorder can emerge as sequelae of disturbed early attachment. Infants learn from caretakers how to evaluate their own behaviour, regulate their impulse to react and soothe themselves in distress. Healthy individuals can largely perform these functions for themselves as adults.

Failure of early attachment interferes in learning these skills and puts the individual at risk of developing dysfunctionalities rooted in the relative absence of these abilities. Individuals who have not learned to calm and soothe themselves in early attachment relationships are at increased risk of turning to maladaptive means of self-soothing, such as substance abuse, or promiscuous sexual activity.

There is an emerging consensus regarding the classification of attachment first characterized by Ainsworth and Blehar (1978). In addition to the three categories defined by the seminal studies in this area, Main and Solomon (1990) defined a fourth category. The original three patterns of attachment classification are secure, avoidant and ambivalent and the fourth is disorganized/disoriented attachment. While there are efforts under way to develop valid and reliable standardized procedures for the purposes of classifying interaction patterns between a child and a caregiver, the primary and accepted methodology remains systematic observations of parent/child interactions. Moreover, any conclusions based on the observations of parent/child interaction, to be more informative, must be placed into the context of the parent's own history and attachment experiences with a view to controlling for false negative or positive findings.

Findings

Under this category of analysis, the findings support a conclusion that the mother lacks the capacity necessary to establish a secure attachment with the child and thereby the capacity to establish a true psychological relationship with her. Moreover, the findings under this category of analysis support a conclusion that the probability is virtually non-existent for the mother to accept, let alone mitigate, her deficits in this respect. She is certainly highly unlikely to do so in time to bring about improvements from which the child could benefit, especially during this most crucial formative stage of her life. The recommendation under this category of analysis, therefore, is that in the best interest of the child, she be designated as a Crown Ward without Access to the mother for the explicit purpose of being placed for adoption.

The primary evidence in support of the conclusion and recommendation under this category of analysis is the finding that there is a marked probability that the mother sustained an attachment disorder during her formative stage of development. This formulation is based on the findings that she was reportedly an extremely colicky baby and a difficult infant. The challenges she posed in this respect likely contributed to the maternal grandmother's self-reported episode with depression, a dysfunctionality that is in part characterized by diminished emotional and physical energy. In this state, the maternal grandmother's ability to respond to a challenging and difficult child likely was considerably compromised. The finding that the maternal grandfather was prevented from compensating for the maternal grandmother's limitations due to his prolonged illness and subsequent death further supports this conclusion. The maternal grandmother's statement that her daughter has never felt herself to be loved underscores the conclusion of a marked attachment disorder.

When the formulation of an attachment disorder was discussed with the maternal grandmother, she presented as receptive of the idea. Initially, however, in spite of the maternal grandmother's past efforts in counseling and a review of literature pertaining to the nature of her daughter's problems, she still presented as blaming herself for failing to meet her daughter's basic needs. Reluctantly, and after some discussion, the maternal grandmother acknowledged that hers was an innately unusual child with special needs that would have challenged even a hypothetically ideal parent The maternal grandmother indicated a beginning acceptance that inspite of her career, related training and experience, her expectations with respect to managing her daughter's behaviour without considerable expert assistance was quite unrealistic. Similarly she acknowledged as unrealistic her expectation that there is some readily available Mental Health intervention that could bring about a timely and discernable change in her daughter's current functioning.

Invariably, neither a person being assessed nor collateral informants attribute dysfunctionality to an attachment disorder. This type of formulation is not in the popular vernacular and the significance of it has only recently been recognized in the Mental Health field. As such, the existence of an attachment disorder is most often concluded inferentially as evidenced by the later-life negative consequences described by Fonagy (1995). As indicated in the preceding literature review, relevant under this category of analysis, an attachment disorder often becomes evident in adolescence when it is manifested in a number of ways, including disruptive behaviour, borderline personality, relationship problems, and turning to maladaptive means of self-soothing such as drugs, alcohol abuse or promiscuous sexual activity. Without doubt, the mother has exhibited all of these later-life negative consequences. Therefore the documented and reported behaviours of the mother combine as supporting evidence of the conclusion that she has an attachment disorder of significant proportions.

Unless recognized and addressed with tenacious commitment and expert assistance, an attachment disorder will be perpetuated inter-generationally. The quality of the mother's relationship with her infant, therefore, is not determined by the physical realities of conception and birth, but how she responds to the child, which in turn is determined by her formative stage experiences. The mother's personality structure and related behaviours in this case are antithetical to establishing a secure attachment with her child. This is revealed by her own Affidavit whereby she admits that the relationship she had hoped would develop with her daughter failed to occur. By her statement, the mother confirms that she cannot do what is reported in the literature as essential to establishing a secure attachment. Inadvertently, she has admitted to lacking the ability to attend with persistence to the day-to-day physical emotional and stimulation needs of the child. For example, instead of focusing on the child, she reported spending so much time organizing her apartment and working that she abdicated all responsibility for the child to the maternal grandmother. Her statement and reports also reveal that she lacks the ability to recognize the unique characteristics of the infant and to utilize a variety of approaches to managing her behaviour. Moreover, her expectations of the child are not informed by an awareness of the child's developmental level and unique temperament. Her documented communication style with the child is most inappropriate insofar as it is better suited to that which occurs between adult peers. Failing to respond to the child in a manner that is mindful of these factors invalidates the child and communicates to her a negative sense of self which is part of the etiology of an attachment disorder.

The hypothesis that the mother sustained an attachment disorder during the most crucial formative stage of her life is further substantiated by the interaction pattern that was observed between herself and the child. The formulation is also reinforced by the information provided by the maternal grandmother. Both data sources reveal a marked probability that the mother has failed to establish a secure attachment with her daughter. While the childcare arrangements have certainly served to compromise the attachment process between the mother and the child, this is not the etiology of the outcome. Moreover, had the mother's dysfunctionalities not intervened, she certainly has the innate cognitive intellectual capacity with which she could have, in short order, addressed the concerns about her parenting and thereby would have prevented the exacerbating consequences of her child being cared for by others.

In spite of the mother's obvious conceited effort to engage with the child positively during the observed supervised access visit, two significant findings further confirm the above formulations. First, there was a marked absence of reciprocal intimacy between the mother and the child. This, in spite of her use of endearing terms to address the child and in spite of the mother's hugs and kisses, to which the child did not respond. It was not until the very end of the visit that on request, the child gave her mother a reluctant goodbye kiss.

The second observation pertains to the mother's profound difficulty with respect to remaining focused. She virtually "flitted" from one activity to another, lacking the ability to focus herself, let alone an easily distractable infant, on a game or activity. While the mother talked a number of times about changing the child's diaper, she did not attend to this task until the very end of the visit. Furthermore, she brought out the child's snack quite late into the visit and was essentially unable to structure her behaviour on consuming the food. The mother's difficulty with respect to maintaining focus was also evident in her inability to appreciate the time limitations, failing to start tidying the room and thereby producing a hasty termination of the access visit.

It is noteworthy that there were several brief instances of the child responding to the mother. These interactions likely serve as reinforcing events for the mother and likely are the basis of her idealized expectation that having the child in her care and control will be a source of great satisfaction for her. Such an idealized expectation is consistent with her dysfunctionalities. In denial she minimizes the physical and emotional effort required by parenting and her significant difficulties responding to the challenges, even at the best of times, let alone at a time of crisis.

In summary, under this category of analysis, the findings support a conclusion that there is a profound probability the mother will inadvertently continue to perpetuate her attachment disorder with the child. She is unaware and likely is in denial of this propensity. Even if she were to accept this as a debilitating problem, her capacity to tenaciously focus on ameliorating it at this time is virtually non-existent. In spite of any initial effort on her part, she can be expected to rapidly lose focus on this vital issue of parenting. Furthermore, under this category of analysis, the child was observed to already manifest the beginning presence of an attachment disorder with the mother, largely attributable to the intergenerational perpetuation of this phenomenon and less so to the fact that the child has not been in her care for some months. Therefore, not only will the child require remedial effort to counteract the attachment disorder that she has already sustained but also will require concerted effort to ensure that she establishes a secure attachment with primary caregivers before the completion of her most crucial formative stage of life.

Reflections on the Child

It is quite probable that the child's natural predisposition is markedly similar to that of her mother. This formulation is based on acts of defiance observed during the access visit and on the reports of Child Welfare workers involved in this case. The workers related instances of the child aggressively acting out against the maternal grandmother and the workers. Furthermore, during the interview with the maternal grandmother, she reluctantly acknowledged that the child was beginning to reveal propensities similar to that of her mother, in fact, around the same chronological age.

In the best interest of the child, therefore, especially given that which is at stake, namely her optimal growth and development and realization of her also likely considerable innate cognitive intellectual potential, it would be functional, albeit not necessarily absolutely accurate, to consider her to be identically disposed as the mother. Accepting this to be the case will serve to ensure that every effort is made to rescue her from a fate not unlike that of her mother. To rescue her will require recognizing the presence of an extremely challenging problem and a requirement for significant expert intervention capable of ameliorating the emergence of later-life negative consequences the same as those of the mother. From a clinical perspective, depending on who parents the child, she will either realize her innate considerable positive cognitive intellectual potential and become a significant contributing member of society or repeat the same, perhaps even more troubled, behavioural patterns of her mother. In this case, the child's fate is highly unlikely to lie anywhere in between these two extremes.

B) CRITERIA OF A GOOD PARENT

Effective parenting that produces adaptive adults has been well researched and extensively described in the literature. Maccoby and Martin (1983) provide a review of the research in the areas of parenting and children's competence, parenting and moral development, and parenting and self-esteem. Fisher and Fisher (1986), in their empirically based summary conclude that open, straightforward, two-way communication is crucial, along with a consistent, fair disciplinary style. Schetky and Benedek (1980) described the positive parent as one who demonstrates the capacity for empathy, regards the child as a separate being, provides reasonable and consistent discipline, acts as a buffer between child and environment when appropriate, sets limits, shows flexibility and provides a good behavioural model.

Belsky, Learner and Spanier (1984), in their review of the parental influences in childhood, arrive at some of the same conclusions. They find for example, that the child's school success and overall intellectual development are enhanced by parents who are "nurturant without being too restrictive, responsive yet not overly controlling, stimulating yet not too intrusive." Such parents were reported to provide "an orientation toward independence, and a family structure that expects and rewards independent behaviour". They further concluded that Baumrind's (1967, 1968, 1971) authoritative parenting model of setting clear limits and expectations results in enhanced self-esteem and socioemotional competency and that discipline is most effectively provided by loving and nurturant parents and when "it relies upon a process of reasoning or induction, and is consistently enforced and varies systematically".

Derdeyn and his colleagues (1982) constituted the American Psychiatric Association's task force on clinical assessment of child custody issues. They concluded that the most significant variables to be considered are, attachment and the child's needs and the parent's capacity to parent, as well as their personality structure.

Chess and Thomas (1987) introduced the concept of "goodness of fit". They defined various styles of parenting of which the "secure parent'" or the best adjusted parent is most likely to enhance goodness of fit.

The preceding criteria of a "good parent" appear repeatedly in the literature. Current studies reinforce the earlier findings, expanding on them and describing further the profound responsibility, skill, knowledge and sensitivity required to raise children to become adaptive adults. The best example of the most current thinking about parenting is Coloroso (1994). She describes three kinds of families: the brick wall, the jellyfish, and the backbone type. The most effective parents are said to be those with a backbone perspective. Tenets of this parenting perspective are firmly grounded in the literature of the past two decades. Optimal parents are like the backbone of a living, supple spine that gives form and movement to the whole body with a structure that is present and firm but also flexible and functional

Parenting, therefore, is no simple task. To be effective, it cannot be instinctive or a repetition of the parents' own experiences as children. It cannot simply rely on what the parent thinks or believes. Because it is an onerous responsibility it must be informed by good knowledge and practical skill, as well as by a willingness to develop these abilities continuously. Most importantly, competent parenting requires personality features, emotional and cognitive functioning conducive to applying in a predictably consistent manner the knowledge and skills that promote a child's optimal development.

An examination of the literature that pertains to groups of individuals who are at high risk for deficient parenting is also imperative in every case. Specifically, these groups are alcohol and drug addicted and severely emotionally disturbed parents. Such parents are identified as running a higher than average risk of producing inadequate or dysfunctional children. Nevertheless, insofar as Parenting Capacity Assessments are not based on a medical model of disease whereby dysfunctionalities are "curable" through medical intervention (taking something out or putting something into an individual's body), there is a unanimous consensus in the literature that DSM labels are not particularly useful with respect to parenting capacity determinations. Moreover, there is a consensus in the literature that DSM labels should not automatically disqualify a parent, even parents who are not being pharmacologically treated for their "mental illness". The reason for this is that no label is able to convey the specific individual manifestations of a disorder, nor can a label accurately describe the severity of that disorder or the conditions under which symptoms are likely. Rather than relying on a diagnostic label, the literature recommends considerations with respect to precipitating factors, chronicity of the disorder, how the particular set of symptoms affects parenting and, most notably, what supports are available to a parent and how remedial is the disorder. Motivation of the parent to seek assistance is also considered to be a key variable. (Schulz, Dixon, Lindenberger and Ruther 1989).

In the process of investigating the pattern of parenting that negatively impacts on a child, Russell, Anderson and Blume (1985) have clearly identified through their review of the literature that alcoholic families are characterized by chaotic organization, unpredictable parental behaviour, poor communication patterns, inconsistent discipline, inadequate attention given to the socialization of children, tense home atmosphere, increased probability of violence and neglect, and higher than normal rates of sociopathic behaviours. The parenting of drug addicts is similarly characterized.

The parenting characteristics of deficient, essentially abusive, parents have been defined and validated by the work of Garbarino and Gilliam (1980) and Gaines, Sandgrund, Green and Power (1978). The pattern that emerges is consistent. Deficient/abusive parents, as a rule, are prone to depression, are immature and dependent, lack in self-esteem and are likely to use anxiety and guilt-provoking techniques with their children. They also have poor child management skills, are inconsistent in discipline and make unrealistic demands of their children. Furthermore, their profiles include impulsivity, higher than normal levels of emotional distress, poor frustration tolerance, physical and psychological unavailability, an immature need for love and affection which the child is frequently expected to fill and deficits in awareness of the child's needs. In brief, these deficiencies are remarkably consistent in their contrast to the positive parenting characteristics identified and established as a sound foundation on which a determination of a good parent is based.

It is noteworthy that the abuse perpetrated on children is more often not of a physical nature. While the general misconception is that abuse refers only to physical or sexual impropriety, a more accurate characterization is far more inclusive. In fact, the Canadian Incidence Study of Child Abuse and Neglect, in its examination of 135,500 cases over a three-month period in 1998 found that almost sixty percent of the problems involved neglect and emotional maltreatment. The conclusion of this particular study is that there are a lot of children harmed through various means by various adults and caretakers that do not reach the front pages of newspapers but are, nevertheless, profoundly negatively affected. Therefore, the consensus of this particular report is that emotional maltreatment, verbal threats, intimidation, terrorizing or routinely making unreasonable demands on a child, as well as neglect of all sorts is equally as abusive as any physical harm perpetrated on them. Exposure to family violence was especially concluded to be abusive to children insofar as the earlier its occurrence and the more profound its nature, the greater the probability of children progressively enacting these patterns throughout their lives. Therefore, while the terms deficient/abusive are used interchangeably in the literature to characterize parents, in the best interest of protecting the rights of children, the emerging trend is to place emphasis on the fact that all maltreatment of children is essentially abusive insofar as, to various degrees, it mitigates their optimal growth and development to become adaptive, autonomous, independent adults.

In determining the existing dysfunctionalities of individuals that mitigate their optimal parenting of a child, the concomitant task is to determine their capacity to bring about discernable improvements in time to be of benefit to a child, especially one in the most crucial formative stage of development This is the focus of the last category of analysis. Suffice it to say here that accepting the assumption that all dysfunctionalities are amenable to some remediation, under this category of analysis the most salient determination is less of capacity and more of timeliness. Moreover, every determination of timeliness must be informed by the availability of relevant expert resources and the assessed individuals current ability to commit and constructively use the services. Individuals in denial and who see themselves as essentially at the mercy of their environment are unlikely to make timely improvements without first resolving these obstacles to engaging in a change process.

Findings

Under this category of analysis, the findings support a conclusion that the mother's functioning is significantly removed from the criteria which characterizes a "good parent". She, in fact, was found to approximate more that which is characterized in the literature as a "deficient/abusive parent". As a function of her formative life experiences, which failed to meet her special basic needs, the mother was found to have acquired profoundly dysfunctional characterological traits and concomitant behaviours. These findings are contraindicated to a child in her care being parented optimally to become an autonomous, independent, adaptive adult. Moreover, insofar as a salient feature of her dysfunctionality is to employ the mechanism of denial to defend against the unpleasant reality of her circumstance, the a prospects of her admitting, let alone addressing with tenacity, the dysfunctionalities that obstruct her constructive use of marked cognitive intellectual potential was found to be so remote as to warrant a recommendation that the child be designated as a Crown Ward without Access for the sole purpose of being placed for adoption.

All the information collected and analyzed supports the conclusion and recommendation under this category of analysis. There is no one finding that is more significant or important than any other. This case, in fact, represents a classic example of the tragic later-life negative consequences to unmet primary needs during the most crucial formative stage in an individual's life. This case also represents a classic example of the profound impact environmental conditions have on the development of an individual in spite of that individual's innate cognitive intellectual potential which a well-intentioned, educated, articulate and responsible parent, in spite of her best efforts, was unable to promote satisfactorily.

The mother was temperamentally, innately predisposed to challenge her primary caregiver. This was further exacerbated by her considerable cognitive intellect, which made it even more difficult as she grew older for the maternal grandmother to reason with her in the process of setting limits. She was always more than capable of devising rationalizations to justify her emotionally based pursuits. As articulated by the mother, the maternal grandmother was indeed constantly trying to control her, but to no avail. As opposed to viewing these efforts on the part of the maternal grandmother as evidence of parental responsibility towards a child to whom she had an emotional commitment, the mother conceptualized her efforts as a stifling of her expression of self and as a stifling of her pursuit of autonomy and independence. It is extremely important to note that at no time did the mother articulate during the assessment process, nor is she noted by anyone as even remotely aware of, the parental responsibility to set limits in order to protect children from physical, emotional and moral harm.

Consistent with that which is known about the development of personality, there is evidence of an emerging escalation of dysfunctionality in the mother's behaviours. Her transgressions initially were troublesome only to her family but eventually became troublesome to her community, including the police. By the time her deviant behaviours brought her into conflict with authorities, her dysfunctional characterological traits were well established and served as profound obstacles to realizing the positive success of which she is capable by virtue of her considerable innate cognitive intellectual potential.

The finding under the first category of analysis of an attachment disorder sustained by the mother underscores the profoundly life-enduring consequences the first few years of life have on personality structure. Virtually all the later-life negative consequences, as described in the literature, are, in fact, manifested by the mother in this case. Furthermore, much of that which is described as characteristic of deficient/abusive parents applies to the mother.

Prior to defining the later-life manifestations of the mother's early negative experiences, and in order to establish the resilience of the mother's dysfunctionalities to change, first it is important to examine the dynamics of her personality structure.

In spite of the maternal grandmothers' best efforts, her failure to respond to the mother's special needs and her unique innate propensities inadvertently communicated to her a parental devaluation of who she is in her own right as a person. For example, she resented how she was dressed for school and how she was forced to wear her hair. This, to her, was instinctively indicative of the degree to which she felt her special nature to be unrecognized and unappreciated. A significant consequence of this is the development of her negative self-image. Failing to acquire a positive self-esteem, the mother was further predisposed to engage in troublesome behaviours. Insofar as academic achievements came easily to her, she could not even take pride in them. As such, she placed no value on something that took no effort on her part to achieve.

An addictive characterological personality trait was established in the mother as a result of a poorly defined sense of self, a negative self-image and unmet emotional needs specifically pertaining to attachment. This propensity, as is classically the case, began to manifest itself soon after puberty. It would not be unreasonable to conclude that now, as a function of her addictive characterological personality trait, the mother has become addicted, with alcohol likely being the drug of her choice. Her habits in this respect are unlikely attributable to youthful exploration and acting out. The documented frequency and severity of her alcohol abuse supports this conclusion. Moreover, the profound alcohol-induced instances of loss of touch with reality further confirm the conclusion that, as a function of her addictive characterological personality trait, the mother has reached the inevitable: namely being physiologically and psychologically addicted. Her disagreement, therefore, with having a substance abuse problem, specifically the use of alcohol, should be highly suspect. Unless she has been consistently involved in a community-based self-help program, her claims ought to be considered as typical manifestations of denial employed by individuals with an addictive characterological personality trait.

In spite of the fact that the mother was exposed through the efforts of the maternal grandmother to a variety of potentially cognitively stimulating activities, the positive consequences associated with such experiences have not been realized in this case. This is a highly unusual occurrence that is attributable to at least two factors. First, whatever efforts were exerted to help the mother reflect on experiences, and through this construct progressively more adaptive meanings, was clearly insufficient to produce positive results. Second, individuals such as the mother who are essentially emotionally driven invariably do not benefit even from the richest of experiences since they lack the ability to maintain the focus that is an absolute prerequisite to constructing meaning through which cognitive development occurs. The mother's "immature behaviours", as described by the maternal grandmother, from a clinical perspective, represent in essence marked cognitive developmental deficits that are extremely disproportionate to her obvious innate unrealized cognitive intellectual potential. Her history, documented behaviours and clinical presentation also are consistent with a classification of the mother's cognitive developmental perspective as characterized by instrumental hedonism. At this perspective, the primary emphasis is on the immediate satisfaction of needs through the path of least resistance. While there is no doubt the mother knows the difference between right and wrong, at this level of reasoning she is driven by her emotional needs and, at best, to avoid possible negative consequences she has fleeting considerations with respect to what she can get away with.

The profound use of denial as a defense mechanism is a tactic available to cognitive developmentally deficient individuals. To understand this, one has to reflect only on the ability of children to daydream and to engage for protracted periods of time in fanciful games of pretend. As the infant matures (i.e., constructs progressively more adaptive meanings to experiences), the ability to create fantasy/denial is gradually diminished. In developmentally deficient individuals, however, this ability is fully retained and is at the basis of the individual's denial, as for example of a drinking problem, in spite of overwhelming evidence to the contrary which, includes at times even vehicular homicide while intoxicated.

From time to time, the mother has been considered to manifest symptoms of depression, although this was not particularly evident during the process of this Parenting Capacity Assessment. The dynamics of this disorder are relevant, especially with respect to how they impact on parenting. Understanding this dynamic may also help to explain, at least in part, the maternal grandmother's failure to establish a secure bond with the mother. Essentially, the diagnostic label of depression refers to the suppression of anger. The anger often is directed at a significant other. Due to dependency needs (which certainly applies to the mother) and in some instances due to social mores, as for example, a mother's prescribed feelings towards a child, the open expression of anger is forbidden to the individual. To suppress the negative emotional state of anger requires increasingly more psychic energy, which makes individuals rather docile and concomitantly progressively less responsive to their environment. Clearly, compromised or diminished responsiveness to the environment in which there is a dependent child, especially an infant, is a profoundly contraindicated state to good parenting.

From time to time, suppressed anger, may come to the surface. When it does, its manifestation is markedly disproportionate to any precipitating event, leaving the observer bewildered as to what could possibly justify the rage exhibited by an individual. This is a well-documented pattern in this case. Witnessing the mother's outbursts, especially if there is an equal response by the object of her rage is profoundly contraindicated to the best interest of a child. It is a well-documented phenomenon that children exposed to outbursts of rage and violence invariably repeat the same pattern. Moreover, the earlier children are exposed to such outbursts and the more violent the outbursts are, the earlier and more violently they will exhibit this in their own lives.

From a clinical perspective, therefore, the mother's developmental deficits are significant contributing factors to her situationally determined emotionally driven behaviours. This influences virtually everything that she does, including her substance use and abuse and absence of commitment to any course of positive action. Insofar as her behaviours are situationally determined, the only thing that can be expected of her is the unexpected. Such profound lack of consistency, inability to focus and inability to be predictably attentive are considerable obstacles to relating to the child as a separate, unique entity. In the literature, this is considered to be a significant descriptor of "deficient/abusive parenting".

It is noteworthy that the Society and the maternal grandmother both wanted this Parenting Capacity Assessment to define what is the nature of the mother's dysfunctionality. In fact, the Society specifically asked what "mental health issues", if any, compromise the mother's capacity to parent. These questions amount to asking for a diagnostic label, diagnostic labels which in fact have been provided previously by assumedly competent physician specialists in psychiatry. While the labeling of one specialist is held to be suspect by the maternal grandmother because the specialist spent only a brief amount of time with the mother, applying a diagnostic label by a Mental Health practitioner in this particular case was not a difficult undertaking. The mother's history, behaviour and presentation even if brief, readily lend themselves to clinical formulations. Formulations which, in this case, have been quite consistent among the various Mental Health professionals who have encountered the mother prior to this Parenting Capacity Assessment.

Notwithstanding the consistent classification of the mother's dysfunctionalities, this case represents exactly that which is referenced in the literature with respect to the inability of DSM-IV diagnostic labels to convey the manner and degree to which a disorder can impact on an individual's ability and capacity to parent. This case also represents one of the worst examples of the enormous disservice that is entailed in simply providing a diagnostic label without explanation and elaboration, regardless of the context in which it is done so. A diagnostic label, as such, is revealed to be virtually useless to anyone other than another physician specialist in psychiatry who likely will use the label to initiate primarily a pharmacological intervention. Alternatively, a label may be of some service for a counselor but invariably even then it is the dynamics which are the salient considerations insofar as these determine what interventions will be introduced to address a specific dysfunctionality.

This case, therefore, warrants at least a brief explanation of the most consistently applied label to the mother's condition, namely Personality Disorder, specifically of the Borderline classification. It is noteworthy that the mother clearly meets the criteria for such a classification as is evidenced by the descriptors of this condition. Therefore, perhaps the child's maternal grandmother was expressing less a desire for a definitive label and more her wishful thinking that her daughter's disorder was something less severe and more easily amenable to intervention. The Society, on the other hand, could be considered as simply requesting in their Terms of Reference a confirmation elaborated by explanation and information with respect to possible viable interventions.

A Borderline Personality Disorder is defined in the literature as a pervasive pattern of instability in interpersonal relationships, self-image and affects, and an equally pervasive pattern of impulsivity beginning in early childhood and present in a variety of context. Virtually all the following criteria as listed apply to the mother and substantiate the classification by physician specialists in psychiatry of her dysfunctionality as a Borderline Personality Disorder.

1. Frantic efforts to avoid real or imagined abandonment;
2. A pattern of unstable and intense interpersonal relationships characterized by alternating between extremes of idealization and devaluation;
3. Identity disturbance: markedly and persistently unstable self-image or sense of self;
4. Impulsivity in at least two areas that are potentially self-damaging (e.g., spending, sex, substance abuse, reckless driving, binge eating);
5. Recurrent suicidal behaviour, gestures or threats or self-mutilating behaviour;
6. Affective instability due to a marked reactivity of mood (e.g., intense episodic dysphoria, irritability or anxiety, usually lasting a few hours and only rarely more than a few days);
7. Chronic feelings of emptiness;
8. Inappropriate intense anger or difficulty controlling anger (e.g., frequent displays of temper, constant anger, recurrent physical fights);
9. Transient, stress-related paranoid ideation or severe disassociative symptoms.

The clinical formulations based on the findings of this Parenting Capacity Assessment and the clinical formulations of other Mental Health professionals, specifically physician specialists in psychiatry, also are confirmed by the results of the standardized instruments administered to the mother under supervision. Her approach to completing the Minnesota Multiphasic Personality Inventory-2 was a co-operative one and, as such, she produced a reliable and valid profile. The single elevation is on Scale 4. This is a measure of antisocial tendencies and behaviours which are void of empathic considerations for the welfare of others. Individuals who score similarly to the mother are also found to have rebellious attitudes towards authority figures, and to have stormy family relationships, blaming their parents for their problems. In spite of any innate cognitive intellectual potential, they often show a history of underachievement in school and a poor work history. If married, individuals such as the mother tend to have marital problems. Invariably, people in this group are viewed as impulsive, and as constantly striving for immediate gratification of impulses. As such, they do not plan well and often act without considering the consequences to their actions. They are found to be impatient, to show limited tolerance of frustration, to exercise poor judgment and to take risks others avoid.

Individuals who produce a pattern of responses on the MMPI-2 similar to that of the mother also are viewed as immature, childish, self-centered and selfish. In social situations, they are seen as ostentatious and exhibitionistic. Consequently on first impression they are viewed as extroverted, outgoing, talkative, energetic, spontaneous and self-confident. In short order, however, they reveal themselves as insensitive and interested in others only in terms of how they can use them for their own purposes. While initially likeable and able to create a good first impression, in time, they reveal themselves to be shallow and superficial in relationships. They seem to be unable to form warm attachment to others.

Individuals whose response patterns produce elevations on Scale 4 also are found to be hostile, aggressive, sarcastic, cynical, resentful, rebellious and antagonistic. They are often found to display aggressive outbursts, to engage in assaultive behaviour and to show little guilt over their negative behaviours. Many individuals with this profile type may feign guilt and remorse when in trouble. Consistent with that which is reported in the documentation reviewed for the purposes of this Parenting Capacity Assessment, those with high elevations on Scale 4, are often diagnosed as personality disordered.

The MMPI-2 profile produced by the mother is further elaborated by her cognitive developmental perspective as determined by the Defining Issues Test standardized scale. On this instrument, she barely recognizes the benefits associated with a reference group perspective. This invariably is indicative of functioning at the previous stage orientation. This stage orientation as evidenced also by numerous behavioural reports reviewed in the file materials is characterized by instrumental hedonism or the pursuit of immediate gratification through the path of least resistance. An elaboration of the mother's pre-conventional stage 2 cognitive developmental orientation is provided in Appendix C.

The Raven's Progressive Matrices, which is a culturally unbiased test of cognitive intelligence, reveals the mother's innate intellectual potential to fall above the superior range. This is well above the ninety-five percentile. Unfortunately, her innate cognitive intellectual potential is essentially unrealized even in spite of the fact that her critical thinking is also considerable as evidenced by the Watson-Glasser scales on which she scored in the seventy-five percentile. Therefore, while she reveals herself to be more inclined to be proactive, as evidenced by the Rotter Locus of Control results, that is to say, to purposefully pursue a well-defined objective, as a function of her dysfunctionalities and developmental deficits, her energies and abilities are directed into satisfying her immediate needs as opposed to producing results which are sustainable and have broad and long-term positive consequences.

Seldom is there such internal logical consistency found in the clinical presentation of an individual. Tragically, the nature of the mother's dysfunctionality is complex and not readily amenable to intervention. This will be discussed in further detail under the last category of analysis. Suffice it to say that all that is known about the mother defines her as that which is characterized in the literature as a "deficient/abusive" parent. The implications of the findings under this category of analysis is that while she has the innate cognitive intellectual potential to score in the top percentile on an examination after completing a parenting course, it is her application of the knowledge and skills that is in question. Moreover, without first bringing under control various aspects of her dysfunctionalities, past underachievement predicts that it is highly unlikely that she could apply herself with persistent commitment to a parenting educational program. It is, therefore, imperative to stress that the issue is both learning knowledge and skills as well as their application. In this particular case, the tragedy is that the mother is clearly a profound academic/career underachiever and with great probability can be predicted to be likewise as a parent.

C) SOCIAL SUPPORT NETWORK

Research on child abuse reveal that a significant proportion of abusive parents live in social isolation, have unmet emotional needs and are unable to maintain composure under stress. An adjunct to being isolated and unable to trust people is an inability to ask for help (Heifer & Kempe 1976; Spinetta 1978). Without a social network, such individuals do not thrive, do not learn new information and related skills, and do not develop a more adaptively comprehensive cognitive perspective of their world. Their insular lifestyle and concomitant lack of stimulation invariably produce a deterioration of functioning and increasingly place children in their care at high risk. To become involved and to stay involved in a social network that is supportive requires aptitudes and a sense of self that is acquired during the formative years in an individual's life. In fact, recent literature has identified the ability to engage in co-operative activity to be determined very early in life. Without such experiences the neurological basis for such behaviours is lost forever (Wright, 1998; Chugani, 1998; Katz & Schatz, 1996).

Because many abusive parents do not trust people, they do not share their problems with others and do not ask for help when they need it. As a consequence, stress builds up to unmanageable levels and dysfunctional behaviours are exhibited. A temporary social network created by involvement with Child Welfare Agency personnel and programs is not sufficient (Breton 1979). A true facilitative social network must be a permanent or a quasi-permanent support system to which a parent can turn in times of stress.

Research, in fact, has demonstrated that the incidence of child neglect and abuse is significantly lower for individuals and their families who are active participants in a broad social network. Moreover, in the long run, getting non-coping parents involved in a positive social network has been demonstrated to produce a higher return than involvement of professionals or social welfare funded services with a family (University of Toronto, 1980).

Establishing and maintaining a supportive social network requires a well-defined level of interpersonal skills of the same order that is required for establishing an emotional bond with an infant. Empirical studies of infant-mother interaction suggest that skills for relationship building are already activated, developed and in use at the point of achievement of interpersonal attachment in the very young infant. If this emerging capacity is nurtured environmentally, it forms the basis for the development of social skills for interpersonal relationships of all kinds.

Therefore, insofar as the attachment process establishes the first interpersonal relationship in an individual's life, it is considered to influence all subsequent relationships (Scheaffer 1971). This, in turn, determines the person's growth and development since, an expanding social network exposes individuals to a variety of events that challenge them to construct meaning from experiences that are increasingly more comprehensive and therefore adaptive.

Parents with a weak or virtually non-existent supportive network (among many deficiencies) will certainly lack interpersonal skills, which is also manifested in the quality of the relationship they have with their children.

The findings under this category of analysis, while presented separately, correlate with the findings under the previous sections of analyses, illustrating the later consequences of attachment disorders, as well as the consequences of acquiring characterological personality traits and/or developmental deficits that inhibit the socialization of individuals into the norm. It is, therefore, not surprising that the findings under this category of analysis reveal marginalized individuals essentially alienated from the mainstream of society if there were significant negative findings in the previous two categories of analyses. The reason for including it as a separate category in a Parenting Capacity Assessment is to identify even tangential positive affiliations. These might justify a faint hope for fostering affiliation with a social support network. Such fellowship might eventually be the genesis of an acceptance of responsibility and, through this acceptance, engagement in a self-improvement process capable of generating advancements in parenting knowledge and skills, as well as their consistent application.

Findings

Under this category of analysis, the findings reveal the mother, as a function of the nature of her dysfunctionalities, as lacking the capacity to establish meaningful relationships that can evolve into a viable positive social support network of the type and intensity described in the literature as essential to optimal parenting. At best, the mother is concluded to be capable of brief self-serving relationships. While she may have many acquaintances, the findings under this category of analysis predict that she is more likely to become increasingly isolated and more likely to experience an increasing frequency of interpersonal conflicts. All of this is contraindicated to the best interest of the child and supports a conclusion and recommendation that the child be designated as a Crown Ward without Access to the mother for the explicit purpose of being placed for adoption.

The mother's own attachment disorder establishes the most significant finding in support of the conclusion and recommendation under this category of analysis. Insofar as the attachment process establishes the first interpersonal relationship in an individual's life, it is logically consistent that this will influence all subsequent relationships. This is the basis of intergenerational perpetuation and exacerbation of attachment disorders, as well as relationship difficulties of all types. As revealed by the maternal grandmother, the mother always had difficulties establishing and maintaining friendships. At best, the maternal grandmother could recall only one relatively persistent relationship in her daughter's life, one which eventually also ended with an altercation and a subsequent police investigation. While the mother can list in her Affidavit potential supportive individuals, there is no objective evidence that she has any meaningful relationships beyond the superficial contacts that characterize the interpersonal style of individuals with the mother's dysfunctionalities.

Tragically, the mother's attachment disorder was unrecognized and consequently not specifically addressed. This negatively affected the development of her interpersonal skills and explains the transient, superficial relationships in her life. Moreover, interpersonal conflicts, persistent experiences of rejection and external devaluation of her all serve to destroy her ability to trust. Without this ability, the mother is highly unlikely to share issues concerning parenting with others in a meaningful manner. Unfortunately, the mother can be expected to defend herself instinctively, by withdrawing progressively more from relationships in order to avoid further rejection and negative appraisals of who she is from the perspective of others.

The very nature of the mother's dysfunctionality is to approach relationships with unrealistic expectations of being rescued by someone who will solve all her problems and to blame others for her difficulties when these expectations are not realized. This propensity is not only counterproductive in romantic relationships, which invariably disappoint the mother as best evidenced by her relationship with the father of the child, but also does not bode well for any meaningful non-romantic relationships. She is unlikely to trust anyone, including the maternal grandmother, to share problems, especially pertaining to parenting issues. Therefore, it would not be unreasonable to predict that without long-term expert intervention, the mother will turn increasingly inward. Invariably, this is associated with escalating frustrations that have been described in the literature as the genesis of child neglect and abuse. Concomitantly, in isolation, the detection of neglect and abuse becomes increasingly more difficult and by the time it does become evident, often irreversible harm has been perpetrated on a child.

In light of the explanation of the dynamics involved in a Borderline Personality Disorder and the findings of this assessment, it should be no wonder that the mother has had persistent relationship difficulties and that she is increasingly inclined not to trust others. This is also evidenced by the mother's considering the information provided by the maternal grandmother to be malicious fabrications and the maternal grandmother's actions to constitute betrayal. Certainly the maternal grandmother's interpretations of events are quite different from that of the mother. These same dynamics now and in the foreseeable future also mitigate against the mother becoming involved with a community-based self-help program such as Alcoholics Anonymous. The very essence of this and other twelve step programs is the fellowship through which individuals gain and maintain their resolve to persistently control a debilitating, life-enduring addictive characterological personality trait.

The mother's cognitive developmental perspective, characterized by instrumental hedonism, is also contrary to the establishment of meaningful relationships. At this pre-conventional level of reasoning, relationships are essentially transient contacts initiated for self-serving purposes or for the purpose of instrumental reciprocity. While only one stage removed from a more comprehensive and thereby more adaptive reference group orientation, the time required for the mother to reach this stage of reasoning can be expected to be markedly protracted since progress is determined not only by the construction of meaning in response to instances of cognitive conflict but also by the stimulating experiences inherent in meaningful relationships. The mother's cognitive developmental perspective, therefore, can be predicted to remain, for now and the foreseeable future, fixed at her current stage of reasoning. This is inconsistent with establishing meaningful relationships described in the above literature review as essential to benefiting from the parenting experiences of others through candid sharing and dialogue around specific and broad issues pertaining to children.

In spite of the mother's ability to be quite charming for brief periods of time, in spite of her physical attractiveness which can be a source of positive attributions and in spite of her significant innate cognitive intellectual capacity, the nature of her dysfunctionalities poses formidable obstacles to establishing and maintaining meaningful relationships. Invariably and inadvertently, her limited capacity to tolerate stress, her unrealistic expectations of others, and her substance abuse, to name only a few dysfunctionalities, alienate her from others. Instances of alienation reinforce her sense of rejection and low self-esteem. This establishes a vicious cycle that is profoundly antithetical to becoming involved in a positive social support network. Left to her own devices, which essentially has characterized her functioning for the past six to eight years, the mother has been unable to accomplish any sustainable objective. The same can be said of her potential to parent without the benefits of a positive social support network comprised of individuals in the pursuit of an improved quality of life for themselves and for their children. Without reservation, therefore, this category of analysis also supports the conclusion that the interest of the child will be served best by designating her as a Crown Ward without Access for the explicit purpose of being placed for adoption.

D) EVIDENCE-BASED EXPECTATIONS FOR ACQUIRING AND APPLYING PARENTING CAPABILITIES

The axiom that people become more like themselves with the passing of time is grounded in the empirically demonstrated phenomenon of characterological traits. Most psychometric instruments, including the MMPI-2, incorporate several indicators that define resilient personality structures. Cattell in 1966 and later the elaboration by Spielberger (1979) expanded on this aspect of personality structure by adding the phenomenon called state. In general personality states are regarded as temporal cross-sections in the stream of life. Emotional reactions are particular examples of personality states (Spielberger 1972). As such, an emotional state exists at a given moment in time and at a particular level of intensity. Although personality states (e.g., anxiety or anger) are often transitory, they reoccur when evoked by specific stimuli and they may endure over time when the evoking conditions persist.

In contrast to the transitory nature of emotional states, personality traits can be conceptualized as enduring differences among people in specifiable tendencies to approach the world in a certain way (for example, with anxiety or anger) and to react or behave in a specified manner with predictable regularity. Campbell (1963) referred to this as "acquired behavioural dispositions". These dispositions are believed to be the result of early-life experiences that dispose an individual both to approach the world in a particular way and to manifest consistently predictable tendencies. The stronger the trait, the more probable that the individual will experience more intense elevations on the related state in a particular situation.

Clinicians in the pursuit of promoting personality change or the amelioration of negative consequences to an event such as trauma, in recognition of this phenomenon, rely on psychometric instruments as well as their informed judgment to make predictive formulations otherwise known as prognosis. Personality focused psychometric instruments, such as the MMPI-2, incorporate into the clinical scales probability statements regarding prognosis, specifically with respect to an individual's response to resolution-oriented clinical interventions. Invariably, findings which pertain to resilient personality structures are designated as having a poor prognosis as evidenced by the lack of gains made by similar individuals.

While the prognosis for change is dismally poor for all characterological traits, some traits are even more resilient than others. Cognitive intelligence, hostility and addictive propensities are some of the most resilient permanent characterological traits. Aggressive propensities is the second most stable personality trait after cognitive intelligence. Aggressive behaviour once established, seems to continue into adulthood even after many interventions to stop it. Most violent adults were aggressive and troublesome children. Such children grow up to be violent adolescents and adults in a predictable and recognizable way (Robins, Tipp, Przybeck, 1991; Olweus, 1979; Loeber 1991). Nevertheless, some individuals, in spite of poor prognosis, appear to be no longer plagued by a dysfunctional trait. The best examples are individuals who achieve and maintain abstinence from all intoxicants for decades. It is vitally important to note, however, that the change in behaviours is not indicative of a change in the addictive propensity trait. The change is attributable to specific deliberate and persistently applied, well-defined tactics with which the individual gains control over the behavioural manifestations of a trait. If the tactic is abandoned (e.g., participation in self-help, twelve-step program), invariably the individual relapses.

Therefore, without evidence of a significant, deliberate and persistent tactic to override the debilitating behavioural manifestation of a trait, with the passage of time, individuals do become more like themselves than they were before. People do not "mellow" with age unless they were "mellow" to start with. Although physically pugnacious individuals may become less so with age due to diminishing physical ability they will continue to act out, even in nursing homes, as long as they are alive.

The motivation to gain control over the dysfunctional behavioural manifestation of a trait is significantly determined by an individual's development of an ability to experience a broad range of emotions. A conscience or empathic ability are significant requirements. In Alcoholics Anonymous there is a saying that "a sober alcoholic is a drunk with a conscience". Individuals with diminished capacity to experience all but the most severe emotions invariably cannot sustain their effort to use an override tactic such as a commitment to participation in a twelve-step program (Rada 1978; Greenspoon & Bakalar 1976).

This category of analysis in the methodology for conducting a Parenting Capacity Assessment poses the challenge of defining the etiology and dynamics of a primary caregiver's dysfunctionalities and, on the basis of this, defining reasonable expectations with respect to a parent's potential to bring about improvements in a timely manner. There are three broad categories into which dysfunctionalities can be grouped. The first entails characterological traits which include the later-life negative consequences of an attachment disorder sustained during the most crucial formative stage in an individual's life. At best, these consequences (traits) can be brought under control but never eradicated from the personality structure of the individual. The second grouping pertains to developmental deficits. Under this grouping individuals are either "stuck" at a pre-conventional perspective, which is dysfunctional for adults, or are in a protracted transition from one stage to another, which is equally debilitating to individuals and a source of great trauma for anyone who is involved with them. With expert intervention, both of these developmental conditions can be successfully addressed by promoting the development of increasingly more comprehensive and thereby adaptive cognitive perspectives and concomitant behaviours. While possible to accomplish, this requires a great deal of expertise, time and effort. The third grouping pertains to acute mental and emotional disorders which are amenable to intervention and eradication, some even if they have already achieved a chronic status. Under this category of analysis, therefore, terms of reference pertaining to type of intervention and projected timeliness of potential benefits are addressed.

Findings

The findings under this category of analysis are particularly worrisome and support a conclusion that there is a marked probability the mother's dysfunctionalities will persist, likely escalating, exacerbated by her substance abuse and by episodic periods of despondency. Furthermore, especially during periods of irrationality, she can be predicted to experience extreme anxiety regarding the future. While it is possible that some crisis or accumulative negative consequences will produce a critical mass that will precipitate a change, at this time this is considered to be highly improbable and certainly so remote as not to justify experimenting with the child's inalienable right to optimal growth and development to become an autonomous, independent, adaptive adult. Under this category of analysis, Crown Wardship without Access to the mother for the sole purpose of placing the child for adoption, while an intrusive measure, is submitted to be the determination that is in the child's best interest.

The mother's cognitive developmental deficit is the significant finding in support of the conclusion and recommendation under this category of analysis. The deficits allow the mother to rely on the immature mechanism of fantasy creation with which to abdicate responsibility for her problems, readily blaming others while denying any responsibility beyond transitory lip service for seeking assistance: lip service which invariably is engaged in for self-serving purposes. It is extremely important to recognize that a person in denial genuinely believes in the fantasy that they have created about themselves and their circumstance. Furthermore, that person genuinely believes that sooner rather than later they will be vindicated or at least will be given yet another chance to prove their virtues. This cognitive/emotional perspective is absolutely antithetical to seeking assistance or engaging in any concerted effort to bring about changes in thinking, emotional volatility, substance use and abuse and general functioning. In this case, why would the mother bother to pursue such a time-consuming, difficult, often emotionally painful process since she genuinely does not believe herself to be in need of such involvement? In a profound state of denial, there is an equally profound resistance to doing that which to others objectively makes imminent, rational sense, especially in light of all the negatives that have happened and continue to occur in that person's life.

To promote cognitive development in individuals whose perspective has fixated at a pre-conventional level of reasoning is the focus of intervention programs best delivered in institutional settings. Therapeutic communities in which substance abuse is addressed incorporate this specific objective, as do "justice-based" communities in which convicted felons with behavioural and substance abuse problems are placed. A great deal of expertise and concerted effort is required over a protracted period of time to make discernable developmental gains that will no longer support the creation of fantasy with which individuals can deny personal responsibility for the negative circumstances of their lives. At this time, such a resource program is unlikely to be available to the mother. Even if she were incarcerated and such a program were offered to her, it is highly unlikely that she would avail herself of the resource for the very reasons that she is in desperate need of this type of intervention. She simply does not believe that she needs it.

Promoting cognitive development and/or addressing the psychodynamic defense mechanism of denial/resistance through weekly counseling is, at best, an extremely lengthy process and, more realistically, an impossible task.

Assuming for the sake of argument that for some unknown reason the mother accepts the reality that she has significant dysfunctionalities and, in accepting responsibility for the circumstances of her life, she begins to pursue a course of intervention with which to bring about improvements in her functioning, without assistance there is little, if any, hope of bringing about change. In this extremely hypothetical scenario, therefore, she will require the assistance of a trained Mental Health professional. Regardless of the modality of intervention used by the professional, it will invariably incorporate the development of a therapeutic relationship. Moreover, insofar as a major component of the mother's "Borderline Personality Disorder" entails emotional liability, impulsivity, and a pattern of intense and chaotic relationships, the treatment of her disorder will be extremely difficult, requiring not only expertise but also a considerable commitment of time. Many clinicians, in fact, are skeptical about the treatment of this disorder. Their skepticism is based on the well-documented fact that by definition, personality disordered individuals find it difficult to co-operate and collaborate, much less take responsibility for their own behaviour. This is particularly true for borderline disordered individuals who typically enter treatment for the express purpose of feeling better rather than making changes in their lives. They want to have their abandonment feelings assuaged, their worries soothed, and the problem of daily living resolved. In therapy, as in all relationships, their secret desire is that someone all-powerful and all-nurturing will "make up" for their chaotic and rejection-ravaged life. In short, they believe that it is someone else's responsibility to make everything better for them. It is certainly not their responsibility because from their perspective they did not create their problem-strewn lives. In the therapeutic setting, that "someone" is the clinician. This approach does not bode well for the establishment of a therapeutic relationship.

Nevertheless, there is an emerging hopefulness among some clinicians that patients who suffer from a Borderline Personality Disorder can and will respond to effective treatment strategies. The treatment strategies are multi-focused, involving the use of medication with which to stabilize mood fluctuations, augmented by cognitive behavioural strategies. The required expertise, however, is difficult to identify, let alone to readily access. Moreover, while authors such as Dr. Len Sperry M.D. (1999) advocate for a more optimistic prognosis for the treatment of personality disordered individuals, at this time the necessary collaboration among various disciplines is difficult, if not impossible, to achieve. In this particular case, to further carry the extreme hypothetical scenario, even if the mother were to attend at a counseling resource, by the time necessary arrangements could be made, the very nature of her dysfunctionality would cause her to disengage from the process and instead pursue some intense immediate emotional need gratification.

It is imperative to keep in mind that the perspective of emotionally driven individuals is that if it feels so strong, it must be right. Such a propensity does not bode well for the prospects of bringing about meaningful change through vigorous effort. Certainly not in time to benefit an infant who is in the most crucial formative stage of life.

The Scale 4 elevation produced by the mother on the MMPI-2 instrument, which is consistent with her characterizations by physician specialists in psychiatry, also confirms an extremely poor prognosis for change in the foreseeable future. Individuals with high scores on Scale 4 are invariably viewed as unable to profit from experience and as lacking in definite goals. They show an absence of deep emotional response to others and invariably fail to form a treatment relationship. They tend to be unmotivated and report feeling easily bored and empty. The treatment prognosis is usually considered poor as they are resistant to change and therapy. They tend to blame others for problems and to intellectualize their limitations. Although they may, from time to time, agree to treatment to avoid punishment, such as jail or some other unpleasant outcome, they are likely to terminate counseling before change is effected.

The screening instruments for substance abuse included in the mother's Affidavit should be recognized as quite transparent and reliant on the ability of individuals to evaluate accurately the reality of their circumstance and to report this in a candid manner in the context of seeking assistance. Moreover, contrary to the mother's claim, the brief letter from the assessor cannot be considered as indicative of an absence of an alcohol abuse problem. What it indicates is that the mother did not believe she had a problem that required follow-up appointments. The findings of this assessment support with great confidence a conclusion that the mother, as a result of her formative stage experiences, acquired an addictive characterological personality trait which predictably has been manifested by her well-documented episodes of substance abuse. Moreover, this represents only that which is known. Perhaps the physician specialist in psychiatry's characterization of the mother as a "consummate liar" was a response to her misrepresentation of her substance abuse insofar as individuals with this characterological personality trait predictably make false claims about their substance use pattern.

To reiterate, characterological traits, by definition, are life-enduring features in an individual's personality make-up. As such, individuals cannot be "cured" of their dysfunctional traits. Instead, once an individual accepts responsibility for dysfunctional propensities, through the persistent life-long application of override strategies, that individual can bring the trait under predictable control. The best example of this is the life-long participation of individuals in community-based self-help programs, such as Alcoholics Anonymous. Therefore, without the mother accepting that she has an alcohol abuse problem and without participating in a meaningful manner in a self-help program such as Alcoholics Anonymous, her claims of abstinence and/or control over alcohol should not be accepted at face value although from time to time, she may be sincere in her desire to achieve this.

In summary, even if through some inexplicable event the mother were to achieve cognitive developmental gains which no longer support her creation of pleasing fantasy and, through this, denial of responsibility for her circumstance, her characterological trait dysfunctional propensities would require protracted and intense effort to be brought under control. Moreover, this assessment report is highly unlikely to have any therapeutic value for the mother. There is overwhelming evidence that she has been confronted numerous times before with the reality of her situation and her dysfunctionalities. In spite of this, she has been quite successful in maintaining her creation of fantasy and through this, a denial of personal responsibility for her problems. Therefore, the prospects of the mother bringing about any discernable change in how she views the world and how she behaves is so remote as to support overwhelmingly a conclusion that, in the child's best interest, she should be made a Crown Ward without Access to the mother for the sole purpose of being placed for adoption.

Discussion

This case represents a classic manifestation of later-life negative consequences to formative stage deficiencies. This case also represents a classic example of an unusual child (the mother) with significant innate cognitive intellectual potential posing parenting challenges beyond the capacity of her primary caregiver to respond competently. As a result of these and other failures during the mother's first decade of life, instead of realizing a myriad of positive potentials possible through her innate cognitive intellectual capacities and other talents, virtually the exact opposite has occurred. The complexity of her problems, as well as their magnitude, is such that physician specialists in psychiatry have classified her condition as consistent with the broad category of a Personality Disorder, specifically of the Borderline type. While this diagnostic label has little meaning for non-Mental Health professionals and the use of a label does not convey the impact a disorder has on parenting its definition clearly characterizes the mother. The findings of this Parenting Capacity Assessment are consistent with the descriptive and explanatory criteria of dysfunctionalities classified as personality disorders. The most salient aspect of the findings is that dysfunctionalities such as those of the mother are profoundly resistant to change, certainly not in sufficient time to be of any discernable benefit to the child in whose best interest this Parenting Capacity Assessment was conducted.

The findings pertaining to the child support a conclusion that, as a function of her natural innate propensities and life experiences to date, she, too manifests virtually identical propensities to those of the mother when she was the child's age. Given the potentially devastating consequences of believing otherwise, in her best interest this formulation should be accepted at face value, although it may not be absolutely accurate. In so doing, the child should be provided with optimal intervention to prevent that which is otherwise inevitable, as opposed to discovering later that she too has become profoundly dysfunctional. If, indeed, the child has the mother's positive natural innate cognitive intellectual potential, in the right environment, nurtured and facilitated, it would not be unreasonable to predict for her a markedly positive life characterized by incremental successes and equally incremental contributions to the community in which she lives.

In conclusion, hopefully this assessment will not be mistakenly interpreted as in any way finding blame for what has transpired in the life of the mother and her child. Hopefully, this assessment will help to explain more fully the etiology and the nature of the mother's dysfunctionalities with a view to rescuing her child from an identical destiny. Certainly the maternal grandmother cannot be blamed for how the mother turned out insofar as even the most competent and informed parent would have been extremely challenged by her special nature. Furthermore, from a clinical perspective, it is inappropriate and incorrect to blame the mother, regardless of her innate cognitive intellectual propensities. While she must first accept responsibility for her dysfunctionalities before any change can be expected, paradoxically, given the dynamics of her dysfunctionalities at this time and in the foreseeable future, she cannot be expected to accept responsibility for her problems. Therefore, while compassion for both the maternal grandmother and the mother is a natural emotional response, ultimately the child's inalienable right to optimal growth and development must be the primary consideration in this case. In fact, this is the only viable consideration available and capable of producing positive results.

Recommendations

Pertaining to the Child

1. In the best interest of the child, Amanda, with a view to protecting her inalienable right to optimal growth and development to become an autonomous, independent adaptive adult, she should be designated as a Crown Ward without Access to the mother for the sole purpose of being placed for adoption in a timely manner.

2. Insofar as the child, Amanda, has already sustained some harm with respect to attachment issues and with respect to being exposed to the mother's violent outbursts, she will require extraordinary, sustained effort on the part of competent primary caregivers to establish a secure attachment and then to nurture this tenaciously so that it can evolve into a true psychological relationship which is a prerequisite to optimal growth and development. Therefore, her adoptive parents will not only need to understand the nature of the harm already sustained by the child but also will need considerable support to mitigate this while simultaneously promoting and establishing a secure attachment with her.

Pertaining to the Mother

1. The mother's reaction to the findings of this Parenting Capacity Assessment, as well as her reaction to the extent to which the findings of this assessment confirm the opinions of Mental Health professionals previously involved with her can be predicted with great accuracy. She will negate and discount the conclusions and, through this, the recommendations pertaining to the child. It is, therefore, imperative to recognize that reasoning with her and expecting positive responses from her are unlikely to produce meaningful results. Any hope in this respect should be tempered with concerns for the welfare of the child.

This case, therefore, especially requires structure and well-defined limits, enacted in a timely determination of the child's status.

Hopefully the mother's predictable negative response to the findings, conclusions and recommendations of this Parenting Capacity Assessment will not be supported by the maternal grandmother. This is a concern, and could protract the child's unresolved status, especially given the maternal grandmother's wishful, albeit unfounded, expectation that the nature of her daughter's dysfunctionalities are not as profound as others indicated and that the problems are more amenable to intervention than what experience has proven so far. Hopefully, this Parenting Capacity Assessment will serve to enlighten the maternal grandmother and help her to act in the best interest of her grandchild who can still be rescued from the destiny into which she was born, through timely and decisive action.

To realize these potential desirable outcomes it will be necessary to carefully review with the maternal grandmother the content and meaning of this report.

2. Every effort should be made to debrief the mother about the findings of this Parenting Capacity Assessment in the interest of compassion, fully recognizing that her existing ability to accept the results by virtue of her dysfunctionalities will be seriously compromised.

In spite of the intent of this Parenting Capacity Assessment to present a clear well-defined rationale for the conclusions and recommendations provided, it is recognized that invariably there are areas that require clarification and elaboration. These can be provided in writing and if necessary augmented in person upon request.

APPENDICES

APPENDIX A

Terms of Reference Posed by the Society and Concise Answers

1.   What specific Mental Health issue, if any, is involved regarding the mother's ability to parent?

The question implies a possible belief that there is a simple answer of a singular nature with an equally simple, singular resolution. The four categories of analysis used in the methodology of this Parenting Capacity Assessment reveal quite the contrary. Moreover, the nature of the question is such that it disregards the complex and many-faceted symptoms of the dysfunctionality revealed by the mother in an escalating manner throughout her life. This case especially exemplifies the disservices created by the use of a diagnostic label without explaining its meaning, impact on a person's functioning and, more importantly, how the dynamics of the dysfunctionality effect on an individual's capacity as a parent.

The body of this report, defines the complexities of the mother's dysfunctionalities and the degree to which these are resistant to amelioration, now and in the foreseeable future.

2.   What is the prognosis for the mother should she receive appropriate treatment for her Mental Health issue, if any, is diagnosed?

The nature of the question implies a belief or speculation that the mother has an acute disorder that is readily amenable to intervention and that through some intervention the disorder can be eradicated. The nature of the question discounts the progressive challenges posed by the mother as well as the progressive manifestations of her dysfunctionalities since approximately the age of fifteen. While physician specialists in psychiatry have labeled her as manifesting a Borderline Personality Disorder among other related dysfunctionalities, the mother also reveals a variety of negative characterological personality traits which, at best, can be brought under control but never eradicated from her personality make-up. This process cannot begin, however, without first promoting considerable cognitive developmental gains in the mother's perspective of an order that is incapable of sustaining her creation of pleasing fantasy which is the basis of her denial. Under the fourth category of analysis in this report, the dismal prognosis to bringing about timely improvements in the mother's cognitive perspectives, emotional state and concomitant behaviours is fully detailed and placed into the context of her early-life experiences and the later-life negative consequences these have had on her.

3.   What treatment would be recommended for the mother and for what duration?

First and foremost, the mother must experience cognitive developmental gains of an order that cannot support the present creation of fantasy and, through this, sustain the use of denial with which to defend herself against accepting the role she has played in the creation of her own misfortunes. This is discussed at length under the fourth category of analysis in terms of the resources that are required to bring about such gains. Essentially, she would have to be institutionalized and placed in a highly specialized therapeutic community program for at least six to twelve months. Such programs are difficult to identify, let alone access. This is especially a problem in this case since the mother is unlikely to commit herself to exerting effort to obtain that which she believes she does not need.

Assuming that the mother's denial could be resolved or even assuming that she could be motivated out of an interest to have someone solve her problems, the expertise that is required to successfully address Borderline Personality Disorder dynamics is not readily available and certainly not easily accessed. Moreover, the previous assumptions are simply that - assumptions. They are without any basis at this time. As such, the assumptions only represent wishful thinking that is contrary to everything that is known about the mother and everything that is known about the complex dynamics of her dysfunctionalities. These comments are best understood in the context of the findings and conclusions described under the fourth category of analysis in this report.

4.   Would the mother's Mental Health issue negatively impact on her ability to parent her child?

All that is known about the mother's history, personality structure, cognitive and emotional functioning, as well as her concomitant behaviours, are all profoundly contraindicated to what is described in the literature as characteristics of a "good parent". In fact, under the second category of analysis in this report, she was found to approximate more closely the characteristics of what is described in the literature as constituting a "deficient/abusive parent". While her intentions are likely genuine and heartfelt from time to time, tragically her dysfunctionalities have been and likely will continue to be for the foreseeable future formidable obstacles to achieving sustainable accomplishments, personally and as a parent. She has been a profound underachiever in all aspects of her life and there is no reason to believe this will be any different with respect to her intentions to optimally parent her child. A persistent theme in the findings of this Parenting Capacity Assessment, is that it is imperative to note that the mother's dysfunctionalities represent characterological traits that cannot be eradicated from her personality structure. At best, once recognized and accepted as dysfunctionalities with tenacious commitment for the duration of her life, the negative trait propensities may be brought under deliberate control. In this case, however, certainly not in sufficient time to be of any discernable benefit to her child, who is in the most crucial formative stage of life. These formulations are elaborated extensively under the second category of analysis used in the methodology of this Parenting Capacity Assessment.

5.   Would the child's safety be compromised if she were in the care of the mother on a permanent basis and unsupervised?

Most certainly the child's physical safety would be compromised if she were in the care of the mother on a permanent basis and unsupervised. Likely the risk would come from neglect, although given the mother's episodic rages and given her propensity to be socially isolated, it would not be unreasonable to predict that her escalating frustrations might eventually be physically acted out on the child also. While invariably such acts are rationalized as disciplinary measures, they can and do escalate to unimaginable degrees, eventually normalizing for both the parent and the child the use of violence as a response to situations. The potentiality of this occurring in this case is not remote. Moreover, any good intentions expressed by the mother should be considered in the context of this report's findings that she is essentially emotionally, as opposed to rationally, driven. These concerns are significant and greatly support the conclusions and recommendations of this report.

6. What is your recommendation for long-term permanency planning for the child?

An answer to this question must be prefaced by the formulation that even if not absolutely correct, the child should be considered as having the same negative and positive propensities as her mother. In so doing, this will precipitate measures with which to prevent her from repeating the intergenerational legacy to which she would otherwise be destined. Amanda was found already to manifest the same propensities as the mother, a formulation which was supported, albeit tentatively, by the maternal grandmother. To mitigate against the harm sustained by the child and the escalating later-life negative manifestations of early formative stage unmet needs will require considerable knowledge, skills, tenacity, commitment, maturity and emotional stability of an order that will challenge most people, let alone the mother. In the absolute best interest of the child and in order to protect her inalienable right to optimal growth and development to become an autonomous, independent, adaptive adult, she should be made a Crown Ward without Access to the mother for the sole purpose of being placed for adoption in a timely manner. If indeed, the child has the same innate cognitive intellectual potential as her mother, in the right environment, it would not be unreasonable to predict that she will enjoy considerable and progressive success and, will likely make significant contributions to the community as a productive contributing citizen.

APPENDIX B
Documents Reviewed

1. The Affidavit of mother dated the 3rd of October, 1999;
2. Letter from J. Brown, M.A., Counselor at Innercity Services pertaining to the mother's assessment for addictive behaviour;
3. A review of a standardized instrument used to determine addictive propensities;
4. Letter by the mother's counsel requesting information regarding the addictions assessment;
5. Counseling session note dictated and signed, dated April 2000;
6. Counseling session note dictated and signed, dated May 2 2000;
7. Letter by Social Worker pertaining to the mother attending two counseling sessions dated March 2000;
8. Letter by the mother's legal counsel to the Social Work Therapist;
9. Handwritten notes prepared by the mother pertaining to her plan with respect to support systems available to her in the community, including names, phone numbers;
10. Psychiatric consultation report dictated and signed by the specialist, prepared at the General Hospital, April 1999;
11. Psychiatric Hospital discharge note dictated and signed by a Case Manager, April 1999;
12. Discharge summary note from the General Hospital after an overnight stay by the mother, dictated by the treating physician and signed June 1998;
13. Approximately 120 pages of case notes;
14. Protection Application to Consent filed on April 1999;
15. Agreed Statement of Facts dated June 1999;
16. Counseling session note dictated and signed, dated May 1999;
17. Psychiatric consultation report signed and dated May 1999;
18. Mental Health Service discharge note dated May 1999;
19. Mental Health Services psychiatric consultation report dated April 1999;
20. Mental Health Services psychiatric consultation dated February 1999;
21. Pathology report pertaining to induced abortion dated August 1998;
22. Mental Health Services discharge note dated May 1998,
23. Psychiatric consultation report dated March 1998;
24. Plan of Care re: the child signed August 1999;
25. Affidavit of the Child Protection Worker employed by the Child Welfare Agency responsible for the case dated June 1999;
26. Psychological assessment note dated March 1999;

27. General Hospital Triage records dated June 1998;
28. Police event report pertaining to disturbance created by "mentally ill person";
29. Police event report pertaining to an assault incident;
30. Police event report pertaining to a motor vehicle accident;
31. Police event report related to impaired driving;
32. Police event report pertaining to impaired driving;
33. Police event report pertaining to domestic dispute;
34. Police event report pertaining to property damage;
35. Police event report pertaining to domestic dispute;
36. Police event report pertaining to disturbance involving an altercation:
37. Police event report pertaining to a domestic dispute;
38. Police event report pertaining to harassing phone calls;
39. Police event report pertaining to domestic dispute;
40. Police event report pertaining to domestic dispute;
41. Police event report pertaining to domestic dispute.

APPENDIX C
Stages of Cognitive Development

Cognitive development occurs in an invariant hierarchical sequence. There are three levels of reasoning, each having two different stage perspectives. The characterization of each stage perspective has been empirically validated as cross-culturally relevant. The degree to which stage development occurs has been similarly cross-culturally validated to be determined by the breadth, depth and richness of experiences to which individuals are exposed and the facilitation they receive in their construction of meaning to that which they encounter. (Kohlberg, 1984)

LEVEL ONE: PRECONVENTIONAL REASONING

STAGE ONE – Punishment and Obedience Perspective

What Is Right
It is right to be obedient, to avoid breaking rules backed by punishment. Rules therefore must be obeyed for their own sake and avoiding physical damage to persons and property is paramount because transgressions are punishable.

Reasons for Doing Right
The reason for doing right is to avoid punishment which is meted out by figures of authority who have superior powers.

Social Perspective of Stage One
The social perspective of Stage One is an egocentric (self-centered) point of view which precludes consideration of the interests of others. At this stage there is no recognition that the interest of others differs from the self nor is there an awareness of any relevance between two points of view. All actions are considered from a physical perspective rather than in terms of the psychological/emotional interests or consequences on others. The perspective of authority is often confused with the perspective of the self.

STAGE TWO - Instrumental Hedonistic Perspective

What Is Right
It is right to follow rules only when it is to your immediate interest. It is right to act to meet your immediate interests and needs. It is right to let others do the same. It is right that all exchanges be equal in kind and that all agreements be strictly abided by.

Reasons for Doing Right
The reason to do right is to serve your own needs and interests.

Social Perspective of Stage Two

Right is relative to each situation and is essentially defined by the path of least resistance and considerations for "what can I get away with".

LEVEL TWO: CONVENTIONAL REASONING

STAGE THREE – Reference Group Perspective

What Is Right

Living up to what is expected by people close to you or what people generally expect of those in a role as a son, brother, friend, parent, etc. "Being good" is important and means having good motives, having concern about others.

Reasons for Doing Right

The need to be a good person in your own eyes and those of others. Desire to maintain rules and that which supports stereotypical good behaviour.

Social Perspective of Stage Three

The individual is aware of shared feelings, agreements and expectations which take primacy over individual interests. Relates points of view through putting the self in the other person's shoes.

STAGE FOUR – Social System Perspective

What Is Right

Fulfilling the actual duties to which you have agreed. Laws are to be upheld except in extreme cases. Right is also contributing to society, the group or institution.

Reason for Doing Right

To keep the institution going as a whole, to avoid a breakdown in the system or the imperative of conscience to meet defined obligations.

Social Perspective of Stage Four

Takes the point of view of the system that defines roles and rules. Considers individual relations in terms of place in the system.

LEVEL THREE - POST CONVENTIONAL REASONING

STAGE FIVE – Social Contract Perspective

What Is Right

It is right to uphold rules in the interest of impartiality and because rules represent a social contract. Some nonrelative values and rights like life and liberty, however, must be upheld in any society regardless of majority opinion.

Reason for Doing Right

The reason for doing right is to protect the welfare of all, based on a feeling of contractual commitment to do so. Laws and duties are expected to be based on a rational calculation of overall utility, "the greatest good for the greatest number".

Social Perspective of Stage Five

At Stage Five there is an integration of perspective by formal mechanisms of agreement, contract, objective impartiality and due process.

STAGE SIX – Universal Ethical Principled Perspective

What Is Right

It is right to follow self-chosen ethical principles. Particular laws or social agreements are usually valid because they rest on such principles. When laws violate these principles, one acts in accordance with the principle. Principles are universal principles of justice: the equality of human rights and respect for the dignity of human beings as individual persons.

Reasons for Doing Right

The reason for doing right is based on a belief that as a rational person one ought to have a personal commitment to universally valid moral principles.

Social Perspective of Stage Six

The perspective of stage six is that social arrangements are derived from a moral point of view. Any rational individual is believed to recognize the nature of morality, specifically the fact that persons are ends in themselves and must be treated as such.

REFERENCES

Ainsworth, M., Salter, M., & Witting, B. Attachment and exploratory behaviour of one year olds in a Strange Situation. In B. Foss (ED.), **Determinants of infant behaviour**. (Volume 4), London: Methuen, 1969.

Ainsworth, M., Blehar, M.C., Waters, R, & Wall, S. **Patterns of attachment Hillside**, NJ: Eclbaum, 1978.

Baumrind, D. Child care practices anteceding three patterns of pre-school behaviour. **Genetic Psychology Monographs**, 75,43-88, 1967.

Baumrind, D. Authoritarian versus authoritative parental control. **Adolescence**, 3, 255-272, 1968.

Baumrind, D. Current patterns of parental authority. **Developmental Psychology Monographs**, 4 (entire issue), 1971.

Belsky, J., Lerner, R.M., & Spanier, G.B. **The child and the family**. Reading, Mass.: Addison/Wesley, 1984.

Blair, R.J.R., & Cipolitti, L. Impaired social response reversal: A case of acquired sociopathy. **Brain**, 123, 1122-1141,2000.

Bowlby, J. **Attachment and loss. Volume II**. New York: Basic Books, 1973

Bowlby, J. **Attachment and loss. Volume III**. New York: Basic Books, 1980

Breton, M. Nurturing abused and abusive mothers: The hairdressing group. **Social Work with Groups**, 2(2), 161-174,1979.

Campbell, D.T. Social attitudes and other acquired behavioural dispositions. In S. Koch (Ed.), **Psychology: Study of a science (Vol. 6)**. New York: McGraw-Hill, 94-172, 1963.

Cattell, R.B. Patterns of change: Measurement in relation to state dimension, trait change, liability, and process concepts. **Handbook of multivariat experimental psychology**. Chicago: Rand McNally and Company, 1966.

Chess, S., & Thomas, A. **Know your child: An authoritative guide for today's parents**. New York: Basic Books, 1987.

Chugani, H.T. A critical period in brain development. **Preventive Medicine**, 27, 184-190, 1998.

Clarke-Stewart, K.A. Infant day care: Maligned or malignant? **American Psychologist**, 44, 266-273,1989.

Coloroso, B. **Kids are worth it**. Toronto: Summerville House Publishing, 1994.

Daly, M., & Wilson, M. **Homicide**. Hawthorne, N.Y.: Aldine De Grayter, pp 89 - 91, 1988.

Davidson, R.J. Dysfunction in the neural circuitry of emotional regulation: A possible prelude to violence. **Science**, 289, 591-594, 2000.

de Bellis, M.D. Developmental traumatology Part I: Biological stress systems. **Biological Psychiatry**, 45, 1259-1270, .1999.

de Bellis, M.D. N - acetylaspartate concentration in the anterior cingulate of maltreated children and adolescents with PTSD. **American Journal of Psychiatry**, 48, 51-57, 2000.

Derdeyn, A.P. **Child custody consultation: Report of the task force on clinical assessment in child custody**. Washington, D.C.: American Psychiatric Association, 1982.

Fisher, S., & Fisher, R.L. **What we really know about parenting**. Northvale, N.J.: Jason Aronson, 1986.

Fonagy, P. **Attachment, reflective self and borderline states**. In S. Goldberg, R. Muir & J. Kerr (Eds.), Attachment theory social development and clinical perspectives. Hillsdale, New Jersey: Analytic Press, 233-278,1995.

Gaines, R., Sandgrund, A., Green, A.H., & Power, E. Etiological factors in childhood maltreatment: A multivariat study of abusing and neglecting mothers. **Journal of Abnormal Psychology**, 87, 531-540, 1978.

Galatzer-Levi, R., & Karaus, L. **Scientific basis of child custody**. New York: Wiley, 1999.

Garbarino, J., & Gilliam, G. **Understanding abusive families**. Lexington, Mass.: Lexington Books, 1980.

Goldstein, J., Freud, A., & Solnit, A.J. **Beyond the best interests of the child**. New York: Free Press, 1973.

Greenspoon, L., & Bakalar, J.B. **Cocaine: A drug and its social evaluation**. New York: Basic Books, 1976.

Hare, R. Without conscience: **The disturbing world of the psychopath among us**. New York: Guilford Press, 1993.

Heinicke, CM., & Westheimer, I.S. **Brief separations**. New York: International University Press, 1965.

Heifer, R., & Kempe, C.H. **Child abuse and neglect: The family and the community**. Cambridge, Mass: Ballinger, 1976.

Hendrix, H. **Getting the love you want: A guide for couples**. New York: Harper, 1990.

Jones, T. Right frontal EEG asymmetry and lack of empathy in preschool children of depressed mothers. **Child Psychiatry and Human Development**, 30,189-204, 2000.

Katz, L.C., & Shatz, A. Synaptic activity and the construction of cortical circuits. **Science**, 247, 1133-1135,1996.

Kohlberg, L. **The psychology of moral development**. San Francisco: Harper Rowe, 1984.

Levy, T. M. (Ed.) **Handbook of attachment interventions**. Toronto: Academic Press, 2000.

Loeber, R. Antisocial behaviour: More enduring than sociable? **Journal of the American Academy of Child** and Adolescent Psychiatry, 30(3), 393-397,1991.

Lowery, C.B. The wisdom of Solomon: Criteria for child custody from the legal and clinical points of view. **Law and Human Behaviour**, 8, 371-380, 1984.

Maccoby, E.E., & Martin, J.A. Socialization in the context of the family: Parent - child interaction. In N.P. Mussen (Ed.), **Handbook of child psychology**. (Fourth Ed.), New York: Wiley, 1983.

Main, M., & Solomon, J. Procedures for identifying infants as disorganized/ disoriented during the Ainsworth strange situation. In M.T. Greenbert, D. Cicchetti & E. M. Cummings (Eds.), **Attachment in the preschool years: Theory, research and intervention**. Chicago: University of Chicago Press, pp 121-160,1990.

Olweus, D. Stability of aggressive reaction patterns in males: A review. **Psychological Bulletin**, 86(4), 852-875, 1979.

Parry, R.S., Broder, E.A., Schmitt, E.A.G., Saunders, E.B., & Hood, E. **Custody disputes: Evaluation and intervention**. Toronto: Lexington Books, 1986.

Piaget, J. **The moral judgment of the child**. New York: Free Press, 1965.

Pollack, S.D. Recognizing emotion in faces: Developmental effects of child abuse and neglect. **Developmental Psychology**, 38, 679-688,2000.

Reid, W.H. **The treatment of psychiatric disorders**. New York: Brunner-Maxel Inc., 1989.

Rest, J., & Kohlberg, L. The hierarchical nature of stages of moral judgment. In L. Kohlberg (Ed.), **Recent research in moral development**. New York: Holt, Rinehart & Winston, 1980.

Robins, L.N., Tipp J., Przybeck T. Antisocial personality. In L.N. Robins & D.A. Regier (Eds.), **Psychiatric disorders in America**. Toronto: Collier MacMillan, 258-290, 1991.

Rohman, L.W., Sales, B.D., & Lou, M. The best interest of the child in custody disputes. In L.A. Whitehorn (Ed.), **Psychology and child custody determinations: Knowledge, roles and expertise**. Lincoln: University of Nebraska Press, 1987.

Russell, ML, Anderson, C, & Blume, S.B. **Children of alcoholics: A review of the literature**. New York: New York, State Division of Alcoholism and Alcohol Abuse; Research Institute on Alcoholism, New York; and Children of Alcoholics Foundation, 1985.

Schaffer, H.R. **The growth of sociability**. London: Penguin, 1971.

Schetky, D.H., & Menedek, E.R (Eds.) **Child psychiatry and the law**. New York: Brunner/Mazel, 1980.

Schutz, B.M., Dixon, E.B., Lindenberger, J.C., & Ruther, N.J. **Solomon's sword: A practical guide to conducting child custody evaluations**. London: Jassey-Bass Publishers, 1989.

Shamsie, Jalal. **Troublesome children**. Etobicoke, Ontario: Institute for the Study of Antisocial Behaviour in Youth, 1995.

Shore, A.N. The experience-dependent maturation of a regulatory system in the orbital prefrontal cortex and the origin of developmental psychopathology. **Development & Psychopathology**, 8, 59-87,1996.

Sperry, L. **Cognitive behaviour therapy of DSM-IV personality disorders**. Ann Arbor, Michigan: Brunner-Mazel, 1999.

Spielberger, C.A. **Preliminary manual for the state-trait personality inventory** (STPI). University of South Florida, 1979.

Spielberger, C.A. Anxiety as an emotional state. In CD. Spielberger (Ed.), **Anxiety: Current trends in theory and research**. (Vol. 1) New York: Academic Press, 1972.

Spinetta, JJ. Parental personality factors in child abuse. **Journal of Consulting and Clinical Psychology**, 46 (6) 1406-1414, 1978.

Sroufen, L., & Fleeson, J. Attachment and construction of relationship. In W. Hartup & Z. Rubin (Eds.), **Relationship and development**. Hillsdale, N J.: Erlbaum, 51-71,1986.

Wright, R. **The moral animal**. New York: Pantheon Books, 1994.

University of Toronto, **Helping networks and the welfare state**, 1980.

Van der Kolk, B.A., & Filser, R.E. Childhood abuse and neglect and loss of self regulation. **Bulletin of the Menninger Clinic**, 58,145-168,1994.

Williams, G. C. **Adaptation and natural selection: A critique of some current evolutionary thought**. Princeton N.J.: Princeton University Press, 1974.

Zanarini, M.C., Reported pathological childhood experiences associated with the development of borderline personality disorder. **American Journal of Psychiatry**, 154, 1101-1106, 1997.

INVOICE

A.T. Polgar Associates Inc

CONSULTANTS IN ORGANIZATIONAL AND INDIVIDUAL BEHAVIOUR

678 Main Street East
Hamilton, Ontario
L8N 1M4
905-545-8944

Alexander T. Polgar, Ph.D.
Director

June 26, 2001
Shannon Whittaker, B.A., M.S.W.
Family Service Supervisor
Child Welfare Agency of Brown County
300 King Street
Mainway, Ontario
K2C2M9

Parenting Capacity Assessment conducted in the best interest of: Amanda Jones d.o.b. 05 September 1999

Clinical Hours

23 January, 2001	Phone contact with the mother	.25 Hours
13 February, 2001	Phone contact with the mother	.25 Hours
27 February, 2001	Phone contact with worker	.25 Hours
06 March, 2001	Assessment Interview with the mother	4.00 Hours
07 March, 2001	Observation of the mother with the child	2.00 Hours
07 March, 2001	Interview with Workers	1.00 Hours
13 March, 2001	Interview with maternal grandmother	2.00 Hours
	Review 190 pages of documents @ 3 min/page	9.50 Hours
	Score and interpret standardized instruments	2.00 Hours
	Dictate 76 page report @ .5 hr./page	38.00 Hours
	Edit 76 page document	4.00 Hours
Total Clinical Hours		**63.25 Hours**

Administrative Hours
06 March, 2001   Supervise administration of standardized   3.00 Hours
                     instruments to the mother
                     Word processing   15.00 Hours
Total Administrative Hours   **18.00 Hours**

Travel
06 March, 2001   Return travel   2.00 Hours
07 March, 2001   Return travel   2.00 Hours
06 March, 2001   Return kilometers 142
07 March, 2001   Return kilometers 142
Total Travel Hours   **4.00 Hours**

Summary
63.25 Clinical Hours @ $XXX.00/Hour
18 Administrative Hours @ XX.00 /Hour
4.00 Hours of Return Travel @$XX.00/Hour
284 km Return Trip @ $.00/km (Treasury Rate)
GRAND TOTAL _____

INDEX

H

Hedonism 141, 144, 147
Heredity 78
Hierarchy of caregivers 35, 40
Home visits 63
Hostility 55, 71, 148
Household, cleanliness 41
Hyperactive 43
Hyper-arousal 79
Hypothesis 29, 31, 39, 125, 136

I

Idealization 117, 143
Immature 43, 119-121, 139, 141, 144, 150
Immediate 15, 16, 30, 56, 60, 61, 67-69, 74, 124, 125, 134, 141, 144, 151, 163
Implications 8, 17-21, 24, 30, 41, 42, 54, 66, 68, 74, 76, 98, 107, 121-123, 126, 145
Impulsivity 55, 75, 77, 82, 88, 139, 143, 150
Inalienable right 2, 60, 90, 149, 153, 159
Inconsistencies 23, 27, 90, 125
Incorrigibles 64
Independence 56, 61, 137, 140
Independent 11, 15, 18, 49, 66, 84, 128, 138-140, 150, 153, 159
Individuality 5, 6, 47, 61
Individuation 39, 50, 114
Inference 97-99
Innate propensities 129, 141, 152
Inquest 91
Insecure 37, 38, 41, 71
Insensitive 144
Insight-oriented psychotherapy 75
Institutionalized 84, 158
Instrumental reciprocity 60, 68, 147
Intellectual 24, 29, 48-50, 56, 57, 64-68, 117, 120-125, 128, 129, 131, 136, 137, 140, 141, 144, 145, 147, 152, 153, 159
Interaction,parent/child 17, 19, 29, 33, 36-42, 69, 71, 79, 80, 102, 103, 121, 130, 133, 134, 136, 145, 169
Interaction pattern 17
Intergenerational 6, 29, 39, 40, 50, 51, 56, 71, 76, 79, 102, 137, 146, 159
Interpersonal 29, 67, 69, 87, 133, 143, 145, 146
Interpretation 7-11, 13, 14, 20, 27, 31, 33, 51, 62, 71, 91, 105, 122, 126, 128
Intervening variable 39, 42, 73, 82, 125
Intervention 1, 3-6, 14, 15, 18, 23-25, 29, 36, 44-47, 49, 53-55, 57, 59, 62, 64, 65, 73-82, 84-87, 91, 103, 110, 112, 117, 119, 120, 122, 124, 126, 128, 135, 137, 138, 143, 145, 147, 149, 150, 152, 154, 157, 169
Inventory 54, 59, 74, 101, 102, 111, 121, 144
Invoice 103
Irrational 56, 127
Isolation 52, 60, 67, 69, 71, 81, 87, 111, 145, 147

Issues,salient 2, 7, 13, 14, 18, 31, 38, 41, 42, 56, 60, 70, 72, 85-87, 93, 112, 120-124, 126, 130-134, 138, 142, 147, 153

J

Judicial 3, 8, 57, 73, 84, 91, 93
Justice 8-10, 89, 150, 165

K

Knowledge 3, 4, 11, 12, 19, 21-25, 33, 41, 45, 4-49, 52, 55, 56, 59, 60, 61, 63, 67, 68, 74, 76, 79, 80, 84, 86, 90, 93, 94, 97, 118-124, 129, 138, 145, 146, 159

L

Labeling 10, 11, 57, 58, 59, 142
Labels, DSM 10, 24, 57, 58, 59, 110, 112, 113, 122, 138, 143, 170
Language, mastering 1, 37, 42, 78, 105
Later-life consequences 20, 29
Law, business of 2, 9-11, 16, 104, 169
Laws 9, 165
Learning disabilities 51
Least intrusive measures 5, 13, 15, 35, 103
Legal 6-9, 30, 31, 41, 60, 73, 93, 94, 122, 161, 169
Legislation 19, 35, 103, 120
Letters of Referral 7
Limbo 15, 26, 91
Logic 99
Longitudinal studies 34, 69, 119

M

Maladaptive 19, 24, 31, 46, 50, 51, 65, 69, 78, 84, 128, 134, 135
Maltreatment 18, 59, 61, 81, 112, 139, 168
Marital problems 144
Marshmallow experiment 56
Maturation 30, 169
Mature 24, 44, 119, 120
Medical model 45, 46, 57, 58, 138
Mental 2, 4, 10, 15, 24, 46, 56, 57, 59, 63, 64, 86, 92, 93, 108, 110, 120, 125, 138, 142, 149
Methodology 1-31, 36, 38, 44-46, 49, 66, 73, 91, 93, 94, 97, 99, 103, 105, 113, 115, 117, 120, 134, 149, 157, 158
Michigan Screening Profile of Parenting 102, 109
MMPI-2 54, 57, 59, 72, 77, 85, 144, 148, 151
Monotropy 35
Mood 51, 76, 124, 143, 151
Moral development 137, 168, 169
Morality 35, 134, 165
Motivation 10, 35, 67, 84, 120, 149
Multiple attachment figures 35
Mysticism 11, 86
Mystique 22

W

SANDRIAM

PUBLICATIONS

CPSIA information can be obtained
at www.ICGtesting.com
Printed in the USA
BVHW011452231121
622354BV00005B/48